Cecilia Bartoli

Also by Kim Chernin from The Women's Press:

Womansize: The Tyranny of Slenderness (1983)
Crossing the Border: An Erotic Journey (1994)

Cecilia Bartoli

The Passion of Song

Kim Chernin
and Renate Stendhal

Published in Great Britain by The Women's Press Ltd, 1998
A member of the Namara Group
34 Great Sutton Street, London EC1V 0DX

First published in the United States of America by HarperCollins
Publishers, Inc, 1997

For photo credits see page 235.

British Library Cataloguing-in-Publication Data
A catalogue record for this book is available from the British Library.

ISBN 0 7043 5081 5

Designed by Irving Perkins Associates

Printed and bound in Great Britain by CPD (Wales) Ltd

For our dear friend Claire Picard,

la passionata assoluta di Cecilia

Sometimes we do not know what we are doing. But even more than ever, I now think we are enlightened by God, or whatever it is above us. . . . Many times after a performance I'd say to myself, How did you do that, how did you dare that? It was music that supported me. There is that last thing you add from yourself, from your soul, from your heart.

REGINE CRESPIN

Contents

Acknowledgments

⚜

Hugh Van Dusen, our editor at HarperCollins in New York, made this book possible. We are deeply grateful for his friendship, his profound love for opera, and his editorial guidance.

Kate Ekrem's creative style of editing, managing crises, and solving problems has saved the day on almost every second day.

Beth Vesel, our agent, was an inexhaustible source of encouragement and support.

Amy Ryan is one of the very best copy editors in the business. We have been grateful to have her at our side.

For their encouragement and help with our research, we are grateful to David Gockley, Director, Houston Grand Opera; Ava Jean Mears, Resource Center Director, Houston Grand Opera; Robert Cole, Director, Cal Performances, Berkeley; Elizabeth Rullier and Françoise Maviel, Institut National de l'Audiovisuel (INA); Brigitte Schubert Riese, Norddeutscher Rundfunk, Hamburg; Laurence Viriot, Opera de Nancy et de Lorraine; Professor Carlo Tabarelli, La Scala; Martin Korn, Opernhaus Zürich; Loretta Ricci and Anna Lungo, Radio Televisione Italiana (RAI); Sabrina Signoretti, Rossini Opera Festival, Pesaro; Dr. Peter Dusek, ORF, Vienna; Paulus Wunsch, ARTE, Strasbourg; Catherine Heuls, Opéra National de Paris Bastille; Dr. Gisela Prossnitz, Salzburger Festspiele; Prof. Norbert Flechsig, Süddeutscher Rundunk Stuttgart; Archiv der Wiener Konzerthausgesellschaft; Helga Appel, Schwetzinger Festspiele; Renate Dönch, Wiener Staatsoper; Irina Kubadinow, Wiener Festwochen; Dr. Kerstin Schüssler, Bühnen der Stadt Köln; Jim Owen, Star Classics (San Francisco); Dan Ashby; and Susan Gilchrist.

For his generous hospitality and informed musical conversation we are indebted to Martin Winrich Becker, Kammermusikpodium, Braunschweig.

For their reading of the manuscript, heartfelt thanks to Odile Attalin, Robert Cole, Tobey Hiller, Michael Rogin, Lillian Rubin, Jeanne Stark-Jochmanns and Janet Sullivan.

Special thanks to Catherine Gallagher, with whom the ideas in this book were discussed at length and in depth.

And most especially our thanks to Luca Logi, archivist of the Teatro Comunale di Firenze, for his warm welcome, his erudition, sound advice, inspiring conversation, and painstaking reading of the manuscript.

I

A Feather on the Breath of God

The First Three Concerts, 1991–1993

*P*eople with worship in their hearts tend to end up at Sunday concerts. I attend such concerts as regularly as some people go to church. If it is not raining, I park near Oxford and University and walk across the Berkeley campus to the concert hall. On Sunday, February 24, 1991, I was taking my usual walk through the campus with Renate Stendhal, my usual companion.

Next to the chancellor's residence, close to the path, there is a grove of old trees with a small brook, a wooden bridge. We always stop here to prepare ourselves for the music that is coming. On that day, a light mist rained down from the trees as we brushed against them. It had been a cold, severe morning, without wind. Here, under the trees, a brittle sunlight moved over the green rocks. I have taught myself not to expect too much from life, except where music is concerned. But I have to be receptive.

Most singers arriving from Europe have been thoroughly discussed before people in Berkeley have had a chance to hear them. Rarely is one asked to respond directly to a musical event without some advance warning of how to take it. I am nervous in situations like this, afraid I may be swept away by a miracle of my own making. On this particular Sunday, I was inclined to feel protective toward the twenty-five-year-old singer from Italy who would soon walk out onto the stage. The Berkeley audience on Sunday afternoons is an elite gathering of musicians and connoisseurs; the sheer musical knowledge contained in the room seems to create a second order of acoustic sensitivity, superimposed on the clear sound-space the hall provides. I have often thought of it as a collective hearing that makes it possible for me, although not a trained musician, to apprehend musical subtleties and complexities that otherwise might elude me. The young coloratura mezzo, whom no one knew, would be put to a strenuous test in this college town.

Coloratura has always meant to me a fireworks of cool vocal agility, but I love the mezzo voice with its dark, redemptive plangency. Coloratura roles, with their highly ornamented, embellished line, are the most technically exposed in the soprano repertoire. Ideally, they demand a perfected breath control, an artfully phrased line, an almost offhand ability to send forth a radiant shower of perfectly matched tiny notes, an absolute beauty of tone and timbre.

The concert began precisely at 3:00.

Cecilia Bartoli walked briskly out onto the stage. She made an impression, at first glance, of shyness, beauty, dark-eyed exuberance, stored tension. I had seats in the first row, almost touching distance from the stage. From here I could feel the visceral preparedness with which she crossed the stage, walked in front of the piano, positioned herself, swallowed, clasped her hands, gathered her forces.

The first part of her program would present a collection of love songs from the seventeenth and eighteenth centuries, music with which most of the audience would be familiar. The first song, *"Tu ch'hai le penne, amore,"* by Giulio Caccini, began with these words: "Oh love, you who have wings/and know how to spread them in flight/go quickly in flight/to where my heart lies."

I had heard this song before, yet instantly felt that something unaccountable had now happened to it. Had I really heard it before? A penetrating vocal intensity had transformed the simple love song into an irrepressible outpouring of longing and desire. There was an odd confusion, as if text and music had been fused in a molten expressivity, so that one could not say where the text ended and the music began. There was something in this voice, penetrating, darkly mysterious, that brought me close to tears. But then I became minutely aware of certain pronounced characteristics of the voice: the fully developed sumptuousness of the lower register, the warm vibrancy of the middle range, which at times seemed burnished with a late-afternoon light. The top was limpid, powerful. The voice rose from velvet through dark gold to a silver transparency.

No twenty-five-year-old singer, of whom we had not yet heard, could possibly be capable of this much ease, artistry, technical mastery, expressive maturity. Perhaps I was making it up? The audience, taut with anticipation, was suspended in a concentrated listening as each glowing note emerged, the legato so smooth the notes seemed to grow out of one another. Was this really happening?

A profound connection had been established between singer and audience. She was good and then some, she knew it, and now she knew that we knew it, too. Her nervousness vanished, the dark eyes flashed with a perceptible gratitude, the voice opened out beyond what seemed possible, shimmering with the silver agility of liquid mercury. If one could stop a drop of water falling through a splinter of light, one would have caught the quality of descending radiance that closed the phrase. She was a singer of awesome technical accomplishment whose expressiveness imparted a kind of devotional intensity to the simplest classical love song. Since then, trying to describe Cecilia Bartoli to friends who had not yet heard her, I said that they could grasp the essence of the singer if they were able to imagine a sensuous, embodied angel, standing quietly on a concert stage as she reported back to God about the mysterious joys and sorrows of human existence.

ℭecilia Bartoli performed in Berkeley five times from 1991 to 1995. At her first performance, in Hertz Hall, on that rainy Sunday afternoon in January 1991, the small concert hall was not more than half full. That year, her manager had difficulty booking her first American season. She returned to Italy with one thousand dollars after expenses. By 1992, word of the singer's artistry had spread, and Bartoli's performance, in the same small hall, was well attended, although I was still able to buy extra tickets for a friend only a few days before the concert. By 1993, when Bartoli came to Berkeley again, her concert had been moved from Hertz to Zellerbach, the largest concert hall on campus, which holds a good two thousand people. The following year, there were five hundred names on a waiting list that had been started a few days after the concert was announced. In 1995, when Bartoli performed in Berkeley for the first time with an orchestra, every important music lover, reviewer, and musician in the Bay Area had tried to buy a ticket. After the concert, a select dinner was held at the Garden Court at the Palace Hotel, where the master chef had created a new dish, Ravioli Bartoli.

The young singer who had sung four years earlier to a half-filled house on a rainy Sunday had since become a world sensation. She was the best-selling classical artist since Luciano Pavarotti, her recordings had won numerous awards, she had been featured on popular and prestigious magazine covers, her concerts regularly sold out within a few hours of being announced.

Her detractors claimed she was the product of clever publicity and media hype. They mentioned her early publicity photos. Bartoli had been dressed provocatively in black leather, a promotional device that was regarded as an exploitative approach to a very quiet young girl. Others thought her record company was misrepresenting the young singer as a concert artist; Bartoli, they claimed, had the perfect recording voice but they wondered how the voice would fare in concert halls or opera houses, where her vocal shadings and dynamics might be inaudible. Some critics attributed her success to the huge amounts of money that must have been spent by London/Decca to plug their new artist. Her first record was released in 1989, early in her career; prior to its release she had appeared as an unknown singer at the Maria Callas Gala in Paris and in only three operas. The CD cover offered her as a young fashion prima donna in large, dangling diamond earrings, wearing black lace against bare skin, red suede gloves, and a haughty, cool, disengaged expression. For Bartoli's detractors the explosion of her career could be attributed to the exploitable Italian beauty of the young singer; also, but perhaps less significantly, to the small, lovely voice, enhanced by flattering recording techniques.

Bartoli enthusiasts experienced her as a radiant natural beauty, with a vibrant, expressive personality and a darkly mysterious voice, which could execute with ease the runs and trills and roulades of the demanding coloratura arias of Mozart and Rossini. I myself was squarely placed with the Bartoli rhapsodists. Black lace and leather, and the vast sums of money supposedly spent to promote the artist, could not account for the impression Bartoli made in concert on her audiences. The publicity might get them there but would not bring them back a second time or account for the enthusiasm of people who attended their first Bartoli concert knowing almost nothing about the singer. The capacity to invoke in her listeners a state of heightened musical rapture seemed to me the distinctive quality of the young artist. More circumspection about a singer who had yet to prove herself in the world was advised by many of my friends, but I thought the appearance of a beautiful voice on the world stage was worthy of careful study and attention. These, I was convinced, could best be accomplished through a willing surrender to the admiration that the young artist evoked. My enthusiasm for the singer, which seemed to call into question my powers of judgment and assessment, was, I felt, an appropriate medium for appreciating an artist whose outstanding gift was the power to inspire rapture.

*　*　*

Bartoli is a child of the theater. Born to parents who both had highly promising international operatic careers, she spent her childhood, along with her brother and sister, backstage at the Rome Opera, where her parents had become singers in the chorus. Bartoli's mother, Silvana Bazzoni, a lyric soprano, could not continue a solo career after the birth of three children. Little has been told about the demise of her father's solo career.

As an adolescent, Bartoli trained to become a tour guide. Then she developed a passion for flamenco dance. Her father, who regarded flamenco as a hobby, paid for the lessons. But Bartoli took her dancing seriously and gave up school and all other interests to pursue it. In time, the legend of Bartoli may set down this passion for flamenco dance as the emergence of the imperative giftedness that was soon to make itself apparent through her voice. Flamenco may also have been her first step out of the family's tight-knit unhappiness. Her parents had never gotten along: her father was temperamental, impulsive, given to outbursts of rage; her mother was practical, down-to-earth, stubborn. Money was scarce, shoes were handed down from one child to the next—a detail Bartoli has mentioned in virtually every interview she has given. When I spoke with her in 1993, she said (seriously) that her fame and success pleased her because they gave her the chance to work with the best musicians in the world and to buy lots of shoes.

For a young girl from her background, flamenco dance was not a plausible career. She would have to make a living; the family certainly couldn't support her. The crisis was resolved with singing lessons. Little by little, the strenuous training began. The young woman created her voice and with it the confidence to make possible, by the time she was nineteen, an appearance on *Fantastico,* an Italian television show that presents young singers, puts them through their paces, and lets the audience decide which of them has the best voice. Bartoli lost the television competition but received an invitation to sing in an homage to Maria Callas at the Paris Opera. Then there were requests from the world's most famous conductors to work with her: an invitation from von Karajan to sing the mezzo solos in Bach's B-minor Mass, a performance of the Mozart Requiem with Barenboim in Paris. The career was moving, but it had not yet become a sensation. She made an appearance at the Rossini Opera Festival in Pesaro, performed Cherubino with the Zürich Opera. She specialized in recitals. She recorded a few discs with Philips, Teldec, and Erato, then got

an exclusive contract with London/Decca. She made her London debut at
Wigmore Hall in 1989. In July of 1990, a few months before she came to
Berkeley, she made her American debut in the Mostly Mozart Festival in
New York. Some reviewers risked being (highly) impressed; many pre-
ferred to wait until the young singer's voice developed. In 1993, when
Bartoli performed for the third time in Berkeley, her fans had begun to
whisper that she was the most important mezzo coloratura of the last hun-
dred years.

The term "mezzo-soprano," when first used in the mid-nineteenth century, referred to the dark, mellow, velvety qualities of a voice, not to its
range. Agility and flexibility, the capacity to embellish the vocal line, were
expected of all singers. Today, few of the singers we call mezzo-sopranos
can reach either the low G or the high C Rossini could take for granted in
his dark-voiced singers. Bartoli, who effortlessly exhibits great agility and
flexibility through a magnificent range, extends a vocal tradition that has
been dying out. She joins the great names of Supervia, Stignani, Tourel,
and Simionato from an earlier era and arrives on the scene at the very
moment Teresa Berganza and Marilyn Horne, who kept the tradition alive
during the sixties, have come to the end of their careers.

All this is impressive, but it is no guarantee that the voice is anything
other than an overnight sensation that will, in turn, fall apart overnight.
The meteoric rise and fall of young opera singers forms its own legend.

From what I could see of her onstage during her second Berkeley concert in 1992, she seemed unchanged—natural, expressive, inspired, highly
responsive to the audience's response to her. Would this rich artistic gift be
able to protect her from the dangers of too much, too sudden fame? These
dangers are also legendary: the temptation to sing too often, to sing roles
for which the voice is not suited or not yet ready. To travel too much, to
exhaust a luxurious young instrument before it has a chance to develop.
How would someone so young, relatively inexperienced in the world,
respond to the critics who questioned whether her voice was large enough,
who insisted she would never be able to perform opera on the stage or fill
a large hall with that uniquely penetrating voice? There were the goading
questions that asked where the voice was going, as if it had to go somewhere and were not already, in itself, a remarkable accomplishment. If the
few years of her early career had brought Bartoli her partisans, they had
also given rise to the doubters, the journalists who name her musical ability "narrow," a "miniature," although by the age of twenty-six she had

inscribed the adolescent Cherubino with an eternal love-longing, charged up Rosina with fiery temperament, touched the enduring core of love as the scorned wife in Bajazet, imparted a haunting sorrow to the great requiem Mozart wrote, when he was dying, in the belief that the mysterious benefactor who had commissioned the work was himself the angel of death. One reviewer, detecting (or imagining) minor imperfections in her dazzling ornamentation, warned, "Prepare to bail out. This girl is getting reckless."

Meanwhile, the "reckless" girl is a woman who spends a year studying a new role, breaks recording dates if she has not mastered the expressive details of a role, stays up until three in the morning listening to Haydn.

Would she last? Was it all a question of hype, as many journalists and rival recording executives were claiming? Was the voice immature, the technique uncertain? It was hard for me to imagine that anyone asking these questions had heard Cecilia Bartoli.

But then again, what did *hearing* mean? Was the cool, detached, watchful state the best possible way to listen to a singer, as some of my friends advised? Was it better, as they claimed, to purge oneself of emotion, in order to keep oneself from being swept away? In Bartoli's name, we debated the meaning of tears.

I thought tears registered the deepest possible response one could have to an event. My friend Cathy thought that crying was a barrier to deeper feeling. I argued that being swept up and swept away was in itself a form of knowledge. My friend Tobey thought it easy to be mistaken in a rapid-fire response. For herself, she would prefer to hold back and think over the emotion an event had called up. She felt comfortable with Wordsworth's idea of emotion recollected in tranquillity. Philip thought that most people were suspicious of strong feeling. He too had heard Bartoli's first Berkeley concert and had rushed out the following day to look for her recordings. He agreed with me that there were some things (we included love and music and god among these things) that could be apprehended only through a capacity for surrender.

Whenever Bartoli's name came up, we debated the old questions: Was emotion to be tamed through reason? Was reason to be instructed by strong feeling?

When, during the following years, we invited a group of friends to listen to our Bartoli recordings, who among us might be likely to know her best? Was it the enthusiasts, who declared after every song that she was the equal to any singer they had ever heard; or perhaps the vocal coach, who was certain Bartoli was taxing her vocal resources—she had heard a note here and there that proved this; or again, our friend the historian, who considered Bartoli excessive and later confessed she reminded him of his dark-haired excessive mother; or my friend the literary critic, who didn't hold much with tears but wept through our entire concert?

Perhaps a so-called excessive response, complete with strong statements and loud declamations, was the only apt response to a remarkable event— as were clapping loudly, getting to one's feet, rushing down to the stage, shouting out the singer's name after a performance.

My friend Augusta thought some of us preferred our debate to actually listening to Bartoli; when she was moved, she told Renate, she found that she had no need for words and preferred to sit in silence. Odile, who is French, suggested we come back the following weekend to analyze Bartoli further; Sophia, a German, thought we should all spend the night and go on listening; our friend who had been an opera singer explained to the man sitting on the floor next to her the meaning of the words Bartoli had been singing; Louise, an art director who is always eager to learn, wrote them down on a paper napkin. Lillian, a writer and sociologist, leaned over to read them with her. Amy, editor-in-chief at *San Francisco Focus* magazine, suggested I write a book about Bartoli; other friends protested that the singer had only been out in the world for a few years; Renate reminded us that Bartoli had had a career in Europe before she appeared in the United States; I thought a book about the singer should be written in a pitch of high ecstasy, in language that would approximate the rapturous quality of the singer's voice. At this, everyone laughed; we then went back to hearing Bartoli again.

*C*hristopher Raeburn, the man who launched Bartoli's career, heard her for the first time at a "sausage-machine" audition (also called a "cattle-market" audition) in Milan. Singers of forty different nationalities were present; they came on, one after the other, "did their little bit" for the various directors of opera houses and heads of record companies and opera festivals, then stepped down. Raeburn, one of the most highly esteemed producers in the business, who had been active through virtually the entire development of recorded opera over the last forty years, was there representing London/Decca. Producers for London/Decca work on staff. In other companies, producers tend to be freelancers under pressure to produce immediate economic returns with little opportunity to foster artistic development. If Raeburn was interested in Bartoli, he would bring her to a recording company that balanced its commercial interests with serious artistic considerations. An agent had told Raeburn that there was a particular artist who might interest him. Her name was Cecilia Bartoli. Raeburn remembers the occasion, vividly—and no wonder. He was about to hear, for the first time, a voice for which he would be prepared to stake his professional reputation.

"Cecilia was nineteen years old. It was phenomenal. She was absolutely extraordinary. We had been looking for just such a mezzo; we were going to record *Il Barbiere*, and I had always wanted to do an Italian *Barbiere* with an Italian, not with an international cast. We were looking around for a proper Italian Rosina because, to my mind, there were lots of Rosinas floating around and they were not suitable. And suddenly this one just appeared out of the blue. I had done Teresa Berganza's very first Rossini record. I'd recorded Marilyn Horne's first Rossini record. So there'd been a certain line of education for me through these artists. But of course neither of the other two were Italian. And now, at long last, here was someone who for me was absolutely the Rossini ideal.

"Rossini was completely natural for her. She didn't have to struggle for anything or work at anything. For her it was just getting up in the morning and doing what she had to do. It was wildly exciting for me; this was something I had dreamed of for so many years but I had never experienced. Certainly it was the voice, which was unique. But it was also her way of singing, her way of expression. To me it seemed an extension of her natural way of speaking. Her whole being represented this Rossini ideal to me and I immediately thought that singing Rossini was probably an extension of what she must have been like as a person. At that time I'd never spoken to her in my life. I didn't know her. But as a singer she was remarkable because of her naturalness and ease. She was already an absolute virtuoso. Her coloratura was exceptional. Her intonation was marvelous. And there were phrases she could do...she took these phrases all in one breath, she'd never thought of taking them any other way. But it was very interesting to me. Because no singer I had heard before had ever taken these phrases in one breath. For her it was completely natural. This was Cecilia."

Bartoli sang "Cruda sorte," from Rossini's *L'Italiana in Algeri* and "Di Tanti palpita," from *Tancredi*. Raeburn was "spellbound." He wrote in his notes, "Very remarkable indeed. VVG [Very very good]."

"I didn't ask questions about where or how she had been trained. It seemed such an unbelievable talent that I immediately knew I wanted to work with her. That's really how it was. I had no doubt that she was the ideal Rosina. I recommended her very strongly to the head of Decca at the time. I also recommended, on the strength of what I'd heard, that we should do a record with her of Rossini arias. I thought we should stake a claim. I didn't want the other gramophone companies to jump the gun. I knew instantly what we had found, absolutely."

"This is the end of my career, but having worked with all nationalities, for over forty years, I find her an absolute synthesis of all that I really believe in. Her singing, acting, her presence . . . she represents the standards I believe in. She is the ideal, a golden-age singer. Cecilia, for me, embodies the whole Italian tradition."

Cecilia Bartoli has an exceptional ability to inspire people to take risks. Her career has been supported by powerful, well-placed men in the music business who have immediately recognized her gift and have gone out of their way to further her career. She has gathered around her men like Christopher Raeburn, her producer; Jack Mastroianni, her manager; the conductor György Fischer, her frequent accompanist, as a charmed circle of father-protectors. She works closely with Philip Gossett, the Rossini scholar, who helps her research and discover music that will be suitable for her voice. With her mother firmly in place as guide and teacher, these men, I imagine, complete the family circle, standing in for the father in Rimini who is no longer living at home.

Jack Mastroianni, Cecilia's manager, first heard of Cecilia through Christopher Raeburn, who played him the Rossini arias tape, which they had just finished recording. (It was this tape that Raeburn had decided to produce with Bartoli the first time he had heard her sing at the audition in

Milan.) Mastroianni was then representing only established singers. His list included Kiri Te Kanawa, Mirella Freni, Marilyn Horne, Hildegard Behrens, Eva Marton. He had never before taken on a "young unknown" and felt that the connections he had in the musical world were only suitable for famous singers. "It would be like retooling a factory," he said when I talked to him about his professional relationship with Cecilia. "I would have to create new contacts and I didn't have the capacity to do that."

Nevertheless, Raeburn played him the Rossini tape, and Mastroianni was "overwhelmed." Raeburn suggested he meet with Bartoli; Mastroianni agreed. She was in Pesaro; he had business there anyway. A few days later he called her and arranged for her to sing for him. The next morning "she and her mother appeared, and they were a couple of minutes late because the accompanist who was supposed to play for her had conked out. And so she dragged in somebody off the street. Literally, somebody who was just godawful. It was painful to hear him. In Pesaro you're at a festival, there are a whole bunch of musicians there, but some of these people just can't manage a lot of fast notes. This guy was having a lot of problems accompanying Cecilia and after a while it was just impossible. So she had him step aside. She sat down and started to play for herself.

"Well, I must say, her eyes, the expressiveness of her eyes, and the character of the singing, and the maturity of the sound of the voice and the sparkle and that individuality—and I was just overwhelmed. Right away I knew I wanted to work with her. If I had to retool I would retool. So I said, 'Well, how can I help you?' And she said, 'Well, things are just beginning to happen for me, and I'm real excited, but at the same time, I want to concentrate on my music, I don't want to have to deal with the business. I'd like somebody to coordinate everything on the business side.'"

At the time Bartoli met Mastroianni, she had already met some agents who worked at the same agency, but she did not have a signed contract with them. They had asked her for some pictures and her schedule; she had sent them and never heard from them again. So far as she and Mastroianni were concerned, she was free; she was looking for an agent to represent her and a manager to take over her business.

Mastroianni said to her, "If you're interested in a world management situation, I'd be willing to speak to you about it. But I don't want to rush you and I don't want to push you, so why don't you take a few weeks, we'll talk then and see what you want to do."

The few weeks passed, Cecilia decided to work with Mastroianni. His agency has a policy that when the artists they represent make decisions of this kind, everyone at the agency abides by it. Then, unexpectedly, the agents who had originally met with Cecilia claimed that Mastroianni had violated agency rules and should have informed them that he had spoken to her. Although they had no contract, they refused to release her; she was part of their list and they would not let her go. It became, as Mastroianni describes it, a very unpleasant situation within the agency. He decided, very reluctantly, to step aside.

"But I thought, God, this breaks my heart, if for nothing more, for the career and the livelihood of an artist with so much potential. It just breaks my heart. I knew this was not just a twenty-one-year-old. This was Venus coming in on the shell, out of the foam, on the waves. But what could I do? I was asked to step aside, and I didn't speak to her until the following August, almost ten months later. I figured she probably wouldn't want to speak to me after what I had just put her through. So I didn't call, I didn't make any effort to contact her, but in August of '89 I got a call from a mutual friend saying that Cecilia would like to speak to me about world management. I said, 'Well, as long as she's with my colleagues, there's nothing I can do about it. I regret it, I really regret it, but there's nothing I can do.' The friend said to me, 'Don't you know? She fired them last month.' So all of a sudden there was no conflict, she was free, and we went forward. We had a meeting. On the ninth of December we signed a contract. These were absolutely memorable events.

"Our working together was not an easy birth. But the rapport between us was always immediate. Now I said to her, 'I need to earn your trust. We both need a mutual trust in one another. I don't want to displace your regional representatives. Do we want to give them a period of time to see what they can do, how they cooperate, how they coordinate, how aggressive they are on your behalf?' Cecilia has a tremendous sense of ethics and morality. She wanted to give them a chance. So I said, 'Fine, six months from now, let's reevaluate where we are.' After six months, all but two of the people eliminated themselves because they didn't do anything for her. After another four months one of the others dropped out, and for the same reason. Now, four years later, we have trouble saying yes to all the invitations she gets.

"Back then, I would say to someone I knew, 'Well, I have this most incredible singer,' and they would say, 'Yeah, yeah, we've heard that before.' People working with a young singer are supposed to be selling *shmattes*. You sell dresses, this dress, that dress, you're rewarded by the amount of engagements you get. With people like Freni, Te Kanawa, Eva Marton, you're not an agent, you're a manager, a kind of statesman. But when you have someone who's twenty-one years old people immediately assume you're on the make to book an artist. That is why I didn't think I could work with her when Christopher first mentioned her to me. But after I heard the tape, and after I heard her sing in Pesaro, well, it was very clear to me, I wanted to be able to do something for her. This might sound like Pollyanna. You know *Cenerentola*, just before the final aria? The 'fairy godmother,' who in this case is a man, the tutor Alidoro, says to the two stepsisters, 'Goodness has triumphed.' This is Cecilia, this goodness is Cecilia. When people meet her they immediately want to call her Cecilia. You just can't call her Miss Bartoli. I can assure you, all this is very real, it's not put on."

Rossini's Angelina (Cenerentola) has been marked out as the signature role of Bartoli, whose life and career repeat its rags-to-riches theme. Reality, with its well-known tendency to mirror opera, has also cast other major characters from Cenerentola in Bartoli's life. The part of the tutor Alidoro, who guides his young ward to Angelina, has been masterfully played by Raeburn, who repeats the wise, protective gesture of the older man by sending Mastroianni, in the part of the young prince, to seek out Bartoli.

"You know, when I went to Rome to sign the contract with Cecilia, I said, 'Why, after what our agency did to you, have you come back to me?' And Mamma said, 'You don't have the face of an agent.' They both have a sixth sense for people. You know, I'm blessed. I have a mother who's like that. Cecilia's like that. And I have something to give in return. My best service to Cecilia is to create opportunities for her to shine, not to sit by the phone as one could do now and say, 'Oh yes, oh no, oh yes, the fee is a hundred million dollars,' and so forth. My best work for her is to give her the best opportunities.

"We've been asked to do arena concerts. I ask Cecilia about it. I don't even tell her what I think, but I think it is a horrendous idea. But I don't want to influence her, persuade her, dissuade her. I always want her to think about a proposal and give me her response. But her immediate reaction is one of riotous laughter. She just laughed. She's not after the easy money route. She said, 'That's not what my art is about.' For her, for

Mamma, everything is in perspective. They have a very good sense of what is good for Cecilia. Her voice is slightly higher than your normal mezzo, there's no question about that. But if she had to sing soprano repertoire it would, I predict, become a fatigue on her. So, something like Donna Anna in *Don Giovanni,* which you would think would be her role, is too high for her. The tessitura tires her. The same with Konstanze in *The Abduction from the Seraglio.* Blonde is much more a role in the middle voice, which then goes and pops out and does high E's and things like that. Cecilia can do that, but if she sang the whole time in a high register she would tire her voice. And that's why she is the Blonde not the Konstanze, although everyone thinks of her as the Konstanze, which is the bigger part. It has to do with the physiology of the voice and protecting the voice and not putting it under strain.

"Here you have this absolutely beautiful young person and you know that a lot of pressure will be put on her in the world to do something or try something that is not right for her. But she will not do it. And I think it is my best service to her to find the opportunities that are exactly right for her.

"When I am at the end of my life it's not going to give me pleasure that I had a list of great singers with whom I worked, but the fact that people could trust me. It will give me pleasure that Cecilia could trust me and I did for her everything I could do, everything, my very best for her."

Robert Cole, who brought Bartoli to Berkeley for her debut, had first heard her on a tape sent to him by Mastroianni. "It was not a very good recording," he told me. "It was done in an amateur way, it was kind of fuzzy and creaky. Certainly, it was not a good presentation of the voice. But obviously the technique was so phenomenal. Even the quality of the voice was extraordinary. You could tell that even on a tape of this kind. There just isn't anyone else singing like that today."

Cole decided, on the basis of the voice he had heard on the poorly recorded amateur tape, to book Bartoli for Cal Performances, the prestigious series sponsored by the University of California.

"I'm not a vocal coach," Cole said, "but I was a conductor and I worked a lot with singers. What was striking to me about Bartoli is first of all that her command is total in all registers. She has, it seems to me, no difficulty no matter where she goes, either in the technique or in sustaining this wonderful quality which is really her own. A lot of people who are critical of her in New York are saying, 'Well, the voice is too small, it'll never make it in the opera world,' and so on. But it has a penetrating quality which is really quite phenomenal. I can't think of it as being small. People have gotten so used to some of the superstar voices of today, including Jessye Norman and Pavarotti. These are big voices. And they somehow think that if someone's going to be a star they have to have a voice like that. Bartoli should be singing in eighteenth-century, nineteenth-century opera houses, which are much different from what we have. But that doesn't mean she can't sing in our opera houses. With that penetrating edge to her voice, the voice will always be audible. I think people exaggerate the question of size."

During the intermission of the first performance, Cole went backstage fast and booked her for the next year. That is how she happened to appear, an unknown young singer from Italy, at her first concerts in Berkeley before she had made appearances almost anywhere else in the United States. By the time of the third and fourth concerts, when she was already an international star, she was still performing in Berkeley, although turning down invitations to places that offered more money and prestige. Bartoli was thanking Cole for his early recognition and promotion of her career, for taking a chance on her, for believing in her before all the evidence was in. Bartoli, with her rare ability to inspire her listeners to take risks, has an equally rare capacity to acknowledge the risks they have taken. This acknowledgment, this paying back in spades what she has been given, is essential to Bartoli's appeal as a performer, as we shall see.

*M*aybe hearing Bartoli for the first time was similar to listening to Rosa Ponselle at her Metropolitan debut. Ponselle was born to an Italian immigrant family in Connecticut in 1897. At the age of fourteen, she made her singing debut in a neighborhood movie theater and performed in vaudeville for the next six years. A friend arranged an audition with Caruso when Ponselle was twenty-one years old. A few months later she made her debut with him at the Metropolitan Opera, an unknown singer with little training and a voice of great natural beauty.

Many music lovers still regard Ponselle as the greatest female singer of the twentieth century. I had always wondered what it would have been like to hear her for the first time from a seat high up in the old Met. Hers was a dramatic soprano voice, more powerful than Bartoli's and therefore intended for very different roles, but it possessed the same dark velvet, the expressivity, the effortless legato. Would I immediately have fallen for her voice, recognized its importance, proclaimed it one of the great voices of the age, even before I had left the theater or had read the reviews?

But how would one know? Was it enough to sense the presence of a great artist, to be seized by a musical rapture and be moved to tears? Probably not. Nevertheless, in the weeks that followed Bartoli's first Berkeley concert I could not dismiss the impression that I had encountered a rare musical phenomenon that revealed something about the nature of music itself. I went looking for the Bartoli recordings that had been mentioned in the program, found them easily enough at Tower Records, brought them home, but did not yet play them. I first had to play the concert silently through to myself until I had understood why it had moved me more than any other musical event I had ever attended, although I had been listening to recordings and attending lieder recitals and going to operas since my late teens. Objective research would have to come later. For now, I had to learn from my own subjectivity. If Bartoli was as important as I thought, it would be because of her power to affect her listeners as profoundly as she had affected me.

To hear a great voice for the first time is a serious business. Every lover of vocal music has heard tales about other music lovers who have been smitten by a singer. It is, as Terry Castle described it in *The Apparitional Lesbian*, "a tradition of awe, delight, and comic self-abasement as old as the opera itself." Castle, who is an admirer of the German diva Brigitte Fassbaender, is also a wily collector of tales about the smitten. As a kindred spirit, she seems to relish Queen Victoria's "adolescent passion for the Italian soprano Giulia Grisi," about whom the queen wrote adoringly in her letters and diaries. Geraldine Farrar, Castle informs us, with wry delight, was met nightly at the stage door of the Met by young admirers in their "teens and twenties, casting flowers and love notes in her direction when she emerged."

Apparently, young opera singers made a regular habit of loving older opera singers. Frieda Leider, who would one day herself inspire passionate rapture in her listeners, was, as a girl, passionately devoted to Geraldine Farrar. Farrar in turn loved Calvé; Galli-Curci loved Adelina Patti; Ponselle admired Melba and wanted to take "Melba" as her saint's name at her confirmation. Writers also fell in love with singers. George Sand admired Maria Malibran and adopted male dress so that she could purchase cheap standing-room tickets, which were available only to men, whenever Malibran was singing. And finally, Castle's coup de grâce: A Belgian schoolteacher named Monique Serrure gave up her career when she heard Georgette Leblanc sing Thaïs at the Opéra de la Monnaie in Brussels. "Merely listening to Leblanc's voice, Serrure said, had made her want to serve her—which she did, as cook and housekeeper, for the next forty years."

The transformational power of a voice has been written into opera itself, as the central drama of Strauss's Salome, whose life and destiny are changed forever by the sound of Jokanaan's voice rising from the cistern where he has been imprisoned. His voice arrests her, it calls her, it draws her to itself, it shakes her out of the life she has been living, awakens curiosities, passions, transfiguring ambitions that will destroy him and lead her to an arcane triumph of love over death, through which the opera acknowledges and celebrates the terrifying power of the voice.

A fictional account of this same mysterious moment, in which one encounters a voice with the power to change one's life, launches the ironic narrative of James McCourt's novel *Mawrdew Czgowchwz*.

"In the late summer of 1947 Ralph returned home from a loft party on lower Seventh Avenue, fed up. Flipping on the predawn FM airwaves, he picked up a transcription of the Midsummer Night Prague Festival Gala. A scant hour later he came ranting through the heat to the front door of a particular brownstone kibbutz on St. Marks Place . . . carrying a paper-based tape in both hands as if it were alive. He was smoking two cigarettes. . . . It *had* to be heard, he told them all. Gin-milk cocktails and coffee were made while Ralph went on declaring, nearly pleading, which seemed hardly necessary. He had only the last part of it, but it *had* to be heard."

The voice has to be heard. It cannot be kept to oneself. Its mystery must be shared, communicated, revealed. As for me, I could certainly tell every music lover I ran into that a miracle had taken place on a rainy Sunday at Hertz Hall. I could repeat the name "Cecilia Bartoli," spread the word. Renate, my companion, knew that she had attended a unique concert but seemed reluctant to join in my zeal. I caught her looking at me from the corner of her eye each time I launched into my Bartoli pane-gyric. I saw her smile discreetly, although I never actually caught her in a dismissive shake of the head, whenever I started to talk about the concert and its meaning. When, during the next months, I began to refer to my first encounter with Bartoli's voice as a spiritual awakening, I realized that for some people I had gone too far.

"Once I chose Anna Moffo," Wayne Koestenbaum writes, in a similar vein, ". . . I was set for life. I had a path. I had discovered an altitude, a mission [in which] the states to be savored are absence, sacrifice, and search." (Wayne Koestenbaum, *The Queen's Throat*, Poseidon Press, New York, 1993). Koestenbaum is, like Castle, a writer interested in the con-nection between homosexuality and opera. He is, again like Castle, a great collector of tales about operatic madness. In *The Queen's Throat*, he tells the story of the young girl who killed herself over the singer Mary Garden, having developed a mad enthusiasm for her from having heard her sing. Another overheated story: a young male fan who broke Dame Nellie Melba's autographing pencil into tiny pieces with his teeth. He wanted to pass out relics of Nellie for his "chosen friends." There is also the fan, an admirer of the diva Mrs. Tofts, who "was arrested in 1704 for throwing oranges at Tofts' rival, Margherita de l'Epine, during a perfor-mance."

Here, in Berkeley, after Bartoli's third concert, Sarah Cahill, a reviewer for the Berkeley *Express,* implicitly associated Bartoli with this awed and stricken tradition. "I have a friend who is completely obsessed with Cecilia Bartoli," she wrote. "He has all her CDs and, for a while, she was always the subject of conversation with him, and he would urge anyone who came in his front door to watch a video profile of her, one which he must have seen twice a day." (Sarah Cahill, *Express,* February 5, 1993)

Renate has also experienced a voice that changed her life, many years ago, as an adolescent. She had been listening to the radio and was sud-denly arrested by a dark, strong, strangely penetrating voice unlike any she had heard before. "I knew it was a woman's voice, but stronger, sharper, clearer than any voice I'd ever heard. It had a peculiar sobbing quality and at the same time a distinct androgyny. The clarity was like truth, as if this singer were speaking a hidden truth I needed to grasp."

Renate had just heard Maria Callas for the first time. She rushed out to buy a record, brought it home, immediately invited her best friend to come over to listen. Now, for many days, over many weeks, the two of them spend hours together listening to Callas. During these hours the friend listens attentively. It is Renate who cries. The fact that she can feel so strongly and be moved to tears in her friend's presence is all that matters. In the strength, truth, clarity, ambiguous androgyny, and mysterious sorrow of the singer's voice, Renate has discovered herself.

Therefore she wonders if it is possible to admire a singer the way I admire Bartoli, if you already have had an awakening through another voice. She likes Bartoli, is strongly moved by her and interested in her as an artist. But Maria Callas stands between Bartoli and Renate. To take up another singer feels strangely like an act of disloyalty, or betrayal.

For Koestenbaum, this infatuation with the voice of a singer feels "like throwing the self away, giving up autonomy and production, becoming pure receiver." He interprets it through the language of addiction, as a sickness "that needs to be controlled."

The novelist Brigid Brophy tends to regard it in a similar light. The "infantile situation," she writes, "is recreated in the theatre or opera house. The audience's attention and curiosity is concentrated on the stage" in much the same way the child's curiosity is riveted by the parents in the primal scene. The audience "renounces the power of speech in favour of the persons on the stage and signifies its own feelings only by the infantile methods of inarticulate cries and hand-clapping." (Brigid Brophy, *Mozart as Dramatist*, p. 40)

For Brophy, opera has become the transposed primal scene; fascination is sexual fascination and singing itself, "the prodigies of muscular exertion and the prodigies of breath control," becomes a metaphor "of virtuoso performance in bed."

Paul Robinson, a highly sophisticated reader of both Freud and opera, likewise understands the power of singing through an analogy to sexual performance. "Perhaps it is no accident that we speak of a voice 'climaxing' on a high note, or compare the ascending and declining vocal trajectory of the typical operatic phrase to the tumescence and detumescence of sexual arousal. There is, in other words, an isomorphism between operatic singing and sexual performance. Moreover the actual sound of operatic singing—which opera fans find so inexplicably beguiling—is itself a form of physical vibration. It is, if you will, the body shaking." (Paul Robinson, *Cambridge Opera Journal* 6(3), 283–91)

The love of singing as an addiction, a regression, a haunted yearning for the primal scene; the infatuation with a beautiful voice, a madness that leads to death, broken pencils, oranges and incarceration. All this did not seem entirely to account for my interest in Cecilia Bartoli.

*P*erhaps there is a way to understand the intense response to a great voice as a transformational rather than a sexual experience, as a form of self-expression, rather than regression. The intense focus on an object, which this response shares with addiction, would become, in this version, a longing for the singer as a long-sought ideal, perhaps an idealized form of the self, the one who can call up, shape, and express emotions most of us hold at one remove.

Monique Montaigne, the stepdaughter of Herbert von Karajan, tells a moving story in *The Opera Quarterly* (vol. 9, no. 3, Spring 1993) of awakening to a new voice and the imperative, even driven sense of mission it gave her. In 1990, she heard an anonymous voice singing a few bars of "*Un'aura amorosa*" from *Così fan tutte* over the opening credits of the movie *My Left Foot*.

"I had rented the videocassette," she writes, "and was startled out of my humid August night lethargy by a dark, clarinetlike sound of rare beauty. It was distinct, unique, and unmistakable and I knew that, had I ever heard it before, I would have recognized it."

A few bars sung in a dark, beautiful voice. A startled awakening out of an August lethargy. The listener waits impatiently for the final credits, certain she will be told who the singer is. But there is no mention of the singer. Who is he? Why has she never heard the voice before? This could be the beginning of the obsession that is said to lead to infantile states and violent self-effacements.

Instead, this awakened interest in a singer's voice takes Montaigne on a search for the singer. She makes calls to the studio in Dublin where the film was produced, is given the name Jozsef Reti, a Hungarian. Now she can buy every record he ever made, turn "the doorbell off, the answering machine on, and adjust . . . the headphones" so that nothing can "disturb or interrupt this experience." But she cannot locate a single recording by Reti. She calls every record store she can think of, the Hungarian consulate general, the Hungarian trade office, a Hungarian import company in Long Island City, whose sales manager tells her that Reti had died seventeen years earlier and that all his records were out of print.

At this point, sick with disappointment, Montaigne remembers something that had puzzled her as a child. Her grandmother, with whom she was living, was an industrious woman who kept the classical music station turned on every minute of the day, while she was cooking or mending or knitting. "Only when Richard Tauber sang would she stop whatever she was doing and sit, or stand very still, sometimes smiling, sometimes in tears, often humming along until the song ended. I had learned to keep quiet—though unable to understand why this was necessary—and could never figure out what made her act so strangely. . . . My own 'magic' was still out there, and something in the sound of Reti's voice told me I had just found it."

A voice has to be matched to a listener; even a very great voice does not hold magic for everyone. The sound that awakens the need to search and serve holds a mysterious, emotional power for particular listeners.

Montaigne goes in search of Jozsef Reti. And now, through one of "those astonishing coincidences that are so difficult to accept," a friend of hers discovers Reti at exactly the same time—in a bargain bin at Tower Records. Montaigne soon has two recordings of Reti, listens to them devotedly, continues to be profoundly moved. Karajan, her stepfather, had died more than a year before. He was the strongest influence in her life and his loss had affected her in unexpected ways. For the first time she had become unable to listen to music. Now, the sound of Reti's voice, those few bars over the opening credits of a movie, had brought her back to herself, a person for whom music had been "as much a part of me as breathing."

She had found in Reti a brilliant technique, elegance, and style, but above all a man who could discover in each aria, in every role, the intrinsic identity of the character. As Reti sings them, "Don Ottavio, Ferrando, Belmonte, and Tamino are men of passion, character, and purpose; each has his own color and personality." She, who has been unable to face the death of her stepfather, and has therefore lost the capacity to listen to music, has found in Reti a man who can hold, shape, and express the full range of human emotion. Here, the singer embodies an ideal form of emotional integration, through the developed capacity to say "precisely and empathically just what the character feels, to speak, as it were, the character's profoundest identity." (Paul Robinson, *Cambridge Opera Journal*, vol. 6, no. 3, pp. 283–91)

Montaigne travels to Hungary; she looks up colleagues and friends who knew Reti, makes her way to his grave, where she begins, she says, to accept the death of von Karajan. Now begins her serious work to unearth the material, liner notes, interviews, a discography, reviews, that allow her to piece together a picture of Reti's career, which had flourished and then faded. In 1988, on the fifteenth anniversary of Reti's death, a Hungarian record company had released two CDs, to which reviewers responded enthusiastically. But it was not to last. "Reti had a brief period of posthumous glory and was once again forgotten save, perhaps, by a few connoisseurs."

This story of awakening, search, and dedication ends on a transformative, not elegiac note. "I do not know what it will entail or how long it will take," Montaigne writes, "but I want to change that [obscurity]. Reti was given two gifts: a beautiful voice and a profound musicality. What he made of these gifts sets him apart, and for that he deserves to be remembered."

The singer has found his devotee, he has awakened her, transformed her, and now she can serve him. This is the singer as teacher, guru, and transformational guide.

*S*ome months after Bartoli first came to Berkeley, I reproduced her first concert from beginning to end by taping, in order, the appropriate songs and arias from her four CDs. Now I too turned off the telephone and turned on the answering machine, adjusted the headphones, so that my experience of immersion in the singer would not be interrupted.

Since her appearance here, I had not listened to Bartoli again as an external voice, but had concentrated on my inner impressions of her singing. It seemed somewhat uncanny that I could now hear the voice again, in its mysterious, dark radiance, singing in exactly the same order the same songs I had first heard it sing, as if I had now acquired the capacity for perfect recollection or stunning auditory hallucination.

My task was clear. I wanted to transform my subjective experience of Bartoli into plausible cognitive designations. I had to do this without a professional knowledge of music or a technical musical vocabulary, through a capacity to translate strong emotional impressions into language. I wanted to speak about Bartoli on behalf of the music lovers, to describe, perhaps fathom, the nature of her impact on us.

This time, what impressed me was the eagerness with which Bartoli gave herself over to the music, as if music were a natural extension of her own inner state. *"Tu ch'hai le penne, Amore"* ("You who have the feathers, O love, and know how to use them, fly from my heart to hers, hidden under veils or under the golden waves of her hair"). It was precisely the simplicity of the words, the lyrical purity of the sentiment, that required so much artistry in the singer. Every syllable had to be deeply felt, then inflected with a precise emotional understanding, or the song would fall back into the mundane vocal exercise it often was. I began to feel, as I made my way through the concert, that Bartoli's perfect vocal technique was perhaps misleading. It was there, not for its own sake, but because it allowed her to transmit musically the full range of emotional expression.

Bartoli had mastered the breath technique; she could take it for granted, she could play with it. "Soft zephyrs, breathe lightly on my loved one's pillow," she sang, in perfect imitation of the whispering wind that has been instructed to carry the secret of the lover's passion. It seemed to make no difference whether she sang on behalf of a shepherd or the shepherdess; her phrasing came of itself, shaping its flawless line as if she merely had to put herself out of the way so that the song itself could pass through her. From each song she created a small world, a cameo, a character in miniature. The saucy girl who "takes today a lover as she plucks a fair red rose." The lover driven to distraction, "pinched, teased, annoyed, and chewed up," who cries mercy of love. The knowing girl, wise beyond her years, who holds out for the lover's faithfulness, scornful of prayers, sighs, eloquence.

It was part of Bartoli's mystery, I felt, that a voice so young already possessed such a rich vocabulary of emotion. I appreciated the wonderful paradox of this very young woman singing, with such tremendous conviction, *"Nel cor più non mi sento brillar la gioventú"* ("I no longer feel youth shining in my heart, and you, love, are the cause").

Bartoli's voice brought together youth with experience, freshness with a dark intuitive knowledge of emotional states she herself, in her own person, may never have felt. *"Selve amiche, ombrose piante"* ("Friendly woods, weeping shades, this unhappy lover begs of you some peace for his pain"). Listening, one seemed to have been pried open into depths and crannies of the self one would not have been willing to visit without the formal reassurances of the singer's mastery.

And the voice? The voice that awakens the longing for sacrifice and search? The third or fourth time I listened to the tape, I recalled the beautiful phrase from Hildegard von Bingen, herself a musician and mystic. Bartoli's voice was, I thought, in Hildegard's words, "a feather on the breath of God." The prodigies of breath control, which Brophy and Robinson had described as metaphors of sexual performance, could also be thought of as metaphors of divine inspiration. Breath plays as much a part in spiritual symbolism and poetic expression as it does in sexual behavior. God breathes life into man, the Holy Breath dwells with us, teaches, brings us to remembrance, guides, speaks, declares, inspires. Breath is divine. Breath has power to attune the spheres. Breath is eternity. In Hebrew, the word for spirit and breath is the same. Prodigies of breath control might therefore make a singer an appropriate instrument for the transmission of spiritual meanings.

Perhaps Bartoli's voice had moved me so profoundly when I had first heard it because it had carried a kind of sacred message, a remembrance, through its power to inspire inner states that music could uniquely transmit. This sense of the arcane power of music, which was widely celebrated by classical poets, became a distinctive part of the conversation among the Renaissance musicians who developed opera.

> Now that we have given the definition of music according to Plato . . . and have said what music is . . . let us turn to the marvels of music, in discussing which Damon, the teacher of Socrates, says that, being chaste, it has the power of disposing our minds to virtue and, being the contrary, to vice. . . . [Plato] also tells us that Thales the Milesian sang so sweetly that he not only influenced the minds of certain persons, but also cured illness and the plague. And we read that Pythagoras cured drunkards with music, and Empedocles insane persons, and Socrates a man possessed. And Plutarch tells us that Asclepiades cured delirious persons with the sym-

phony, which is simply a mixture of song and sound. (David Kimbell, *Italian Opera*, Cambridge: Cambridge University Press, 1991, p. 40)

Bartoli, I thought, as I turned on the light and shook myself out of the dream state she invariably produced in me, was herself transported when she sang. Standing on the stage, next to the piano, she seemed at particular moments far away, her eyes closed, lost in reverie, as if communing with the source of music itself. I remembered how, in that first concert, at the end of a song she seemed to wake up to the presence of the audience and dutifully return to herself as we applauded her. Then, warming up to us, she applauded us in return to acknowledge the transport we had shared with her. This movement of intense, devotional feeling between Bartoli and the audience was, I felt, one secret of her power and our enthusiasm. For people who yearn for high beauty and mystery but do not seek it through institutionalized religion, it may be the opera singer of a secular-spiritual age who carries the sacred.

*I*n the summer of 1991, a few months after she first sang in Berkeley, a film was made of Bartoli's recital at the Savoy Hotel in London. In mood, atmosphere, expressive power, and repertoire, this concert is as close to her Berkeley recital as it is possible to come. The film has caught and preserved an impression of Bartoli before she had become a world phenomenon. All the simplicity, purity, and rapture are present in this young artist who has not yet become fully aware of her power and can therefore offer herself without self-consciousness as a servant of music.

Music lovers who missed Bartoli during the early years of her career can enter it directly through this video from London/Decca. Most viewers, I think, will be struck by Bartoli's intense presence as a performer. Skeptics will find it hard to dismiss the rapt quality of Bartoli's voice, face, and gestures. They are particularly arresting in Vivaldi's *"Sposa son disprezzata."*

The aria is composed of a single verse and may well be, even with

repeated hearings and a secure knowledge of Bartoli's expanding repertoire, the single most beautiful song she sings. As filmed, the aria captures
visually and musically the essential quality of Bartoli's art and will repay
serious study for anyone wondering why millions of people are so moved
by her. A local music reviewer, puzzling about her popularity and finding
her "far from one of the great voices of the century," noted that she "pos-
sesses the narrowest repertoire of any singer to achieve superstar status in
our age," since most of what she sings "lingers on the periphery of the
vocal heritage of the 18th and early 19th centuries."

To understand Bartoli's power over her audience, one must experience
the way she allows this so-called narrow repertoire to express its enormous, subtle, wrenching emotional depth. *"Sposa son disprezzata"* makes a
good beginning.

The concert begins. We are in a small, darkened hall, part of the audience, observing the singer on the stage. The recital opens with the lovely
song, *"Se tu m'ami"* ("If you love me"), attributed to Pergolesi but more
likely written by A. Parisotti, the editor of a famous anthology of Italian
arias, who loved to include his own compositions by attributing them to
famous composers. Almost all the *arie antiche* sung by Bartoli come from
this album. *"Se tu m'ami"* will soon be the title song of her album of *arie
antiche,* which has not yet been released. Bartoli seems to relish this song,
perhaps for the young girl's insistence on picking as many lovers as she
likes.

For her second song, the camera moves away to observe the pianist,
György Fischer, her frequent accompanist. As he plays the opening bars
of the song, the camera spots Bartoli standing alone onstage. The camera
moves from behind, slowly, irresistibly drawn to the singer, passes in
front of her, and turns back to face her. She is wearing a simple black
dress; her rich, dark hair is caught up in back of her head so that it falls
luxuriously over her shoulders, a few long wisps straying out to frame her
face. She is very still; her hands are clasped, her eyes focused inward.
There is no trace of nervousness or tension. The beautiful young face is
in repose.

Sposa son disprezzata
fida, son oltraggiata,
cieli che feci mai?
E pur egl' é il mio cuor

il mio sposo, il mio amor,
la mia speranza.

I am a scorned wife,
I am faithful yet insulted,
heavens, what did I do?
Yet he is my love,
my husband, my beloved,
my hope.

Simple, seemingly conventional, the aria expresses a sentiment not likely to appeal to contemporary women. Yet, enclosed within these words, held and supported by a music of unsuspected power, Bartoli discovers a hidden journey. As she sings it, the aria is stretched taut between two words—"*disprezzata*" (scorned), at the end of the first line, and "*speranza*" (hope), at the end of the verse. In twenty-six words Bartoli needs to move her sophisticated, secular audience from despair to a devotional belief in the will of heaven.

"*Sposa,*" the first word. By the second syllable we know that this wife has been scorned. We don't have to wait for the end of the line to figure that out. "*Disprezzata,*" when it arrives two words later, has brought us to the uttermost humiliating depths of this betrayal. But is it possible? She, a faithful wife, insulted? The singer's arms open in a taut, uncomprehending gesture. The voice renders the dark confusion of a devoted woman surrendering to the stark power of her first betrayal. Then, eyes closed, hands clasped over her breast, the scorned wife, as Bartoli creates her, does what she must to go on loving. She must manage to love her husband. She must, nothing else is possible. The seemingly conventional words of resignation and acceptance—"he is my love, my husband, my beloved, my hope"—are not a statement of fact, they are an incantation, intended magically, fervently, to bring about the reality the words evoke.

The verse is now repeated and we find that the inflection of the words has changed. Bartoli has now discovered anger in the wife's declaration that she is scorned; there is a note of outrage working its way into the reminder that she is a faithful wife, a tension of bitterness into her cry to the heavens, a cry that must be repeated two times before the wife can bring herself to the insistent repetition that she loves the man who betrayed her. Yes, she loves him, he is her beloved, her hope. But these lines in turn have to be repeated with a total surrender to the sustained, unfolding, embellished vocal line before they can effect the magical potency of the incantation.

The singer has closed her eyes, her head is bowed. The song has ended, but the singer's mouth remains open, as if these words of prayer, incantation, surrender to heaven must once again be silently repeated. The piano plays the closing bars of the aria. Bartoli does not move. The audience shares with her a moment of perfect silence.

It is here, precisely in this moment, that we can see Bartoli bring herself back. She has a long way to come. She has to move back from the scorned wife to the singer, move back out of her own musical rapture into an awareness that she has an audience and has been observed. She opens her eyes, seems momentarily stunned, slightly dazzled, then hesitantly, as the audience applauds, graciously returns to us.

Play the aria over as many times as you like, watch the film of the recital until it wears out and the emotional impact will not lessen. This song is the essence of Bartoli. It establishes the impossibly high musical and emotional standard to which she must rise in every performance. Understand this and it will be hard to think of her repertoire as narrow or her voice as a miniature.

I lived through Bartoli's second Berkeley recital, in February 1992, in a sorry state. I wanted to be reassured that the singer was as good as she had seemed the first time; therefore I had trouble hearing. To begin with, my taut, overly focused listening deprived me of the ability to take in the expressive dimension of the recital. I was observant rather than receptive, I fixed on details that immediately lost their relationship to the whole. I felt no pleasure when a beautiful note emerged, but followed it with an anxious brooding, as if at any moment it might break or fray and let me down.

Her "Homage to Rossini," on the eve of Rossini's second centennial, had drawn a full house to the same small hall on campus. Many listeners felt they were in on the beginning of a great career. In the following days, reviewers would also prove to be ecstatic. Robert Commanday, the music critic for the *San Francisco Chronicle*, who had a reputation for toughness: "You hear her and you know you are at one of those historic events of vocal discovery. Fabulous. This Italian singer has it all, and in equal proportions—a voice such as comes along maybe once in a generation or two, terrific technique, natural musicality, intelligence, personality and looks. The basic sound is smooth and finely finished, warm and just velvet enough on the sheath. Within there's a resilient, firm-tempered core that is apparent in the keen focus of her voice, and when she draws it out or modulates timbre and shading. Seamlessly, Bartoli's voice passes through its ample range. When she turns on the passagework, she exults in the coloratura . . . the detail concentrated with exact chromatic steps, no sliding, with trills, tight and electrically fast, and with embellishments that are expressive, not merely decorative ornaments."

I quote at length from this review because it is accurate, reflects my opinion of Bartoli from other recitals, and fills in the gap in my perception of this one. I followed Bartoli through the first half-dozen songs barely able to stand the tension of each note. Would the note be round, full, rich, distinct, expressive, glowing? Would it have the capacity to glide into the next? If she was less than perfect, would she still be good enough to justify my first enthusiastic impression? Could she possibly be even better than she had seemed then? What would it mean to seem better?

There were songs from the first concert, others that I recognized from her recordings. (Does Bartoli ever sing a song the same way twice?) Characters spoke through her eyes, the movements of her head and hands. The haughty courtesan of *"La grande Coquette"*; the excited girl of *"La regata veneziana"* cheering on her gondolier; the abandoned women of *"Mi lagneró tacendo."* But were they as vivid as the first time? Was the audience impressed? Was Bartoli as fresh and compelling as she had been the year before?

My attention was troubled by a persistent imaginative intrusion that made it hard for me to distinguish Bartoli onstage from the Bartoli I had conjured up over many months of listening to her in private. Was this the first concert from a year before—the second half of which had also been devoted to Rossini? Was it last night and we were at home listening to Bartoli on CD? Was she going to sing Rosina's *"Una voce poco fa"* from Rossini's *Il Barbiere,* as she had the last time? Would she perform again that strange aria I had never really noticed before, the housekeeper's *"Il vecchietto cerca moglie"* from the same opera?

This year's Rosina, I thought, was taking on a hard edge; she'd been around for a while, grown a year older. The old housemaid was once again a buffa triumph, the roughness of her character showing itself in the hard edges of Bartoli's tone.

As the encores were delivered, I found myself hoping Bartoli would break with Rossini and sing Mozart's Cherubino again, as she had the previous year. During the final applause, when it was clear that the concert was over, I realized that I had been waiting all night to hear two particular songs. I wanted to hear Vivaldi's *"Sposa son disprezzata"* and Pergolesi's *"Se tu m'ami"*; if she didn't sing them again nothing would console me.

I left the recital convinced that Bartoli was a rare vocal discovery, aware however that I had better calm down and get myself into a more receptive listener's mode before I heard her the next time. Would there be a next time? Was she going to come to Berkeley again? Apparently, diva worship had its dangers. If she performed in Berkeley the following year, I might miss the whole event by once again concentrating on it too closely.

When Bartoli returned to Berkeley in 1993, she repeated two songs from her first recital, *"Se tu m'ami"* and *"Sposa son disprezzata."* At that time, I had not yet seen the video of her performance at the Savoy Hotel, but I had already fallen under the spell of *"Sposa."* I had made a repetitive tape of it, so that I could study it, fathom it, figure out the secret of its emotional power. I knew, from the program notes of the first concert, that Bartoli's mother had been her only teacher. I did not yet know the story of Bartoli's family life. As I listened, however, I began to wonder if the young singer's understanding of scorn and insult might have been handed down to her by her mother. When she sang *"Sposa,"* did she sing on her mother's behalf? Did she become her mother?

With this idea, I returned to my interest in the nature of diva worship. The confessional quality of so many arias written for women, then sung and performed by women, suggested that one of the pleasures granted the listener by the diva arose from this induction into the secret emotional life of women, that unspoken life, particularly of the mother, from which the woman is always trying to protect her child. There are very few actual mothers in opera. When an opera singer opens her heart to her audience, there are few children cluttering the stage or the story to keep the audience from a swift, unwitting identification of themselves as the diva's child. The fascination of the great singer would therefore rest, not in its capacity to reduce the audience to regressed and passive children, but to fulfill the childhood longing to be admitted into the mother's secret emotional life. Indeed, mothers in opera show a distinct tendency to risk, kill, or eliminate their children, as if they were enacting opera's secret wish to remove children from the story. Azucena sets fire to her infant son. Gretchen murders her infant in despair. Medea murders her children to avenge her husband's betrayal. Norma decides to murder her children for the same reason. Kostelnicka (the child's grandmother) murders Jenufa's infant. Herodias stands by passively when Herod orders Salome to be killed. Clytemnestra degrades Electra and removes her from the court. The Queen of the Night dangerously tries to turn her daughter into a killer. Cio-Cio-San (Madama Butterfly) murders herself rather than her son, a maternal precedent opera could not easily adopt, as it violently silences her voice and the opera along with it.

The opera heroine most likely to draw her audience of listener-children into her inner life would ideally be childless and lonely and perhaps betrayed. The Countess' *"Dove sono"* in Mozart's *The Marriage of Figaro* is unbearably moving precisely because one could imagine one's own mother, in the darkness of her secret life, whispering a similar lamentation. Perhaps some of the mysterious vocal power of Cecilia Bartoli came from this direct line of emotional transmission from her mother, who might well have taught her, while she taught her singing, more than a perfect technique. If this were true, *"Sposa son disprezzata"* would then be a representative instance of the more general fascination of a confessional aria sung by a woman. Could one explain Bartoli's power over an audience in terms such as these; was she, because of her relationship to her own mother, uniquely capable of this expressive mandate?

There was no way to confirm or annul these fantasies. Immersed in the aria through its endless repetition, I would imagine new, more elaborate explanations for Bartoli's vocal power. Perhaps it had something to do with the tradition of bel canto singing, which had been developed (some say) hundreds of years before the invention of opera. Others regard bel canto as a typical baroque phenomenon, the term itself accurately applied to the repertory from baroque opera to Rossini and thus contemporary with the birth of opera. In the more romantic view, which appealed to me, bel canto techniques of singing had been passed down through an obscure process of evolution whose origins dated back to antiquity. Certainly, by the fourth century, when canons (singers) were ordained into the church to execute the musical service, systematic instruction in the art of singing had been well established. Music, along with sculptures, paintings, and devotional buildings would now glorify god. Perfection in the art of singing had become inherently devotional, a form of worship and prayer.

I now began to imagine Bartoli's mother, who had also been a singer, as part of this ageless tradition that handed down, from teacher to pupil, mature singer to novice, arts and secrets of vocal technique that most modern teachers of singing no longer teach.

There were, I knew, obscure texts describing the methods of the bel canto art. It was a tradition with schools, books, and direct transmissions that have been largely forgotten or neglected in our time and now seem purely legendary.

I had an anecdotal, tale-like sense of this lineage, which I now pieced together through some casual research. Pier Francesco Tosi, a famous singer and composer of the eighteenth century, became one of the most celebrated singing masters of his time. He was the son of a musician, from whom he had learned the vocal customs and traditions of the preceding generation, which he in turn taught to his students. I was also fascinated by the line of masters and schools. Giovanni Battista Mancini, also a famous singing master of the eighteenth century, had been a pupil of Bernacchi, who had studied with Pistocchi, who had founded a school of singing in Bologna. The success of this school, writes Cornelius Reed in *Bel Canto,* "made that city the center of Italian voice culture." When Bernacchi hurt his voice because of what are believed to be the bad teaching methods of his youth, he went to Pistocchi and asked him to restore his vocal capacity. Pistocchi did so, after three years of arduous training in the bel canto style.

Bartoli is one of the few young singers on the world stage today who has been taught to sing without straining her voice. She consistently refuses roles that would be too taxing for her, she chooses with great care conductors and directors who appreciate the qualities and limitations of her voice. This care for the voice as a god-given but perishable instrument is noteworthy in the world of contemporary opera and might, I imagine, have much to do with the tempered wisdom of Bartoli's mother, who must have seen it all and then some during her solo career and her long years in the chorus of the Rome Opera, where she would have had ample opportunity to observe the hazards of a soloist's career.

Could one imagine Cecilia and her mother teaching together some day? Would they establish a school, in which the arts and techniques the mother had taught, the daughter so brilliantly mastered, might be handed down? As teachers in their own school, they would have to persuade young singers to spend months and years on the most basic techniques of singing, before attempting difficult songs. They would stress the attainment of equal power in all registers of the voice, discouraging the eagerness for high notes and big voices, through which so many young singers destroy their potential. They would emphasize the discovery of the unique qualities of the emerging voice, directing it to a repertoire suitable to its size and expressive capacities. Or was this fantasy of a singing school not to be taken literally, but understood as an interpretive guide to Bartoli's symbolic vocal lineage?

I attended the third Berkeley concert with these thoughts about lineage and transmission. *"Se tu m'ami"* was the sixth song on the program. The minute I heard it I felt that I had been right in my various musings and dreamings. Bartoli's voice was a throwback, a carrier of the archaic traditions of bel canto singing, a true mezzo of the velvety, dark old school, not a mezzo by virtue of failing to sing high enough to become a soprano, or low enough to qualify as a legitimate contralto. She had ringing high tones, full and embodied low tones, she had what Rossini regarded as the dark, natural voice of women. Someday, I thought, she would sing opera with original instruments because her voice was itself an original instrument that must have been slipped to her through the mysterious corridors of time.

And then, five songs later, she sang *"Sposa."* A lot of people present in the audience that night must have been listening to Bartoli recordings. A perceptible stir and muted rumble moved through the concert hall as the piano set the first notes of the song. Then the kind of silence fell in which a performer will be compelled to bring forth what is in her, an unforgettable silence that only a great performer can create. She sang *"Sposa,"* I thought, as she had never sung it before, probing the music for the obscure link between betrayal and the capacity to love, bringing out the final florid *"speranza"* as a palpable affirmation of transcendent faith.

That night she sang the eighteenth century—Scarlatti, Pergolesi, Giordani, Paisiello, Caccini, Carissimi, Vivaldi, and Mozart. Was she making it clear to us that she *was* the eighteenth century, that we were to understand her in its terms? If she had wandered out of her age, she had not gone far, but had followed its natural development into Rossini. It seemed clear to me that black leather and lace had little to do with the rise of her career. The enthusiasm of her listeners had to be explained in a more complex and demanding way, perhaps through an understanding of enthusiasm itself. Our word is derived from a cluster of Greek concepts; from *enthusiasmos,* which means "divine possession or inspiration"; from *enthousiazein,* "to be god-inspired"; from *enthousiastikos,* which gives us our word *enthusiastic.* Perhaps indeed Bartoli was the old bel canto dream fully realized. She had been taught to respect the natural qualities of her voice. Her voice rang pure and true in every register, the tones merging imperceptibly into one another, without the least interruption of the breath. She had the capacity to reveal the innermost soul of a woman. She had a deeply spiritual nature and might best be understood as something more even than a singer. Perhaps, whether she knew it or not, her voice was indeed a feather on the breath of god or even that breath itself.

Okay then, I had to meet her. Yes, along with her two million other fans. I wanted to ask her directly whether these ideas about her singing were legitimate interpretive intuitions. As interpretations, they seemed to have been suggested by her appearance on stage, the music she chose to sing, the way she sang it. Should I, in the full grip of my enthusiasm, write her a fan letter?

After the third concert I began to spend a serious amount of time listening to Cecilia Bartoli. A naive enthusiasm might make one into a silly goose, but a serious enthusiasm seemed to promote a disciplined concentration. Bartoli had never recorded the Mozart songs, but songs and arias from the rest of the concert were available and I put together a taped approximation of her recital. My repeated listenings, which often lasted late into the night, confirmed my impression that she had a fine ability to enter a role and bring a character to life, a capacity that now made me impatient to see her in an opera. In her interpretation, during the recital, of Rossini's five settings of *"Mi lagneró tacendo,"* she had given the impression that she was five different women, each responding uniquely to a lover's betrayal. Rossini had composed close to fifty different settings of the text, written from a man's point of view, by the eighteenth-century poet, Metastasio. Some scholars regard these highly experimental chamber pieces as an ironic meditation on the nonsense of music, Rossini amusing himself, in his retirement, by making the same text serve some fifty different musical ends. When Bartoli gets hold of the songs, however, their ironic origins have been transformed by her characteristic emotional authenticity. She sings words spoken by a man to a woman with the unmistakable emotional inflection of a woman betrayed in love (a transgender adventure reminiscent of Brigitte Fassbaender's interpretation of Schubert's *Winterreise,* a song cycle written for a male voice and rarely performed by a woman). In the intimate darkness of my own listening to Bartoli's recording, I felt as if I had been invited into the emotional states of a single woman, who was bringing herself through anger to a muted resignation; to a futile effort to take things lightly; to a lyrical outpouring of feeling, designed perhaps to win the lover back; to a final grim facing of the truth. Yet somehow, through these detailed emotional states, Bartoli had managed to insinuate an almost inaudible sob, so that anger, resignation, lightheartedness, and fatal acceptance were all built up over a ground note of suffering and loss. I felt a definite connection between these songs and *"Sposa,"* and was again struck by the impression that Bartoli had a secret knowledge of the way emotion became music and was then transformed, through the performer, into emotion again.

Yes, I had to meet her. In Europe, she had already performed Rossini's Rosina, Mozart's Despina, Zerlina, and Cherubino. Was I about to go halfway around the world to see her onstage? And having seen her, how would I talk to her? Would I make my way backstage, push through the crowd of admirers to blurt out everything I had ever thought about music in an effort to catch her attention? I was beginning to think that my studious, concentrated listening to Bartoli had taken on qualities of a magical effort. I was trying to make the voice materialize as Bartoli the person, so that I could tell her what I thought about her and find out what she thought about that. It was a dialogue that had to take place. If I had to listen to her recordings for seven hours straight, seven days in a row, for seven weeks, I would do it. If God was, as I often suspected, an intrinsically musical being, I would be able to reach him with this form of prayer.

II

A Conversation

1993

On our way to Houston, where Cecilia Bartoli had just made her American stage debut in *The Barber of Seville,* Renate says, "People can't have a normal reaction to genius. They fall either into idolatry or into panic."

"Panic?"

"The immediate intense worry about losing this treasure that has just appeared. 'What will happen to her voice? Will she keep it? Will it grow?'"

"That's envy. I don't hear any real concern for the voice in that. It's a wish to cast an evil eye, to doom it."

"Well, if it's doomed, then everything is back to normal."

"Why not just go out and worship this great thing that has been given to the world?"

"To love a voice in that way involves the incalculable risk of suffering its loss."

"Some people just can't bear to be swept off their feet. They have to immediately turn and attack the very thing that might transport them."

"Well, that's what I mean by panic."

"Why bother with music if you don't want to be swept up into a rapture?"

"Some people like to approach these things more slowly. But that doesn't mean they have less appreciation once they get there."

On the way to the house where Cecilia Bartoli was living during the weeks she performed *The Barber of Seville* with the Houston Grand Opera, I did not think the interview would take place. When the cab passed a house with a piece of paper tacked to the door, Renate and I both thought the interview had been canceled. When we knocked at the stately home with the right address, when no one came immediately to open the door, I was certain no one would come. God may have loved an enraptured phrase, but he was also known to be a trickster. If my prayer to meet Cecilia Bartoli had been answered, at a time when her agent was broadly turning down publicity requests and had refused outright to give a profile to the *New Yorker,* I could be thankful that my interview for *San Francisco Focus* magazine had been granted. But that did not mean the interview would take place. There was always the last minute, when the best-laid plans could suddenly unravel. It did not seem reasonable to expect that the singer, whose voice I had studied for the last two and a half years, was also a woman who could open a door to a guest cottage back by the pool.

We knock, the door opens, Cecilia Bartoli is there, dressed in a one-piece cotton sunsuit; her dark hair is pulled back from her temples and tucked casually behind her ears. Younger, less glamorous than the stage person, she is wearing no makeup or lipstick. She seems welcoming, shy, polite, not exactly receptive, but suggesting, I thought, a willingness to be so if the interview went well. She offers coffee, we accept, Cecilia Bartoli goes off to prepare it. I find myself cursing the minutes lost to our sixty-minute conversation.

I had prepared for the interview with a notebook full of cross-referenced questions, observations, and comments, most of which I had copied out again on bits of paper torn from the hotel stationery so that I could organize them in thematic piles. I had grouped my questions into the interpretive categories that had been evolving over the years. Mother and daughter. Eighteenth century. Spirituality. The singer as divine messenger. Above all, I wanted to keep myself from blurting out what I was feeling, a habit of mine that cannot be thoroughly disciplined. The notes made an appearance just once during the interview and were never heard from again. They certainly did not succeed in restraining me.

Now that we were all seated I found myself talking in what seemed to me a torrent of words, but which Renate claims was a tolerably slow, reflective pace.

"Well, we're nervous."

"Oh, why?"

"We are very great admirers of yours. We heard you for the first time in Berkeley two and a half years ago. It was an amazing experience because we didn't know who you were. Nobody in the audience knew who you were yet. So you think to yourself, How can this be? This shouldn't be happening. Not to me. Not in my lifetime. I thought I was hearing one of the greatest voices I ever heard."

Bartoli thinks this over, then receives the outburst graciously. She seems to know when someone is speaking the truth, however exuberantly. And then, since I have used up my initial momentum, she says, "When did you arrive in Houston?"

"Yesterday. We came to see you."

"Did you see the performance? How did you get tickets?"

"We called the box office. The man told us the performance had been sold out for months. Then he said, 'Hey, look at this, just now two tickets have been turned back in.' Things like this make you think your prayers have been answered."

"It's a strange production," Bartoli responds. "It's not traditional. The stage is not comfortable, because we have two different levels. It's very hard to walk. Because of that I have to think every time more about my feet, not about my voice. Not every time. But sometimes I really have to be careful when I walk."

Renate says, "That's not the impression it gave."

"Really?" This question is asked with curiosity, a desire to be told the truth.

"Really. One could see that you are a dancer. Even a trained mime. Had you studied commedia dell'arte?"

"No, I haven't studied, but I have seen many productions. My mother, she is a singer. My father, too. When I was a child, my parents took the children to the opera every night. My father was in the chorus. And so maybe for this reason I am comfortable . . . I have seen many singers, many productions."

With these words Cecilia Bartoli has taken on a strangely ageless quality, as if she were as old as music itself. I note this impression; it lasts through the rest of our time together and reminds me of Monteverdi's conviction that music imitates the passions. With her great gift for expressive inflection, perhaps this is indeed the arcane knowledge in which Cecilia Bartoli was born to instruct us.

"Wasn't your mother in the chorus as well?"

"Yes, she sang solo for five years. But after she married, with three children, well . . . impossible for her to continue."

"Did she speak about that when you were growing up? The loss of her solo career?"

"Oh yes . . ."

Here, a silence falls. No one wants to interrupt it, all three of us perhaps thinking about our mothers.

Finally, I say, "Your mother regretted it?"

"Well, she had a beautiful, beautiful voice. She has it now, too. Much more beautiful than my voice."

This woman says what she means. Nevertheless, I say, because I am having trouble taking it in, "A more beautiful voice than yours? You think so?"

"Yes, yes. Because it's a natural voice. I studied to become a singer. She was born with it. That's different."

If ever I have heard a god-given voice, it is that of Cecilia Bartoli.

"Yes," she agrees, "my voice, it's natural. But not compared to my mother. For example, my voice is natural, okay, but I studied to understand the support of the voice, to open the larynx. My mother never did. For her it was just there. When she was fifteen she went to the *conservatorio* to study music. She had the voice already made."

"But we think the same of you."

"Well, in one sense yes. I started to take lessons with her, it was very easy for me to understand. Compared to other singers, yes, you could say it was much faster for me. I spent two or three years studying for the technique and maybe it would take another singer ten years. I study now, too. I have to study. So for me it was easy in this sense, compared to other young singers. But it was still easier for my mother."

"Are you still studying with your mother?"

"Oh yes."

"Is she still your only teacher?"

"Yes. Oh yes. When I was in the *conservatorio* in Rome I had other teachers. A teacher for theory, for piano, for history. I also had one teacher for the voice. But she"—there is a momentary hesitation—"she was . . . a nice person."

"The real learning has come from your mother?"

"Yes, from my mother."

When Cecilia Bartoli is excited, hands, arms, fingers come to life. She laughs, throwing herself back in the chair. She sings a phrase to make a point. The quick light in the dark eyes, which have their own dark voice, gives the impression of an elemental power barely restrained, perhaps out of courtesy to the conversation, not from fear of those elemental forces in herself.

For the first time, I take out my notes. I have written the name of every song on my favorite Bartoli disc, *If You Love Me*. For each song, I have made notes, noted questions, some of which date back to the first time I heard her sing. I have a vivid impression of the moment she walked out onto the stage, how young she was, her shyness. Since then, I have imagined this conversation with her, this very conversation about these songs.

"There are twenty-one songs in this album. Maybe twelve are songs of loss of love and despair. The music is very deep, very melancholy. At the same time, I keep hearing something sacred in the way you sing them. That is what I am so drawn to in your voice. But am I right? Do you have the sense of carrying a sacred message?"

"If I have this sacred . . . ?" She hesitates, then repeats the word, as if she had never before thought to apply it to herself. "This sacred . . . ? I don't know. I love this music, I really feel this music, I love to sing, I like Paisiello, Scarlatti, Vivaldi. It's very important for me when the music is very pure, very pure. It was important for this recording. Many people know this music, but they don't *know* it, they hear the aria many times, but they don't *hear* it. Everyone studies these arias at the conservatories. But to sing them well, that is difficult. There must be a firm legato line but also something very, very natural. This is not an easy balance to find. But I wanted to sing them, I had a special feeling for this music. There are many nuances. I don't know the name for the feeling. The recording company didn't believe in this recording. That is why it was made with piano. Many of the pieces were written for orchestra, but the recording company says, 'We'll see, we'll try first with piano, it's very expensive with orchestra if the recording fails.' So it was a big surprise for me and for the recording company when the recording was a success. For me it's, well, what? It's like a joke! I didn't make a recording of Neapolitan songs. I don't know why these songs are a success, I don't know."

"I think it is something about the emotional intensity. Sometimes when you sing I have the impression it's hard for you to come back to the audience."

"Sometimes I am in another world. It's not hard to come back. Just, well, when the music is finished, I come back slowly."

I come back slowly. Yes, as she has done every time I have heard her sing. Slowly she comes back from another world. That is what I have wanted to know.

"There's something about that other world to which you go. I think you carry the audience there, too. There is something for me so moving about this experience, I can only use the word 'sacred.'"

"Something sacred? Something spiritual? Yes, yes, I understand. But it is hard to respond. Sometimes I myself am transported by the music and sometimes this happens to the public, too. But I don't know if there is a word for this. And that's good. If I have a word, I lose the feeling, perhaps. But sometimes, well, I feel as if . . . it is very funny to try to explain this. As if I am separated from my consciousness, as if someone else is directing it. I can see myself from far away. I am not in my body. But, if I am not in my body, who is in my body?"

"Well, who is?"

"I don't know. But I hope it is a very beautiful young man . . ."

An explosion of Bartoli laughter, during which I remember how easily she moves in and out of arias for nymphs or shepherds, mature women, adolescent boys. The word I would use for what she is describing is "inspiration."

We have been conducting this part of our conversation in French, which Bartoli prefers whenever the talk grows very serious. "*C'est évident,*" she says, "that there is a spirituality. For me, it is very important to think this. If I have to go on the stage, I have to believe in something. I always hope that things will go well and I ask to be helped. I had a professor, a teacher of piano who was also my music professor, and he was very important for me, for my musical life. He died four years ago. And sometimes when I sing I feel that he is there and is helping me. I don't believe that one dies and that's the end of it. I don't believe it. That is not possible. Sometimes it is important not to put a concrete image on a spiritual feeling or thought, but to feel that there is . . . a protector. *Enfin,* I can't touch this with my hands. But there is a spirituality, whether a woman or a man or a star, does it matter?"

"I think what matters is that one finds this spirituality in music. Why else have I come all the way to Houston to hear you? Seriously, I ask myself this question."

She waits seriously for an answer in a silence that seems to become the answer.

"The recital is more pure than opera," she says. "It is very exposed, you must show more states of the soul. The Eternal Father gives me the ability to do this, with my voice. That is why I am here. To give people this joy, this beauty."

And now I wonder if Bartoli herself has a favorite singer, someone for whom she would travel across the country, around the world. Has she had the experience of hearing a great voice for the first time and feeling that she has been changed by it?

"Well, I like very much a certain singer, yes. But she is from the past. I have a recording of her. Conchita Supervia, you know her? Of course, I never saw her. I have a recording of *Cenerentola,* from Czechoslovakia. When I hear her voice, I feel something . . . hard to say in words. I feel, we are the same. I feel, this is what I too have inside me. I feel, I don't know how to say . . . maybe I say, this voice of Conchita Supervia, this is my voice. Of course, I would go to hear her, anywhere. Anywhere. To take pleasure. To learn. If you take pleasure something stays in the mind and the heart and that is a lesson, too."

*B*el canto skills, as Rossini understood them, depended on three crucial elements. First, the voice, the instrument itself, which he referred to as "the Stradivarius." Next, the technical skill of the singer. Finally, the way in which the beautiful voice expressed its technical accomplishment tastefully and with feeling.

Rossini found these qualities in Isabella Colbran, the leading singer of the Teatro San Carlo in Naples when Rossini became the musical director of the city's opera houses in 1815. During the next seven years he created ten operas for the various theaters of Naples, but it was for Colbran, who later became his wife, that the demanding coloratura arias of those years were composed.

Colbran was the daughter of the court musician to the king of Spain. She had studied with Crescentini, one of the leading castrati of his time. From 1801 to 1822 she was regarded as the finest coloratura soprano in Europe. Rossini had first heard her in 1807 in Bologna, when he was a music student. There is no record of his first impression of this voice that a decade later was to inspire his music. Therefore, when I have tried to imagine the adolescent Rossini's response to the first hearing of Colbran's voice, I have placed him in the audience during Bartoli's first performance in Berkeley.

The novelist Stendhal, Rossini's contemporary and biographer, described Colbran as she was in 1815, when Rossini met her again in Naples:

> It was a beauty in the most queenly tradition: noble features which, on the stage, radiated majesty; an eye like that of a Circassian maiden, darting fire;

and to crown it all, a true and deep instinct for tragedy." (Stendhal, *The Life of Rossini,* p. 157)

An echo of this admiration can be found in reviews of Bartoli onstage. "Her dark good looks project grandly across the footlights: a mane of lustrous hair, huge brown eyes, a generous mouth and milky shoulders that enhance a décolletage."(Martha Duffy, *Time,* December 14, 1992)

James Jolly, writing about Bartoli for *Gramophone* (February 1992), wonders whether Isabella Colbran "had a voice to match that of Signorina Bartoli, our newest and most lustrous Rossinian primissima donna [with] a temperament that can be fiery and affecting by turns."

In younger days, Colbran amazed audiences with a dark voice that ranged from G below the stave to E flat *in alt.* In the arias Rossini wrote for her during his Neapolitan years, he regularly sends her down to A flat and even G, but asks her to ascend only occasionally to a high C. Today, we would consider Colbran a coloratura mezzo-soprano with a facility in the higher registers. The chromatic runs, the astonishing vocal leaps, the florid cadenzas and showers of coloratura Rossini wrote for Colbran likewise indicate a virtuosity similar to Bartoli's. But these demanding, dramatic roles that Colbran sang with mature interpretive power during her prime have posed neither interpretive or technical difficulty for Bartoli, who recorded them fearlessly during the first five years of her career, when she was in her mid-twenties (*Rossini Heroines,* London/Decca, 1991).

During my conversation with Bartoli, I could easily picture her as a member of the troupe of the Teatro San Carlo, a majestic theater with an opera company that possessed outstanding singers and a magnificent orchestra. As we talked, Bartoli seemed to me more than ever a being poised between the late eighteenth and the early nineteenth century, carrying the "sense of the brilliance, tonal homogeneity and stylistic address" of the castrati of the old order, while embodying "the new order of singing actresses with brilliantly developed coloratura techniques stretching across several registers of the voice." (Richard Osborne, *Rossini,* p. 11)

But would a throwback know she was a throwback? Would she feel instinctively that she was of the eighteenth century? And how, in a conversation that seems to move with its own winding thematic drift, would I be able to pose this delicate question?

"Many people say the whole musical world is waiting to see how your voice develops over the next ten years. Are you waiting?"

"Well, some people . . . I think people never take pleasure . . ."

Her facial expression takes over where words fail. I see in her eyes—what? An impatience? The imperative need to be understood? Renate and I sit forward, eager to understand what she is about to say. But she remains silent.

"Some people never take pleasure . . . in what's there?"

"People are never happy," she says slowly, deliberately. "It's strange. If you have one thing, they want the other. When some critics write, they say the technique is good, the acting is good, the expression is good, but the voice is a little small. So, I think this is not really constructive. Because if I try, if the technique is not good, I can develop it, I study it. If the acting is not good, I make it better. If some people tell me, Well you have to think about this bar, the nuance here, the nuance there, I do it with pleasure. But if some people tell me, You have to have a big voice, *non é possibile.* It's not possible."

"But it's irrelevant. Your voice belongs to small, eighteenth-century theaters. We still have perfectly appropriate theaters. Covent Garden, Glyndebourne, Ferrara, Teatro Comunale di Bologna."

"In Italian, we have some proverbs. We say, *'Non è possibile di avere la botte piena e la moglie ubriaca.'*"

"It is not possible to have the cask full of wine and at the same time have the wife drunk?"

"Exactly. One or the other. In my case, it's not possible to have a big voice and have the coloratura. I know my limit."

"Is it a limit, or is that where the gift lies?"

"Well, I know why I am here. I am here for Mozart and Rossini and this repertory. I take pleasure in my repertory. You know? You understand? I love Mozart. For me, in ten years, I can't imagine I will stop singing Mozart because I have to sing another composer. Stop singing Mozart? He is an angel from paradise. With Rossini there is something else. He is more earthy, more spicy. I am like this, too. If I will be tired of Rossini, I will be tired of myself. Many people ask me to sing Carmen. I say no. I know my voice."

"Well, I quarrel with anyone who says we are waiting to see what happens to your voice in ten years. To me, your voice is already a fully developed expressive instrument."

"Maybe in some years I will sing Carmen. But for now, no. No."

"The task is to recognize what the voice is, in its own nature. This is the kind of voice, it seems to me, Mozart or Rossini would have recognized immediately."

Cecilia Bartoli claps her hands. She jumps up from her chair, glances quickly at me, then at Renate, sits down again, and leans forward confidingly. "I'm very happy, because now I start a new repertory with Haydn. How can I say? I am here for this music. *Io sono* . . . I am, you know? To be at home? For me, that is the eighteenth century."

"It's fitting that you have come on the scene with your voice and this expressive feeling just at a moment when the serious operas of Rossini are ready to be heard."

"Oh yes, oh yes. Now, we have this renaissance with Rossini serio. *Barbiere* is not the only Rossini. And now I start to sing with András Schiff. We are recording songs of Mozart, Schubert, Beethoven written in Italian, the only songs Schubert and Beethoven wrote in Italian. The text is from Metastasio and from Petrarca. I have special feeling for this music, it is so beautiful, the *combinazione* with the German music and Italian text. The sound is so sweet. I'm very happy. I know why I am here."

With these words I have the impression we have left the interview and entered a conversation. It is made up of the things we say, our response to them, which is for the most part not spoken, our almost musical absorption in the conversation itself, which changes languages, from English to Italian to French, as if refusing to tolerate linguistic obstacles to this unexpected communion between strangers.

*F*rom time to time I find myself peeping around the edges of our talk to take in consciously the personality of the woman with whom I am talking. I have met other (very) famous people, but never before found myself as riveted by the personality as by the artist. It seems to make no difference now that we are restricted to words. I feel the same magnetic spell the voice casts from the stage. I have the impression she too is absorbed in our conversation, which flows in and about the theme of mother and daughter, into odd channels of its own making, and then runs back to mothers and daughters again.

"How is it you are able to have such a strong sense of what's right for you, against all this chatter that goes on in the world?"

"You mean the sense of what I have to do? Well, my mother. My mother is very important in my career. When I start to sing, she directs me, she helps me to know."

"Your mother knew what was right for your voice?"

"Yes. She knew. Many times she says to me, 'Cecilia, you have to try it first. You have to find out for yourself. When you are home, working with a pianist, you can try this role. And if you feel comfortable, okay. If you don't feel comfortable, *lascia maturare.*'"

"Let it mature, let it develop?"

"Yes."

"She's not pushing you then."

"My mother? Oh, no."

"I wanted to ask you about her. She's not just a mother with a daughter."

"Oh, no. For me, she is a great teacher for technique. And not just for technique. For the words, the expression, the meaning. This is interesting. Because, you know? For my mother, I was an experiment. She never taught before."

"You are her first student?"

"I am my mother's only student. She tried with me because my passion was for flamenco, not for opera. When I started to go to flamenco school . . . well, it was not school. It was with a dancer. I started to take lessons, then I completely forgot school, I stopped everything. There was just flamenco."

Because I am a stranger, I do not ask whether this sudden interest in flamenco was also an interest in the teacher. I have read somewhere that Cecilia, at the age of sixteen, took off for Paris with a friend; they ran out of money, had to sing on street corners and in the Métro before they could earn their fare home. In her biographical video on *The South Bank Show,* Cecilia says she began making excursions into Rome against her parents' wishes. I am aware of the interviewer's right to ask provocative questions, but I say only, "How old were you then?"

"Just a little before fifteen. Fifteen, sixteen. And my mother, when she realized my life was only the flamenco, she knew there was no future for me. Because the flamenco in Italy, it's not serious art. Many people think the flamenco is just a hobby. If I want to study flamenco I have to go to Spain, and well, it was a little dream. But not *realizzabile*. My mother knows this. She understands what could make a career. She says to me, 'Yes, okay, if you want to dance, you dance. But you and I, we start to take lessons with the voice.' I say to her, 'No, it's not for me.' I just say, 'No, no, not me, no.' So when I start with her it is something like a joke. 'Well, we'll see.' So I start with her. At first my mother would not let me sing even a simple song. We work on only one note at a time. You know the song by Pergolesi, *'Se tu m'ami'*? Many students start with this song. But my mother, she says to sing this song is very, very difficult. To sing purely is difficult, to sing with meaning, nuance, is difficult. So we work one note at a time and at first I find it very boring. We have months of exercises. Very boring. But one day I hear my own voice come out and I think, Can this be me? Can this be me? I see I have something in there. Something I didn't know before."

Until now, I have been thinking of the effect of a voice on a listener. I never wondered about the singer's first impression of her own voice, that moment when she hears the trained voice newly emerging out of months or years of vocal exercise. But this is also the moment I have been so curious about. What happened, little by little, day by day, that made it possible for the mother to guide the daughter to this first, astonished awakening to her own gift?

"Your mother knew the voice was there?"

"She knew my musicality. She taught me the voice. We worked very hard for the *passaggio,* for the voice to go smoothly from one register to the next. My mother says nothing is more difficult in singing. And she is right. The voice must have the same color, the same tone in every register. Until I learned to sing correctly, my mother did not let me sing even a simple song."

The soprano Renata Tebaldi and her mother were inseparable, living, traveling together, each apparently the central figure in the life of the other. But the Tebaldi mother was a warm, comforting, and devoted companion, never a teacher who had taken on the responsibility for the development of the daughter's gift.

Maria Callas and her mother have left behind their stormy tale of anger, rejection on both sides, open acrimony, dramatic feuds, bitter envy. With most other great singers one never hears a word about the mother, as if she had no relevance in the daughter's career but had simply been left behind when the daughter took off into the world.

Christa Ludwig, the great German mezzo, whom Bartoli admires, had been taught singing by her mother, who had also had an operatic career. Recently, I learned that Joan Sutherland had also been taught by her mother. There may be other such relationships of which we are not aware. The journalist who wrote a major profile of Bartoli for *Vanity Fair*, although invited to the Bartoli home, showed no interest whatsoever in the mother, the determining influence in her daughter's career, but expressed instead a desire to talk to the father, who was no longer living at home, and who had not been Bartoli's teacher.

When Cecilia dropped out of school and took off for Paris, her mother may have felt that her daughter was headed for serious trouble. Perhaps, when Cecilia got caught up in flamenco dance, her mother sensed the emergence of an artistic gift that could not yet name itself. She may have wanted to provide her daughter with an inner discipline, a concentration that could protect her against the hazards of adolescence. She herself has described her method of teaching Cecilia, stressing the need for a singer to develop a strong will, to want to be the best, to achieve the commanding presence, the sheer naked courage required to face an audience. One can easily imagine her brooding about Cecilia, her eldest daughter, who was running wild. She may have spent hours thinking about her daughter's future. In the rare interviews she has given, she has spoken frankly of her wish to see her daughter have the musical career she, the mother, had to sacrifice. The mother as teacher, what a marvelous solution. As teacher, she would be able to free the daughter from the burden of the mother's unlived life. In helping to create the daughter's voice she would also create herself as a teacher. Then she would be able to give, from a mother's intuition, what a great teacher can give—the gift of the self, the calling up of the daughter's own capacities so that they can make their claim on her.

"When I studied with my mother it was not only two hours a day. If I am singing in the kitchen, you know, singing for myself, or in the bathroom, I hear her call out, 'Cecilia, *non e giusto*. It's not correct.' My mother teaches me that I must never force the voice, the sound comes from the breath, the breath rests on the diaphragm, I must sing freely. Sometimes I like to tease her, so I sing something wrong to see if she is listening."

"Was she listening?"

"*Sempre, sempre*. Always listening."

In the laughter that follows, Bartoli says, "When I was a child, in the summer, when the opera was in the Baths of Caracalla, my brother and I made it our playground. We played all over the scenery for *Aïda*. But then I sing music, not opera. Well, one time I sang opera when I was eight. I sang the shepherd in *Tosca*. But just this one time. Because my father asked me. 'Cecilia, if you want to sing the shepherd, why don't you sing?' He promised me a video game. With the money from this role he promised to buy video games. I sang, but he never bought the video games."

"Tell him that he owes you the video game."

"I told him. He got a television. But, well, never the video games."

"Are you still waiting for the video games?"

"No, no. I know my father. When I was eight, I didn't know."

"You believed him."

"Yes, exactly."

"But now you know—what? He makes promises, but . . ."

"Well, it's his character. When he promises, he means it, he wants to buy the video game for you. But he forgets . . ."

"Very different from your mother."

"Oh yes, very, very. It's very interesting, because when I sing, my mother comes and she is a support, really. She never has fear before my performance. My father, no. I don't want him there because he makes me nervous."

"I have the impression he's not living at home anymore."

"Exactly. For this reason he's not in the video. But also for another reason. The people come from the television station in Rome, but father and mother together are not good. They are not good together. So it was much better to leave him out."

"Was he nervous with his own singing, or is this . . ."

"It is when I sing."

"Only for you?"

"Oh yes. For me." Here, she hesitates, reconsidering. "Well, when he sings, in the past, yes he was nervous. I'm nervous, too. Sure, everyone is nervous before a performance. I am always looking for the bathroom backstage. But he . . ." Cecilia Bartoli has thrown herself back in the chair, shaking with laughter. "If my father stays home the day before a performance, he just starts with his *nervosismo*, you know?"

A quick gesture of her hands and shoulders renders the nervous temperament of the father. "My mother and father, it is much better for them to separate. Many people think it's possible to make a marriage. But after they marry, well, it's not. I think my mother was in love with my father for the music, for the voice. It's unbelievable to see my parents very happy with music, when they sing together. But when the music is finished—aagh, like a war. They never had a life together outside of music. Twenty-five years ago, the life was different in Italy and many people don't want to separate. My mother, she doesn't want to separate, maybe she thinks, In the future it will be better. I think this was wrong, a mistake. My mother separated from my father not long ago, a few years ago. I love my father. He has a big sense of humor. He has temperament. He's a dramatic tenor, *molto spinto*. I think with another wife . . . well, my father is naïve, a dreamer. I think for my father maybe it was better to have a naïve wife. My mother has her feet on the ground. She is steady, *costante*. They are not good together. This is not a secret. It is just life."

*R*ichard Stasney, the medical advisor to the Houston Grand Opera, knocks at the door. He has brought Cecilia an umbrella and an opportunity to end our conversation. We offer to leave, she immediately declines. I point out that our hour and then some has gone by. She says that she is not tired.

She is talking about the expressive relationship between words and music when a violent clap of thunder crashes through the guesthouse. Cecilia Bartoli does not look up, does not hesitate for an instant, apparently is not aware of it. Moods flow through this conversation as if they were absorbed in their own passage from somewhere else. What happens outside, beyond this room, to the overcast sky suddenly broken open, to the swimming pool spattered with rain, does not seem to matter. But I have an assignment. I am here to check out my various intuitions about the singer. I turn the conversation back to Bartoli, who gives the impression she would rather talk about music.

"I wanted to talk to you about this song, *'Sposa son disprezzata.'* We heard you sing it the first time in 1991 in Berkeley. We have heard it many times since. There is so much despair in this song. A woman despised, rejected, but still faithful to the husband. When you sing this song you seem transported. For some reason, I associate this song with your mother. Is there anything to that?"

"Well, my mother was there when I studied the song. We discussed the song together. We discussed the words. They are very important. She says to me, 'Cecilia, what do you think this means?'"

I am so eager to hear more about this meeting place of words and music that I find myself speechless. Renate picks up the conversation.

"So you discuss the words," she says, "the expressive color, the meaning? And that's where the emotional impression starts to form?"

"Yes, exactly. We discuss where the music and the words come together."

"Do you imagine that you are *la sposa*?" Renate asks.

"Oh yes, absolutely. It is the only possibility. It is not possible to stay Cecilia and sing *'Sposa.'*"

"But you are not *sposa disprezzata,* scorned, insulted."

"Not yet!"

"You know it's coming?"

"It's coming, it's coming."

We laugh, but there is more than laughter here.

"But is it your mother?" I say. "Is she *sposa disprezzata?*"

"Oh yes, in one sense, yes."

Here there is a reflective pause, a sense of time passing easily. Even in the silence there is the focused concentration that has marked the entire conversation. I have already noticed Cecilia Bartoli's acutely absorbed listening to what is being said. Now I become aware of her capacity to make use of silence. Because I am observing her closely, I notice how completely she gives herself over to the moment. In this, she lacks all trace of the self-absorption one expects to find in a star.

"Well," she says at last, *"'disprezzata'* maybe is not the word. Maybe *'non realizzata.'* Her life is not realized."

Another silence. We let an unspoken impression pass back and forth between us without hurrying to give it form. I remember my early impressions of *"Sposa."* It seems that there is, indeed, in Bartoli's singing the echo of the mother's muted solo voice, that pure, lyric soprano given up to raise children. The restrained sorrow of this never fully realized voice has been part of the mysterious transmission of musical knowledge from mother to daughter. Perhaps this accounts for the maturity of the daughter's expressiveness.

"What do you plan to do in terms of your career, when it's time to marry?"

She looks up with an expression of great curiosity, as if wondering what she will say. "Oh, I don't know. I don't have any plans. I don't think about it. It's not a rush."

"You are not worried about it, although you have seen this in your mother's life, this not being realized?"

"Well, I think that marriage is not really important to me. The most important for me is to have, well, *amour,* to have love, you know? And the children, okay, I would like children. But we'll see. *Amour* first. Because I know. I know children, marriage without love, it's not easy."

"Were your parents angry at each other?"

"My father has a big temperament."

"Does this mean he shouts a lot?"

"Shouts?"

"Loud voice?"

"Oh yes, oh yes. I've never seen an Italian with a small voice. But for the children it's not good. We get used to it. But it's not good. When the mother is afraid, well, it's hard to explain, it's not a quiet situation. My mother's life is inside her, but not lived."

"Does your mother have any students now? Have students come to her?"

"No, she doesn't want students."

"But do students want to meet with her?"

"Yes, yes. Many people want to work with her. And she . . . Well, this is interesting. She doesn't want this. She says, 'It's not possible for me to just experiment with them. My daughter was an experiment, but she's my child.'"

"So she hesitates, she's not confident she could do the same thing for someone else that she did for her child?"

"Yes, maybe she thinks that. But I think it is possible for her. Because she knows voice very well, she has her own method to open the throat." Bartoli opens her mouth and points to her throat. "What do you call this?"

"The larynx, the glottis?"

"Yes, maybe. She taught me how to lower the *gola,* like yawning, with the tongue low." She demonstrates the technique for us, opening her mouth, pointing to her tongue, thrusting her head forward to let us gaze down into the mysterious darkness from which the Bartoli voice emerges. "This way," she adds, "the voice comes with a beautiful sound. So, we practice one note at a time and slowly, slowly, there is a beautiful sound in the full range of the voice."

"But still your mother doesn't want to become a teacher. Maybe you're enough for her?"

"Well, I think it's too bad. Many, many young singers will want to have help, and it's possible for her to help many people, I'm sure."

"Do you talk to her about that?"

"Yes, we talk. She says, well, *'Vediamo, vediamo.'* We'll see, we'll see. But I tell her, Mommy, if you don't want to give the individual lessons, you can give a master class."

I have seen films of Elisabeth Schwarzkopf with her students. She is unaccepting of any but the very highest accomplishments, impatient, sharp, insistent that they produce their best. Some of her students are crushed by this. The best seem brought to the exercise of their highest art, precisely because it is being uncompromisingly demanded by someone who knows what the highest is. I wonder if Bartoli's mother is a teacher of this sort.

Certainly, the mother as teacher would have to draw out from the daughter what was distinct, true, and unique in the child without confusing the daughter's gifts with her own. She would have to recognize the strengths and weaknesses of the voice she was helping to create so that she could guide the daughter to music suitable for her voice, as Silvana Bazzoni had drawn Cecilia to Mozart and Rossini. The work between Cecilia and her mother had been as significant as the appearance on the world stage of the Bartoli voice itself. Is Silvana Bazzoni shy? Full of self-doubt? She could now make a career for herself as a famous teacher. Does she hesitate, as once before, when it was a question of her own career? Is it she who, once again, feels that she must sacrifice herself for her daughter?

"She finally was able to separate from your father," I say, as if this fact has suddenly taken on new meaning. "But that was after you were already studying with her."

"Oh yes, I was at home studying with her and my father was there, too."

I have the feeling Cecilia Bartoli knows what I am thinking. She watches my face. Once again, I cannot bring myself to say things that seem too intimate for a conversation between strangers. But I would like to ask whether the mother's work with the daughter, gradually, over the first several years, made it possible for her to leave the father, as if this work between the two women, which created the daughter's voice, also created the mother's independence.

*R*ichard Stasney checks in to see how we are doing. This time he brings another two umbrellas and invites us to lunch. He tells us that Cecilia has not yet eaten breakfast.

I say to her, "You must be tired."

"No, no, I'm fine."

"You're sure?"

"Yes. When I'm tired, I will tell you. When I'm hungry, I will tell you, too."

But there's still the problem of the plane, our luggage at the hotel. Richard Stasney has seen to all this. A cab will be waiting for us at the restaurant when we have finished lunch. The hotel is on the way to the airport. There will be time to eat, continue our conversation, drive past the hotel, get to the airport on time.

But the conversation is not easy to interrupt. We stand in the lovely small room without taking the final steps to put on raincoats and outdoor shoes. We speak fast now; our time together is coming to an end.

She picks up her coffee cup from the floor next to the chair, places it carefully on the wooden table. She says, thoughtfully, as if there had been no interruption and she had not already said it before, "I say to her, 'Mommy, if you don't want to give the lessons individually you can give the master class . . .'"

"Why do you think she hesitates?"

"I don't know. I don't know. Yes, it is a big responsibility. And I think she is afraid—what if the student does not understand? Yes, that is the reason."

"She knows she can communicate the teaching to you . . ."

"Yes, to me . . ."

"Because you are her daughter?"

"Exactly. This is what I wanted to explain before. I am her daughter and, well, I know. We work hard but at the same time I know. So we work hard, but also it is very easy. She says to me, 'Cecilia, come over here, we try something.' I say, 'No, no, I'm busy.' 'Cecilia, come here. We'll do some exercise, we'll start with something easy.' She teaches me the breath is the most important. The breath is a technique; the control of the voice, but also part of the emotion, the expression. Okay, we start with something easy. But after the easy, well . . . With new students, new people, she doesn't know if she can teach them. Maybe she thinks, There cannot be a big teacher if this teacher did not have her own big teacher."

I recall the image that came to me when I began to listen to Bartoli's recordings, the bel canto lineage of teacher and student, masters and disciples transmitting a knowledge that had been built up over the centuries through the study of voice. It seems to me that Bartoli's mother, who has trained her daughter to the exacting standards of bel canto, belongs to this tradition but may not recognize it in herself. In spirit and technical mastery she might have stepped directly out of those fine bel canto schools, with her respect for the voice's natural endowment and development, her emphasis on the sheer, exquisite beauty of tone, the lack of strain, the mastery of breath, the equalization of registers. When Cecilia's mother has her daughter practice over and over again with a single note, she reminds us of the familiar (if apocryphal) story about singing master Porpora limiting the castrato Caffarelli to a single page of exercises for five or six years. The story probably does not do justice to the breadth of the castrati's musical culture, but it may well point to the thoroughness of the castrati's early vocal education.

"Does she hesitate to teach because she's still working with you?"

"Yes, sure. But this is not really the reason. Because she has time if she wants it. I'm here, for example, and she's in Italy."

"So we don't know all the reasons she hesitates."

"She has retired now. She is receiving her pension. And now she says that she doesn't want to do anything. She has already worked a lot. With her singing in the chorus, and three children, and with a husband who is there but . . . well, she has worked a lot in her life. And so she says, 'Well, now I'll just play *la signora*.'"

We share a laugh about this; also, about the conspicuous relief daughters of our class would feel about the mother's ability to retire, lavishly.

Bartoli says, "But I think her life is still with the music. Yes, that is sure. Maybe now she will have the time to think about becoming a teacher."

"You might have to convince her to take this risk with another person. When I saw the way you and she were working together, in the video, I thought, She's a born teacher. She looks for what is there in the student. She sees the particular gift. She says, 'Come. Bring me that.' My guess would be that she could do it with other people too."

"Oh yes, I think so, too."

"She is fifty-six years old. She could begin a whole new career at this point. But you may have to urge her. Maybe she prefers to travel with you?"

"She travels sometimes with me. But she doesn't get involved with the business. She knows how to draw the line. She knows her limits."

The stage mother, merged with her daughter, using the child to make good the disappointments of her own life, living through her, terrified of losing influence and control, is a common feature of theatrical legend. But the crucial test that distinguishes the stage mother from mother as teacher is the ability to let go, to step back when the time comes, to let the daughter take up her own life.

"My mother knows it is possible for her to give me counsel about music. But not with the business. I have a manager for this. I'm very happy with him. When I started to sing, I have a different agent everywhere in Europe. One agent in Italy, one agent in France, one agent in Germany. It was crazy, because sometimes these people call me for the same engagement. So it was crazy to decide who will get the commission. I also had an agent in America. Mr. Mastroianni is not the first one. I had an agent in the same company. But that one can't do anything for me, he can't get me any engagements. I don't know why. I think some people don't realize which talent they have in their hands. Mr. Mastroianni, he is in love with Rossini and he recognizes the situation. The music world is interested in Rossini and I am interested in Rossini, too. He believes in my voice. He believes in me, in my talent. I don't have to explain to him what I want to do, this is not good for me, this is good. He just asks, 'Cecilia, do you want to do this?' Then I decide. He always supports my idea for the project, for the role."

"So your mother is not the only influence on your musical life?"

"I have my mother, Mr. Mastroianni, György Fischer. I also have Christopher Raeburn, my producer. He understands the voice, he has been here since the time of Tebaldi. When I read from new music or a new role, I ask him, 'What do you think, Christopher? Do you think it's good for my voice, because I would like to try it.' He tells me, 'Yes, Cecilia, you have to sing this role at home, then you will tell me how it feels to you.'"

"So you ask your mother and you ask Christopher Raeburn if something will be right for your voice, but then you try it and make up your own mind?"

"I talk with my mother, we talk it over, we try it together, we see how it feels."

Richard Stasney is back to remind us time is passing. He assures us we can continue our conversation in the restaurant. We walk outside into a light rain. Cecilia opens her umbrella and holds it over us. She tells us her mother will be arriving the following weekend, for the last performances. She asks if we would like to come back to meet her.

"Shall I try to convince her to become a teacher, to give a master class?"

We are laughing at the idea that I could have any influence on her mother, but when the laughter stops, Cecilia is serious again. "My mother's life is with the music. That is for sure. Maybe she rests now and that is okay. But she has her whole life to live. How can she live without the music?"

We are waiting for Richard Stasney to bring the car around. We talk about the San Francisco opera house, which Cecilia has visited and thinks is too large for her voice. She says that her mother takes Cecilia's recitals more seriously than her roles in opera. I tend to agree. Renate is an enthusiast for stage productions; she has fallen in love with Cecilia as a comic actress. Last night she said to me that Cecilia is to opera buffa what Callas was to tragedy. Cecilia points to her throat. "The coloratura is in here," she says. She points to her heart. "The comedy is here, and maybe someday the tragedy, too."

Renate wonders whether there is a role Cecilia would like to sing someday.

"I don't know. I like *Samson et Dalila,* but this is really a contralto role.

So it is only a dream. I can reach this range, but the role is really dramatic. So, well, it's my dream. For now, my voice is not right for this music. Maybe it's not possible. But we'll see. Maybe after I have a baby. Sometimes the voice changes. We'll see."

"Sure, have a baby and sing Dalila," I say as the car drives up.

"Have a baby and give it to your mamma to make another singer out of it?" Renate asks.

"People say singers have a normal life," Cecilia says in French as she closes the umbrella. "It's not true. Singers are gypsies. How can you have a serious love if you are never in the same place? Even friendship is difficult. I see many familiar faces in the audience when I perform, I see students I know from the *conservatorio*. But they don't come backstage after the performance. With the other women in the cast it is also difficult. There is jealousy, of course, the jealousy is always there. Someday I will perform less, maybe I will travel only for six months, then rest and study a new role the rest of the time."

We have been talking for a long time and are looking forward to the restaurant. Cecilia says, "When I am away from Roma the first thing I do is look for a good restaurant. Before the performance I can't eat, I'm too nervous. But afterwards, I eat everything, antipasto, soup, pasta, everything! I like to cook, I like to eat, at home I eat pasta for breakfast. You remember what I say on the video? Well, it's true. Sometimes I think my relationship to food is . . . well, almost sexual."

*O*n our way to the restaurant Richard Stasney plays Mozart's *"Exsultate, jubilate"* on his tape deck. I am in the front seat next to Stasney. Cecilia, Renate, and Stasney's son are in the back. He said that when he picked Cecilia up at the airport he was playing *"Exsultate, jubilate,"* Kiri Te Kanawa singing, and that Cecilia just started to sing along and soared right up into the high C's with no problem in the soprano register.

Stasney, the official physician to the Houston Grand Opera, is an expert in operatic throats. He recently examined Cecilia and thought that her range was formidable, that she could sing anything. He tells me that her vocal cords are fresh and healthy—long and white, without the red spots that indicate strain or forcing. This puts to rest certain stories I have heard from various vocal teachers about how Cecilia is straining her resources when she sings. Stasney adjusts the rearview mirror to catch Cecilia's eye. She has been sitting quietly, humming to herself, communing with her own voice. She acknowledges him with a smile and says, matter-of-factly, "Well, I have the notes also for the Queen of the Night. But the voice is too dark," she adds with a mischievous grin and then throws out a cluster of terrifying high notes from the queen's second-act aria in *The Magic Flute*. A year from now, she will arrive in New York for her debut at Carnegie Hall and will sing a selection from Bellini's *Sonnambula* in the original soprano key, a minor third higher than the expected key, because the correct orchestral parts will not have arrived on time.

In the restaurant, between the choosing of food, the excitement of dining in Houston's finest establishment, and Cecilia's introductions to Richard Stasney's friends who come up eagerly to the table, the conversation continues. I am struck by her concentration. She is polite, formal, gracious during introductions but then immediately returns from them to meet us again at our own level, whatever that is. When you are silent, she is silent with you. When you search for a word, she waits; when you find yourself (once again) suddenly talking about the sacred element in music, she is fascinated by the sacred element, too. The ease with which she moves from a high seriousness to earthy laughter, exchanging tastes of food, exclaiming about the garlic in my spinach salad, reminds me of her voice itself, with its perfectly balanced registers flowing effortlessly one into the other. But this is a conversation built on the musical form of theme and variation. Before long, we all know, we shall have made our way back to mothers and daughters. This time, it is Cecilia Bartoli who takes us there.

"My mother, she will arrive on Wednesday, for the performance. She is curious. I told her about this unusual production, where I have to think about my feet sometimes more than my voice."

"Will she come backstage afterwards and tell you what she thinks?"

"Afterwards? You think she will wait until afterwards?"

Her laughter at this is exuberant enough to catch our waiter. He stands happily with the large plate of pasta, behind Cecilia Bartoli, laughing with her.

I am reminded of some gossip I heard in Los Angeles. A young singer who had performed with Bartoli claimed that the mamma was stern, judgmental, critical, disapproving. In this account Cecilia had been visibly devastated by her mother's criticism after a performance; she lived only for her mother's approval and had developed no real personality of her own.

"My mother, she will be there right after the first intermission," Cecilia adds. "She will say, 'This is okay, that is not good, this went well, that could be better.'"

"And you believe her."

"My mother? Of course. She knows. My mother, she wants only the very good. She won't put up with anything else."

A vision of the old bel canto teachers shows up again.

"My voice is in here," Bartoli says, touching her neck with two fingers. "But I don't know it as well as my mother knows it. If I say to her, 'Mommy, what is wrong with this note?' my mother tells me, 'You do this, you do that, you don't support with the breath.' She knows."

Whose voice is this? This voice trained by the mother, whose teaching was practiced by the daughter, who at times must draw upon the deep, old knowing of the mother, which the daughter shapes in a register, deeper, darker than the mother's own. This amazing voice, which has startled the music world, is clearly the daughter's own unique accomplishment, yet it is equally the product of the days these two women have spent together, studying, rehearsing.

Cecilia Bartoli is smiling with delight about her mother. She performs a little mime of the mother's appearance backstage during the first intermission, the concentrated look, the knowing intensity. Then the wonderful laughter comes again, in which our entire table joins.

Maybe the Los Angeles story about the domineering stage mother is part of the false legend that tends to rise around a great career, as if we were capable only of outworn stories and cannot grasp the complex relationship of the mother as teacher to the daughter who is developing herself through the older woman.

But now the taxi has arrived. There are handshakes with Richard Stasney and his son. An embrace with Cecilia Bartoli, who tonight will be cooking pasta with peas, a Roman specialty, for a cast party. I am hoping we can make it back the next weekend, but you never know. This may be the last time I ever have lunch with my favorite singer.

Now that I am leaving it seems strange that I came all this way to ask the singer questions her voice has already answered. I think I was right in my intuition that there is something archaic in her voice, going back far beyond a single generation, perhaps centuries old, and that this old beauty has been passed on to the daughter through the mother. But the singer herself can only grope toward this knowledge. The sources of her inspiration live, as George Herbert describes it,

Quite under ground; as flowers depart
To see their mother-root, when they have blown
Where they together
All the hard weather
Dead to the world, keep house unknown.

The richness of Bartoli's voice reminds me of a half-heard impression of singing I once detected in the air around the Cycladic harper in the Getty Museum in Los Angeles. He is small, not more than a foot high, a sitting figure of soft, luminous marble. His hand rests patiently on the harp, his head is raised, he is listening. Through this listening, which has lasted three or four millennia now, the music will eventually reach the harp. It is this sound I hear in Cecilia Bartoli's voice, as if she is, at last, bringing to expression the archaic yearning of a breath, a silence.

III

❦

The Barefoot Diva

The Fourth and Fifth Concerts, 1994–1995

There is a photograph of Cecilia Bartoli in Salzburg during an interview in 1993, scampering along next to the river in a summer dress, her sneakers dangling over her shoulder. A year later, in downtown Pasadena, on a small patch of grass, she again whisks off her shoes and begins to run around. "Excuse me," she says to the interviewer, "but it's very important for me to feel the ground under my feet." When Bartoli showed up for an interview with *Newsweek* in 1993, she wore no shoes and no makeup. A year earlier, when she was in Los Angeles with her manager, Jack Mastroianni, they came to a hotel where "there was a whole grassy field. Immediately, Cecilia threw off her shoes and ran. She said, 'Excuse me for doing this, but when I was a little child one of the things that gave me the greatest pleasure was to go to the park across the street and have my feet feel the earth and the blades of grass.'"

If Bartoli is a diva, she is determined to remain a barefoot diva—grounded, steady, good-natured, an enthusiastic participant in ensemble work, ferocious only where the question of musical integrity is concerned. Cynics (and some music reviewers) wonder, How long? How long before she acquires the temperament, the willfulness, the indifference to others, the headstrong self-regard of the stock diva? When her third Berkeley concert sold out within days, I too began to ask myself, How long? It was her health and stamina that concerned me. I had begun to worry that the world would exhaust Bartoli before she had a chance to give the world what was in her. She was generous, spontaneous, warm-hearted, enthusiastic, and she loved to sing. When I thought about Hans Christian Andersen's red-shoed dancer who could not stop dancing, I was happy that Bartoli kicked off her shoes at every opportunity.

We did not make it back to Houston to meet Silvana Bazzoni, Cecilia's mother. I got a bad cold, I had an exam coming up the following Monday, we could have gone anyway, but I decided I had better be responsible and study. Renate found my reasons superficial and unconvincing. The interview had gone so well, she thought that I was afraid to repeat it and fail to achieve the same intense communication. Maybe, she said, I preferred to remain the devoted fan, worshiping from a distance without moving closer to the personal reality of the singer. Certainly, there was something I liked about my role as unknown fan. One meeting, a single charmed glimpse of the singer's personal life, seemed consistent with this status. Anything more and I might lose the capacity to reason about diva worship from the outside. I wouldn't have missed the interview for the world. I felt that my intuitions about Bartoli had been confirmed and that I could now spend years of my life studying her art. But the yearning I felt to draw close to the mysterious source of the singer's inspiration was perhaps more readily fulfilled in the intimate enclosure of my own listening. Her voice, her breath, the expressiveness of her face, eyes, hands when she sang, were the essence of Cecilia Bartoli. But paradoxically, they formed an essence even more available to an enraptured listener than to the singer herself. She was, as she herself described it, transported when she sang. Therefore, when she was not singing, she could only look back on the state of inspiration and wonder about it. Was I afraid I might ruin my relationship to the singer as inspired instrument through an all-too-human discourse with the singer and her mother?

There were many questions I had wanted to ask Silvana Bazzoni when I was on the plane back from Houston. Had there been a moment of first hearing for her, too, a singular instant when she was arrested by her daughter's voice and musicality? Or had she gradually formed an impression of Cecilia's musical gifts over time? When the children were young, Cecilia would sing for her younger sister, Federica, because her sister used to get carsick. Was Silvana Bazzoni listening with a singer's ear as the car drove along the winding road to Rimini? In her interview for *The South Bank Show,* Silvana Bazzoni has spoken convincingly of the inner discipline required to become a singer. She wanted Cecilia to devote herself to music because music refines the spirit. Perhaps, when she began to teach Cecilia to sing, it was this inner discipline and refinement of spirit she wished to transmit to her daughter, especially during that period of flamenco dance, wild trips to Paris, secret excursions into Rome. Or did Silvana Bazzoni suspect that her daughter had the potential to become the outstanding mezzo coloratura of her generation? She has said that she wants Cecilia to give to the world the joy and beauty the Padre Eterno, the eternal father, had given to Cecilia—an expression with an easy, colloquial quality in Italian that cannot easily be rendered in English. Did Silvana Bazzoni feel that she had a responsibility to shape and organize her daughter's life so that she could give herself to the world? Or was the expression intended to be witty and perhaps ironic?

On the plane, I began to think of Cecilia's voice before it became a voice. Then it was a pure potential that might have been ignored; it certainly was unrecognized by her when she was studying to be a tour guide. Without her mother's intervention, her rare gift might have been known only as the musicality of the young woman leading tourists around the fountains of Rome, humming to herself or even, on occasion, suddenly breaking into song.

I did not go back to Houston to meet Silvana Bazzoni, I would now say, because I wanted to listen inwardly to my conversation with Cecilia. The same withdrawal into myself had been necessary after the first Berkeley concert. My conversation with Cecilia was becoming musical as it became memory. Thematic clusters of conversation, partial phrases, interrupted developmental lines played themselves through my thoughts. What Cecilia had almost said, not quite said, perhaps implied or inferred now began to fascinate me. I postponed the meeting with her mother and arranged to see them both in Rome, perhaps in the fall, when I was planning a trip to Europe. I was giving up a rare opportunity. The magic door that had opened to let me in, however intensely, to the singer's life could easily close again. I knew this, but turned back to play through in silence what Cecilia had said about herself.

When Cecilia appeared on *Fantastico,* a top-rated television talent show in Rome, she had sung with an orchestra for the first time. It took courage for a girl of nineteen to make her first public appearance under these conditions. Cecilia had talked about the experience lightly, with cascades of laughter and a shake of her head. At the time, I had been thinking that her daily practice under her mother's exacting standards must have been a good preparation for this first performance. The contestants on *Fantastico* appeared before a live audience, performed with famous singers, returned several times to the show with changes of clothes and repertoire. In the year following *Fantastico* Cecilia would be invited to perform at a memorial concert for Maria Callas at the Paris Opéra, where she would immediately win the support of famous conductors, including Herbert von Karajan. Looking back at *Fantastico,* Cecilia could afford to laugh. But how had she felt at the moment when the vote was announced before millions of viewers? In the final tally, Cecilia's competitor, the sixteen-year-old Roberto Caltriti, had received 12,362 votes to Cecilia's 7,638. In telling us the story, had Cecilia also wanted us to understand how grueling the experience had been?

When Cecilia talks about her first audition with von Karajan her face turns serious; her dark eyes grow darker with the imperative need to summon her powers—but there is no fear in them. The audition took place in Salzburg, a year or so after Cecilia's appearance on *Fantastico*. As she tells it, she walked out onto the stage for the audition, the hall was dark, she could not see von Karajan but heard a rough voice speaking her name from the darkness. As memory, the audition has become a great story. And why not? Von Karajan was impressed, he worked with her in several sessions and invited her to perform the Bach B-minor Mass for the 1990 Easter Festival in Salzburg, an event that never took place because von Karajan had died.

How different was that first audition from the daily exercise of facing up to a mother's exacting standards? Any girl who could rise to her teacher/mother's musical expectations might be well prepared, I thought, for renowned conductors with formidable voices in dark halls. But how had she felt at the time?

Some months after my conversation with Bartoli I came across an interview published in the German newspaper *Die Welt*. From this I saw that I had been right to sense fear, wrong to imagine that it had dominated her experience. She talked about her work with von Karajan and described the terrible anxiety she had felt during every rehearsal. "My whole body shook, although I really had no reason for it. He was in no way strict with young singers. But I simply couldn't stop shaking. Of course he noticed it. It was impossible to overlook. But he didn't say a word."

Bartoli told the interviewer that von Karajan had explained to her how to develop a phrase so that it seems to draw out into the infinite while simultaneously leaving one enough time to be able, at the end of the phrase, to quietly draw breath. I remembered something similar she had said to us about von Karajan over lunch. She spoke with an expression of concentrated intelligence, as if she were, as she told the story, taking in once again this "mysterious secret" von Karajan had taught.

The rough voice in the dark hall, the "frightful shock" of working with the famous conductor, her body shaking visibly from head to foot during every rehearsal. From this encounter Bartoli derives an essential secret of her craft. That is what matters to her, she says. Everything else has become, it seems, merely a good story.

$\mathcal{M}$y idea of what it meant to worship a diva changed after my conversation with Bartoli. Before I met her, she had been a mythical presence with a cultural mission. She had, I thought, stood firmly planted under the watchful protection of a musical god. Now I saw her as a young woman whose innermost development was taking place before the public eye. Because she was a young performer, visibly maturing from year to year, she experienced openly a process of self-exploration and discovery that for most people remains intimate and secret, hidden carefully away from naming or sight, until its growth is assured and its development accomplished. She was young, certainly; she had an ebullient life force and captivating energy; she sprang onto a stage and into music as if she were leaping into her own element.

"A few hours after her plane landed at Kennedy Airport on Monday, the diva did not so much waltz as bounce onto the stage ... where she was the evening's subject in an interview series. . . . She impishly smiled at the audience over jokes and broke into spontaneous song in mid-sentence to illustrate her musical point. Offstage, she wears little makeup, giggles readily and [laughs] infectiously over several octaves." (Diana Jean Schemo, *The New York Times*, September 29, 1994)

In this popular version, Bartoli was able to draw on a seemingly boundless energy, drove an Alfa Romeo, dashed out after performances to late-night parties, slept for twelve hours, woke refreshed and hungry, consumed pounds of pasta, and immediately got down to work. But did this portrait do justice to the complexity of the singer's life and character?

Roger Mills, following Bartoli through a day in her life, describes her at breakfast. "Chatting away at breakfast she is high-spirited, roars with laughter, pulls wonderful comic faces by way of illustrating anecdotes (a drunken Roman taxi driver is particularly impressive) as well as being touchingly solicitous with her mother. Bartoli can produce a breed of rather professional charm with journalists or musicians she doesn't know well, but her natural habitat is bubbly warm-heartedness."

The description is certainly accurate but probably not complete. Mills reports that she "shows every sign of being happy with the hectic international itinerary her enormous gifts have secured her," notes that she gets home to Rome perhaps every six weeks but that she finds living in hotels lonely. (Roger Mills, *Classic CD*, July 1993)

Bartoli had mentioned the loneliness of travel to us, too, and had seemed to dismiss it as a tolerable necessity. But when she showed us around the guesthouse in the garden of Richard Stasney's home where she was living during her weeks in Houston, her joy and relief had been palpable. She had a well-stocked kitchen in the guesthouse, but Stasney was clearly keeping an eye on her. The day after the interview, when I called to speak with her, she was cooking with Stasney in the large kitchen of his home. She had spoken warmly about him as a host, shared an affectionate bond with him, and several times mentioned lightly (it seemed) how much she disliked hotels and loved staying with him.

During the conversation, when she spoke of her host, I had taken in her warmth and expressiveness. Now, however, my silent listening reordered the relative weight of comments in our conversation. I became aware of seriousness and shadows, brief silences with the gravity of a musical pause, and I thought that Bartoli had been telling us that her life was often very lonely. Her mother and sister sometimes traveled with her, a fact that she repeated several times. She had an apartment of her own, but when she was in Rome she ate dinner at her mother's apartment. There were frequent phone calls when she was on the road, and flying terrified her. Sometimes it frightened her so much she could not get on a plane and had to cancel a performance. She hated flying, she had told us when we were leaving for the plane, and we were lucky, she said wistfully, to be traveling together.

A day or two after our interview she thought she was coming down with a cold and might have to cancel her next performance (she recovered). A month later, when Roger Mills spent a day with her in Vienna to interview her for *Classic CD,* she was wearing a strong-smelling linen-seed poultice, "an old singers' remedy for colds" Silvana Bazzoni called it.

Bartoli is no different than other singers when she regards a cold as a catastrophe, tries not to sing at all, says that singing with a cold would not be fair to her, her audience, or to "the gift God has given me." (*BBC Music Magazine,* August 1993)

But I began to worry about those colds. Shortly after her Houston commitments were fulfilled, she canceled a recital in Canada. That summer, during her performance as Despina in *Così fan tutte* at the Salzburger Festspiele she became ill and had to cancel several performances. During the time before she returned to Berkeley for her third recital, I was collecting reviews and articles about Bartoli, some of which dated back to the early days of her career. I noticed that she had also canceled her important

London debut at Wigmore Hall in 1990. In 1992 she had canceled her return appearance at the acclaimed festival in Pesaro (Rossini's birthplace) because of illness.

During the next couple of years, illness would delay her appearance at the Bingham Endowed Series in Jefferson County, Kentucky, where she was to have opened the season. In December 1994, Bartoli canceled her five scheduled performances in the Dallas Opera's production of Rossini's *La Cenerentola.*

John Ardoin interviewed her about the cancellation.

"There has been speculation," he wrote, "among opera followers that Ms. Bartoli canceled her appearances because she did not want to perform in the Music Hall, which is maligned by some for its cavernous size and its uneven acoustics. But Ms. Bartoli denies that is the case.

"'That rumor is totally false for various reasons, one of which is that I loved the experience of my previous appearances with the Dallas Opera. . . . The truth is that, unfortunately, I suffered a knee injury on the stage of the Zürich Opera . . . on top of this I got a very bad bronchitis, which not only prevented me from singing but also from flying.'" (John Ardoin, *Dallas Morning News,* January 22, 1995)

More recently, in the spring of 1996, illness caused her to cancel a recital in Washington, D.C., then cancel and reschedule her debut recital at Carnegie Hall in New York.

Bartoli was not a woman to lightly disregard performance responsibilities, fellow performers, professional arrangements. If she canceled an appearance it could only be because she was ill or exhausted or could not risk damaging her voice. "No one makes me live like this," she had said to us when we talked in Houston. "I don't have to live the rest of my life like this." She repeated this idea, in almost identical words, to Roger Mills a month or two later. "Yes," she said to him, "it can be depressing being away from home and so on, but no one is forcing me to do it. I don't feel as if I have to live like this forever."

A Bartoli silence can be as expressive as words. "I have to live my life now," she said to us when we discussed her heavy performance schedule. "Now," she repeated. "How long do I have?" At the time, I thought she was referring to the predictable career of the opera singer, who will probably retire sometime around the age of fifty and then live on for many years after her voice. In retrospect, I heard the same words through a darker tonality.

"I have always had a premonition I would not have a long life," she said to Walter Price in *Opera News* when she was twenty-six years old. "I don't see myself with white hair like my grandmother. But I really don't think about it often."

She did, however, mention the same idea to Linda Blandford in a long interview for the *New York Times* in 1993. "I think I'm not here for a long time. . . . When I think about my life, I am sure I will not arrive at an old age. But I would rather sing one day as a lion than a hundred years as a sheep."

Bartoli's good nature, patience, warmth, humor, and responsiveness are already legendary. "Someone is always after Bartoli, yet she seldom objects when people pluck at her sleeve. . . . During rehearsal breaks one day, Bartoli was assailed by two writers who wanted instant interviews. Neither had called in advance. . . . She was unfazed as eight people attended a costume fitting . . . one held the pins, one did the pinning and six supervised in three languages. . . . The ordinary mortal wouldn't have put up with it, but Bartoli shrugs. 'I realize this is what happens. You have to accept it if you're on this level.'" (*Newsweek*, October 3, 1994)

Signorina Bartoli works hard, travels frequently, is on the road three-quarters of the year, travels only half the time with her mother or sister, gets colds, is mortal, has strenuous recording sessions, which, she told us, were extremely difficult for her. "People don't understand this," she had said. "People think you can make the perfect recording because you can repeat many times. But the repetition is . . . it is exhausting, the hardest work, *orribile*. With an audience, there is the response, the feeling, so the singing is more natural, more spontaneous. In the opera the story is there and the other singers. In the studio . . ." She had interrupted herself and touched me lightly on the arm. "You will tell this, please, I want people to understand. In the studio, how do you keep the feeling with so many repetitions? But you have to find it again, you have to keep it. But every time when you play it back you think, It could be better."

Jack Mastroianni had talked to me about the Bartoli family. Cecilia, he felt, was well supported by them. "They are a very close family, they always had to struggle to make ends meet financially. Shoes were handed down from brother to sister to sister. The need to survive kept everybody close. In the family they are all very protective of one another. We were on a plane down in the Caribbean, and the sister had an attack of low blood pressure. Cecilia just held her hand, talked to her, fanned her, consoled her, cradled her. This bond is quite incredible. It comes from the mother, it goes back to the mother, it goes to the sister, it goes back to each sister."

There were eight months between my interview with Bartoli and the date set for her fourth concert in Berkeley. During that time I listened to her recordings, played through our conversation in my mind, and worried. Bartoli was less mythic, more human than I had supposed, more poignant and perhaps exhaustible than the saga of the barefoot diva suggested. She was a cultural treasure and I was afraid we might use her up before she had lived out the long life I wished for her and she, perhaps, did not think she would have.

*W*hen you get ready to hear Bartoli again you find yourself preparing for more than a concert. You start working, sometimes weeks, even months ahead of time, to be ready for the experience. After the first time, you already know that you will have to take the risk of throwing yourself open to the depth from which she fetches her song. This need to surrender oneself to the singer's expressive appeal may be the reason fans are consistently more moved by Bartoli than her reviewers, whose responsibilities tend to make them wary and cautious, critical and edgy before the possibility of being swept away. "Bartoli need only close her eyes, clench her fists and launch into one of any number of minor Italian songs," writes Allan Ulrich, of the *San Francisco Examiner,* "and the seduction—of senses, intellect and judgment—is complete." It is possible, however, that you cannot hear Bartoli unless you find this seduction desirable and allow it to keep your senses, intellect, and judgment fully engaged.

The interplay of risk and gratitude, gratitude and devotion, distinguishes Bartoli's relationship to her audience. When Bartoli sings, particularly in a recital, she opens herself to emotions most people rarely feel, or feel only in private, or under the most intimate conditions. We might take it for granted that this is what singers, and particularly opera singers, essentially do. Bartoli, however, does it with a unique kind of personal hazard.

Many people when they hear Bartoli for the first time feel that she is singing directly to them, as if the house had emptied, they were alone in the dark room, and she was reaching out to them through an intimate whispering. When, at subsequent performances, you realize that almost everyone else in the audience feels the same way, you may experience a common bond of enthusiasm with them, as if the singer had transformed a group of strangers into a listening congregation, with each member united to the others by the fervent belief that she is singing only for him. Strangely, the intimacy and immediacy of this experience are in no way lessened by the knowledge that thousands of other people share in it.

The imperative need to give the joy of a great gift accounts for the highly individual impression Bartoli makes as an artist. When I have seen her, Bartoli is never singing merely introspectively, or for the music alone, or for the display of a remarkable technical facility, or because she desperately needs to show herself in public to win love and applause, or because she is at home on the stage or feels alive only when giving voice to a fictional character's deepest yearning. Bartoli sings because she has something to give that she passionately wants the audience to receive. She wants every member of the audience, if possible, to take part in this gift because of the pleasure gifts of this sort bring.

Some years ago, when I began to study her art, I thought I had explained it to myself with the idea that a divine breath passed through her. Now I found myself thinking that this mysterious breath must have awakened in the singer a desire to collaborate fully with its passage into the world. When Bartoli and her mother speak of Cecilia bringing to other people the gift the Eternal Father has given to her, they both mean it.

Bartoli's personal artistic mission makes her need for her audience an essential part of her art. In a wonderfully circular manner, by which singer and listener are brought together, Bartoli's audience makes it possible for her to reach the expressive depth she wants the audience to feel. A performance by Bartoli reveals a continual tension between inspiration and communication (the rapt transport we have seen in her, the slow, gracious return to her audience), both equally important to the singer, both an essential part of her charismatic appeal.

When Bartoli talks about nervousness at the start of a performance, she immediately adds that after the first song or two, the nervousness disappears as she becomes aware of the audience's response. Bartoli applauds her audience after a performance. Some reviewers regard this as itself part of the performance. "Her new habit of raising her hands above her head, Rocky Balboa–style, and of applauding her audience even as they barely begin to applaud her, distract from the characteristic sincerity of her communication." When I have been part of the audience I have felt that Bartoli applauds the people who are applauding her in recognition of our participation in the performance itself. Bartoli comes forward to take her bows. When she straightens up she beats her fist lightly, rapidly over her heart. Another characteristic gesture. The audience loves her? Well, she loves us back, precisely because we have taken the risk of receiving what she has to give.

Opera singers tend to impress us through their mastery of the high style, their skill at artifice, their distance from ordinary life, their power, grandeur, sumptuousness. Bartoli impresses a listener with her ardent desire to communicate. This immediacy, it might be said, is part of every great performer's bag of tricks. Bartoli's willingness to take the risk of expressing herself, so that her audience will be willing to take the risk of responding, and her palpable gratitude when this response is forthcoming, make the exchange between Bartoli and her audience more compelling and mysterious than is usual with most artists.

While preparing for Bartoli's fourth Berkeley recital, I listened to her newly released recording with András Schiff. She had spoken enthusiastically about it during our conversation, fascinated by the Italian texts set to music by Austrian musicians. The CD, when it appeared, some months before her highly anticipated Berkeley concert, indicated that Bartoli had extended her repertoire beyond Mozart and Rossini into the larger, Italian-dominated international operatic culture of the eighteenth century, which Mozart of course represented.

Mozart spent the last ten years of his life, from 1781 to 1791, in Vienna. He moved to Vienna from Salzburg because of the musical opportunities the city offered him. "Vienna was a natural staging-post in the migrations of musicians across Europe, particularly from Italy, the homeland of opera buffa, to St. Petersburg, whither Catherine the Great was inviting the leading opera buffa composers of the age. As the capital of a large empire, ruled by an educated aristocracy, Vienna had quite naturally developed strong cultural traditions, more so in opera than in anything else, owing to the wider acceptance of Italian rather than French or German influences (Austria herself ruled most of northern Italy). As a cosmopolitan capital in the confident days before the French Revolution,

Vienna attracted the great operatic talents of the age." (John D. Drummond, *Opera in Perspective*, p. 193)

Cecilia's recording of Italian texts set by Haydn, Mozart, Beethoven, and Schubert drew her into the exquisite, international musical culture of Vienna, with its predominant Italian influence. She had been surprised, she told us, to discover Austrian musicians setting Italian texts to music, but seemed to feel particularly happy with the combination and strangely at home with it. Long before my conversation with Bartoli, I had begun studying the origins of opera and had followed its development through the eighteenth century, the period with which I thought she might be closely associated throughout her career. I had already imagined Bartoli at the Teatro San Carlo in Naples, performing the prima donna roles in Rossini's operas. Now she had left Italy and arrived (moving backward in time) in the Hapsburg capital of the Austrian Empire, where she could be glimpsed among the elite musical society of Vienna, easily establishing herself among the composers who were creating and evolving the forms of eighteenth-century opera and song.

At the time Mozart arrived in Vienna, Metastasio, whom Cecilia loves, was living there and had "developed opera seria libretto-writing to a fine art. Here too lived Johann Hasse . . . the most prolific of opera seria composers. Calzabigi and Gluck had written their first 'reform' operas in Vienna in the 1760s. At the time of Mozart's arrival, the Court Kapellmeister and Theatre Music Director was Antonio Salieri . . . only six years older than Mozart. Early in 1782 there also arrived in Vienna Lorenzo da Ponte, ex-diplomat and spy, and, some would say, the greatest opera buffa librettist." Joseph Haydn was living at Esterház but visited Vienna "fairly often," where he could hear "some of the best singers in Europe, hired by the Emperor Joseph II." (John D. Drummond, *Opera in Perspective*, p. 193)

It was to this lost world that Bartoli now opened a magic casement, through her recorded performance with András Schiff, whom she had described to us, with considerable warmth, as an unusually expressive and sensitive pianist. The atmosphere of Bartoli's recital on *The Impatient Lover* was recognizably different than anything she had achieved before. Her voice sounded more poised and mature, perhaps because it had found the notably classical restraint required to hold and support lyrical expression, especially Metastasio's.

Metastasio is regarded as the first major poet to have turned his attention to musical drama (David Kimbell, *Italian Opera*, p. 192). "His more popular texts were set dozens of times—the favourite *'Artaserse'* more than eighty times—by composers in every corner of Europe where Italian opera had taken a footing." Throughout his life he had a close association with musicians and understood music "probably better than any earlier theatre poet had done." Characteristically eighteenth century, he had written that "the transports of inspiration should never disturb the equilibrium of reason," a consideration that had clearly influenced Bartoli's performance of the music inspired by his texts.

Metastasio acknowledged the powerful charm of music itself, its power "to enchant, and to illuminate the hidden recesses of the heart," but felt that these powers depended on its "keeping company with the poetry." "'Believe me,' wrote Metastasio to the Chevalier de Chastellux in 1765, 'whenever music aspires at the preeminence over poetry in a drama, she destroys both that and herself.'" (David Kimbell, *Italian Opera*, p. 196)

A musician setting a text by Metastasio or any other eighteenth-century poet, even well beyond the early eighteenth century, when most of his texts were written, would feel constrained to hold the delicate balance between text and music with which Metastasio was concerned. Bartoli, although she had recently discovered these works by Austrian composers, had instinctively sensed this challenge, which informed her interpretations and brought a new gravity to her singing.

Her fans had grown familiar with her interpretations of Rossini, the bubbling, irrepressible comic spirit, the unrestrained, sometimes earthy, sometimes heroic lyricism. We had enjoyed her power to engage Mozart's deft painting of hidden soul landscapes, his peerless musical realization of human character. Now we had to follow Bartoli into a musical repertoire that certainly included Mozart, but asked for new sensitivities, balancings, and shadings.

Bartoli gave the impression, on this new album, that she was exploring the textures of classical simplicity, its richness and startling abundance—then taking it as delicately as possible through Beethoven and into Schubert, where a romantic restlessness and striving began, here and there, to disrupt its precariously poised serenity. Beethoven singing in Italian, with utter simplicity of vocal line. This was a Beethoven Bartoli was born to discover. She found in the brooding, introspective, stormy composer a strangely haunted longing for simplicity and restraint, a quality apparent in all of Beethoven's settings of Metastasio verse, as Bartoli performed them. The album's final Beethoven song, *"In questa tomba oscura,"* to a verse by Giuseppe Carpani, brought out in Bartoli a dark, deep, somber voice, a hushed solemnity that seemed intended to establish that simplicity was the only appropriate vehicle for the communication of serious sentiment. Her vocal shading in this poem, addressed to the ungrateful lover and sung from the tomb by a "naked shadow," takes on an eerie, otherworldly calm, a poise that mysteriously allows both Beethoven and Bartoli to express an emotion that is gravely sad and severely stern. *"Ingrata"* (ungrateful one), the last word of the song, repeated twice, grows in Bartoli's performance from a word of infinite reproach to the even more terrifying final word of an irrevocable judgment.

Schubert presents her with a different task. He too is setting Metastasio, as well as texts that were originally German and had been translated into Italian. It is in the Metastasio verses that Schubert hints at and Bartoli realizes the implicit romanticism of his music. *"Mio ben ricordati"* ("Remember my beloved/if I should die/how much my faithful heart/loved you") sounds appropriately eighteenth century in its serene reassurance of love beyond death. But the second verse, as Schubert sets the words and Bartoli performs them, foreshadows the forthcoming restlessness of romantic yearning. "And if cold ashes/are capable of love/then in the grave/I shall still adore you." Through that dangerous and ambiguous word "if" (both as set and sung), the tensions between the diverging classical and romantic sensibilities of the eighteenth and nineteenth centuries are ominously sounded.

Singing that can realize the troubled currents of a vanished age! A vocal shading and nuance that give to the Schubert songs an almost conscious awareness of nostalgia and farewell, as if their composer knew they were the last Italian texts ever to be set by a Viennese musician. Yes, indeed, I was looking forward to Bartoli's forthcoming Berkeley concert.

"With a display of star power worthy of a true diva—but with none of the attitude—mezzo-soprano Cecilia Bartoli charmed a sold-out house of adoring fans in Berkeley's Zellerbach Hall yesterday afternoon," wrote the reviewer for the *San Francisco Chronicle* about Bartoli's fourth Berkeley recital. "This was no mere recital, it was a full-blown event— with every music-lover in the area who could land a ticket in attendance, and scattered disconsolate admirers milling around outside in search of last-minute serendipity (one hopeful was cagily hoisting a sign inscribed in Italian and English)."

The day before, at Tower Records in San Francisco, Bartoli had spent two hours "accepting compliments and signing her name on CD booklets, photographs and whatever other objects were placed before her" by hundreds of fans who, by the time she arrived, on schedule, had waited for hours to greet her. (Jesse Hamlin, *San Francisco Chronicle,* March 12, 1994)

On the day of the recital Renate and I were politely hailed at the parking lot, a block or so from campus, by a professorial couple who offered us a small fortune for a ticket to the concert.

"You knew this was a Bartoli concert," wrote the reviewer for the *San Francisco Examiner.* "You could tell that 400 yards from the auditorium doors as you ran the gauntlet of hopefuls brandishing signs begging for tickets, at almost any price."

For Bartoli's concert on March 14, 1994, "there were 500 names on a waiting list for a house that sold out last August." Cal Performances, her sponsors, had restricted the ticket sales to people who had subscribed to a regular series. Each subscriber was entitled to two Bartoli tickets. We offered the extras with great ceremony to our closest friends.

On the way to Zellerbach Hall, where Bartoli would be singing to an audience of some two thousand people, we passed excited clusters of Bartoli fans, all of us, I thought, brandishing the same look of pride in having had the foresight to get hold of tickets.

Renate wanted to go backstage at intermission or after the performance to say hello to Cecilia, whom we had not seen since our conversation in Houston. We hadn't made it to Europe in the fall, the intended conversation with Silvana Bazzoni never took place. I had written my article for *San Francisco Focus* magazine and now found that it was being handed out by Cal Performances as part of their press packet. Nevertheless, I felt hesitant about going backstage to talk to Bartoli, shy, not certain of my welcome, unwilling to take the risk. She had become, through all my months of study and listening, so much a part of myself that I was perhaps reluctant to encounter her out there in the world, independent of my wishes, no longer part of my fantasy life, a celebrated singer who might or might not recognize me as the woman who had conversed with her in Houston some eight months before. Renate thought I was being silly but decided, as we took our seats in the third row, close to the stage, not to go backstage after the performance without me.

In Houston, Bartoli had told us how much she liked to see her fans backstage. She always wanted to know how people had responded to the music and if they had similar responses to hers. She thought of the entire concert as a dialogue between herself and the audience and wanted to continue the discussion backstage. She had fans who attended all her concerts and regularly came backstage afterward to say hello. She remembered them, she said, picked up the last conversation with them, was eager to know more about their lives.

Nevertheless, I hunkered down in my seat, closed my eyes, ran through the Beethoven and Schubert songs with which Bartoli would begin her program. I was disappointed that Beethoven's *"In questa tomba oscura"* was not on the program, relieved to find that Schubert's *"Mio ben ricordati"* definitely was. Bartoli was also going to sing Mozart's *"Exsultate, jubilate."* This reminded me of our ride together from Richard Stasney's home to the restaurant, the skies overcast, the jubilation we felt as we drove through the well-groomed streets, Kiri Te Kanawa on the stereo, Cecilia humming to herself in the backseat, then grandly throwing out the high notes of the Queen of the Night.

The second half of the program would include the five settings of Rossini's *"Mi lagnerò tacendo,"* which she had sung in Berkeley before, four Bellini songs she had never recorded, and then would conclude with *"O rendetemi la speme,"* from *I Puritani*. Renate and I had played this aria from Callas's recording of the opera countless times. Renate would now see whether her loyalty to Callas stood between her and Bartoli, and I would get to find out how Bartoli held up against the most expressive singer I had known until I heard her.

Dim lights, last-minute coughing and shuffling, a pitched, excited silence, Bartoli comes out onto the stage in a rumpled pink dress, wearing the tiny pearl earrings she often wears, her hair loose over her shoulders. The audience greets her with more applause than many singers get at the end of their concerts; she acknowledges it with her radiant smile. She is performing today with György Fischer, part of the inner circle of Bartoli advisors. She gives him a quick, secret look of trust and pleasure. I have the impression that most people in the audience have stopped breathing. The first notes are startling, almost unexpected, precisely because they have been so eagerly awaited.

"*Ecco quel fiero istante/Nice, mia Nice, addio!*" ("Here is the fateful moment! Farewell, my Nice!")

I knew exactly what to expect: the refined exploration of the vocal line, the textured nuance of simplicity. I knew where they would sound and almost heard them before I realized that something was wrong. Something was wrong? The tone was as beautiful as ever, the voice full and rich, but the song sounded strangely staid rather than simple, as if it were looking for its expressive purpose and were not yet complete in itself.

Bartoli was often nervous during the first two songs, she had told us that. The audience's response would soon change that, I thought. The two versions of *"L'amante impaziente,"* marked by Beethoven as "calmly questioning" and "restlessly demanding," were the perfect vehicle for Bartoli's vocal shading. On her recording with Schiff, she had found questions within questions within shades of calmness. The restless demands of the second version were articulated with fiery impatience and a wonderfully sumptuous passion. But here, onstage, the two versions seemed to lack expressive color; it was almost hard to tell them apart, they seemed not fully invested with emotion. I opened my eyes to have a look. It was Bartoli all right, but somehow not entirely Bartoli. The gestures were familiar, the expression of her face and eyes were recognizable, yet they seemed to be performed by an accomplished Bartoli impersonator, rather than by Bartoli herself.

Renate pushed against my shoulder; she too had noticed. Had Bartoli been delayed at the plane and sent a representative to stand in for her? The first couple of songs had come and gone. The audience was warmly responsive but the singer continued to seem remote. The Schubert songs, two of them by Metastasio, seemed flat, conventional, as if their pure, simple sentiments were simply inane.

There was enthusiastic applause between the Schubert and *"Exsultate, jubilate."* During the applause I had a bad moment. I thought my fears for Bartoli had all been realized: she had sung too much, traveled too much, was too lonely, had made too many recordings, didn't get home enough, had used up the gift the Eternal Father had given her, had spent it too profligately. Perhaps, as many reviewers had foretold, she was one of those young singers of enormous promise and potential who burn themselves out during their earliest years and fade into obscurity, leaving a handful of recordings behind to remind the world of what they were and what they might have become. This had happened to Souliotis, a singer who had been hailed as the successor to Callas but whose voice, in the middle of a performance one day, simply blew apart. Bartoli's voice was as lovely as ever, in its rich amber darkness, but emotionally it had gone strangely flat. Even in Mozart's ecstatic motet, Bartoli could not quite reach the solemn jubilation that joined words and music in what should by rights have been a natural Bartolian affirmation of man's relationship to the divine.

> *Exult, rejoice*
> *O you blessed souls*
> *as you sing sweet songs.*
> *Because of your song*
> *the heavens resound with me.*
> *The friendly day shines,*
> *now clouds and storms disappear.*
> *An unexpected peace comes to the*
> *righteous.*

Thunderous applause, intermission, people moving out for refreshments, excited conversations in the aisles: it could be that I am missing something here. But no, Renate looks very disturbed, puzzled. She leans over to whisper, our friends come up. People who have never heard Bartoli before are moved to tears; others who know her better feel that she is not quite at her best. I am afraid she has undergone the fate reserved for the most highly gifted—indescribable exaltation followed by the inevitable fall from grace. My friend Cathy comes to sit next to me. She slips her arm around my waist and whispers, "There's still the second half. Even the best singers have off days. Don't worry."

But I am thinking about the origins of opera. I am remembering Daphne and Eurydice, human women who got mixed up with the divine and semidivine and were destroyed because of it—Eurydice dragged into the underworld, Daphne turned into a tree as she fled from Apollo. Was early opera prefiguring in these characters the fate of its later divas, their sacrificial quality? Was Bartoli one of those mythical women placed intermediate between gods and men who could not, in the very nature of things, long survive the tension? Was that why we worshiped divas, sensing in them their doomed perishability, precisely because they gave to us so much of what they had been given?

Bartoli opened the second half of the program with Rossini's *"Mi lagnerò tacendo"* ("I shall suffer mutely my miserable fate, but do not delude yourself, my love, with hopes that I do not love you. Cruel one, why do you continue to make me suffer thus?"). It was a text by Metastasio, with which much of the audience would have been familiar from Bartoli's earlier performances and CDs. The five repetitions would require her to act and shade and differentiate and embody five different moods or characters, as she had done in the past. But would she, who seemed not fully present, be able to do it?

I wanted to creep under my seat but felt this might be taken as a sign of disrespect rather than anxious concern. Something was hammering so hard in my ears that I could not hear the singer. But I could tell, from the forward movement of Renate's body, that something good was happening onstage. I opened my eyes, I opened them wider. Bartoli had come back to her face and eyes, she was inhabiting her own gestures, her voice was packed with emotional color, the five versions presented poignant sorrow, anger, heartfelt regret, even an unexpected tipsy monologue that never quite managed to hide the unbearable pain of the abandoned lover.

She was back, she had returned to us, she wasn't exhausted, used up, spent, as I had feared. And she was about to sing Bellini. My friend had been right, Bartoli had had an off day, been tired or distracted during the first half of the performance. I had been shaken only because I had never before seen Bartoli less than inspired or fully present. Now, having seen her as less than herself, I understood more completely the nature of her power. For Bartoli to be Bartoli she had to give everything she had; less would make her more like any other great singer.

"Bartoli was simply a bel canto dream, a model of limpid cantilena in the recitative. The shaded and even chromatic runs in the cabaletta were golden age material, time capsule stuff," wrote the *Examiner* reviewer, who had earlier been concerned about the seduction of senses, intellect, and judgment.

"With its long, deceptively simple melody, mounting in inexhaustible arches of sound, [*'Vaga luna che inargenti'*] is purest Bellini, a kissing cousin to *'Casta diva.'* Bartoli's performance was extraordinary: sumptuous of tone, unaffected in its gestures and marked by an emotional openness that was haunting to see."

As we were leaving, Renate confessed that she was willing to grant Bartoli a place in her heart right next to Callas; there was room for both of them, with their diverging interpretations of Elvira's mad scene. Callas had used her big, weighty voice to deliver the furthest pitch of Elvira's desperate madness: "Give me back my hope or let me die." Bartoli, with her younger, smaller, more gracious instrument, had reached the universal suffering of the abandoned woman; her Elvira was notably less mad, and therefore even more stricken in a way we listeners could understand. Far back, beyond audibility, were echoes and overtones of all the abandoned women Bartoli had brought to life. The despised wife, the impatient lover, the naked shadow in the tomb, the ever-changing women of *"Mi lagnerò tacendo"*—they were all present in a silent chorus of desperation and distress but were never quite allowed to lose themselves in madness.

People on their feet, thunderous applause, a young man approaching the stage with a single flower, people moving out into the aisles while Bartoli applauded us, as if to say it was we, after all, who had made it possible for her to reach the emotion she had called up in us, singer and audience face to face, thanking each other for our shared accomplishment.

*T*he singer walks out onto the stage. There, she meets the extravagant, even fevered expectation of her audience. None of us knows exactly what has brought us to this pitch or what we want from the woman with the beautiful voice. For some, perhaps, a revelation about the nature of music, an absorption so intense it will amount to rapture, or maybe, more discretely, an insight into the hidden depths of human character. Certainly, at the very least, a full two hours of enjoyment. We seem unmindful of the singer as a young woman who has dedicated her life to the realization of this moment. We may even end by blaming her for our own failure to be moved or transported, no matter how beautifully she sings. Some of us may find that we have become guarded and critical and have spent our time focused on minute, even imagined, vocal blemishes.

The question of size follows Bartoli as if it were her personal demon. She may sing beautifully with an amazing coloratura but the voice, some people say, is small, even tiny, and surely not capable of filling a large American house. This question was raised by local reviewers and members of the audience after her fourth Berkeley concert and would be repeated again the following year. The same question had also concerned reviewers after her Houston debut in *Il Barbiere.* Some reviewers wondered if even there (where the auditorium is not large) her voice could reach the back of the house—where Renate and I had been happily sitting, having no problem hearing.

"And so this heralded stage debut was something of an anticlimax," wrote the reviewer in the *Texas Opera Review,* "not because Bartoli failed to sing well but because one's attention was drawn to the fact that the voice may not be large enough to fill big American houses."

Bartoli sang well; indeed, she sang, according to this reviewer, with "the distinctive articulation of the coloratura, the beautiful bloom even in the lower range, the remarkable agility." Yet somehow the reviewer was distracted during this beautiful singing by thoughts of other places Bartoli might someday sing, unsuccessfully.

John Ardoin, the noted Callas discographer and an early Bartoli enthusiast, heard differently: "While her sound is not large, it is large enough to make an impact, with its perfect blending of registers that span more than two octaves."

Another reviewer for the *Texas Opera Review* was also worried about size and found much to criticize in Bartoli's voice. "Her sparkling personality, strikingly individual phrasing and amazingly nimble if aspirate-prone coloratura suggested Conchita Supervia. But Bartoli's mezzo—dark, creamy, somewhat throaty (many vowels were thick and muddy)—is tiny. . . . One wonders how Bartoli's voice will carry in larger houses."

Where one listener finds mud, another beholds clarity. "She has a coloratura facility that is as fastidious as it is clean and fleet," writes Ardoin, "a musicality that includes an epicurean sense of phrasing, diction so perfect you could take down the words of her part as if it were dictation."

Christopher Raeburn, who has spent the last forty years studying voices, agrees. "When people talk about her aspirating her coloratura, that's implying she puts in an 'H.' She does not. But she articulates coloratura very, very cleanly, and maybe some people don't like that. This is not sloppy coloratura. When Cecilia sings, every note is distinct. Some people may not want that. I find it very cheering to hear somebody with the discipline Cecilia has. But her coloratura is not always the same. In certain parts of Rossini she will make a very, very articulated coloratura. For Mozart, it will be very slightly more legato. All this is conscious. It comes from her. Many singers, when they sing this repertoire, use it as an exercise. Cecilia uses the coloratura as characterization. Her coloratura is the logical, musical extension of her singing and her interpretation. It is all within the idiom and I don't know another singer who does this with such success."

During the months after Bartoli's fourth performance in Berkeley, Lotfi Monsouri, the director of the San Francisco Opera, tried to sign her for the '96 season and was turned down. She had visited the opera house and thought it might be too large for her voice. Bartoli is as careful in selecting a site as she is in choosing her roles—both have to suit her temperament, character, and abilities. When I spoke to Monsouri about this he responded succinctly. In coming years, he said, he would try to arrange a production for her in a smaller place where she would feel more at home.

If American opera houses are too large for Bartoli, we will have to flock to hear her in smaller places, more suited for her voice, the intimate connection she makes with her audience, the music she performs, the period in which it was written. As a fan, it seems obvious to me that if she is bringing the elegance and simplicity of eighteenth-century music back to us, there is no reason it should accommodate itself to how large we have grown.

Bartoli reads her reviews. Some years ago, before she had mastered English, it was a relief, she has said, that she could not exactly understand everything that was written. She was troubled by reviewers who thought her voice too small, puzzled by the inconsistency of their response to her. A few reviewers, John Ardoin and Peter Davis notably among them, had immediately recognized the rare qualities of Bartoli's voice and had described them accurately.

In 1989, before Bartoli had appeared in America, Ardoin wrote: "Cecilia Bartoli—mark the name, it is one to remember. . . . She appears to have it all—voice, temperament, style, security, an extraordinary way with words and a dazzling technique. . . . It is all done with a dark, resonant sound that rises above the staff seamlessly to a glistening, ringing top that would turn most sopranos green. And while scales and embellishments are dispatched with an imperious, etched precision, they always are used expressively to convey dramatic meanings."

Response to music is highly subjective; Bartoli knows that as well as anyone. A young performer, however, comes to knowledge of herself, at least in part, through the world's response to her. It is correct to think of Bartoli as enclosed by a protective wall of mother and trusted advisors. This does not mean she would find it easy to offer herself to the world when it proves to be an unreliable mirror. Her sensitivity and receptivity to her listeners are a crucial part of her expressive gift. She would not change an interpretation because reviewers were critical of it. She sings and acts, she says, because of the way she feels. But what can Bartoli (or any other young singer) make of the abounding confusion and critical contradiction that accompany her performances?

Some reviewers who admire her technique feel that her interpretations all come out sounding "much the same."

Others, by contrast, comment on her expressivity: "She is, most crucially, a communicative singer who, through a combination of vocal gestures and physical bearing, draws the listener into the emotional or dramatic world of the song at hand."

Still others note that she "herself seemed too concerned with the notes to delve into their expressive depth."

Or, by contrast: "The ornaments were never matters of display; they never proclaimed: 'Look what my voice can do. Don't you like it?' Instead, the turns and roulades seemed to be emotion transmuted into sound, eruptions of feeling that could not be constrained by a simple melodic line."

Some reviewers find her a natural successor to Teresa Berganza and Marilyn Horne. Others write that "on first hearing there was little to remind a Berganza admirer of the Spanish singer's warmth, charm and easy command of the florid style."

For others she "might be the next great coloratura mezzo," although they would prefer to wait before declaring themselves. Ardoin, as we have seen, is willing to take the risk, finding her technique flawless, her expressiveness assured. A reviewer for the *Boston Globe*, on the other hand, described her as having a "brittle staccato . . . and a tricky, twittery way with coloratura." The same reviewer worried that Bartoli never sounds young, and found that Jennie Tourel, pushing sixty, sounded "more like a young girl when she sang '*La regata veneziana*'" than Bartoli did.

The reviewer for the *New York Times,* on the contrary, wrote of the "wonderful freshness" of her voice and admired her "scale passages, runs, roulades and trills [which] are cleanly and precisely articulated."

The reviewer for the *Los Angeles Times Mirror* felt that she had a "strong and handsome voice," but that it lacked the "unique, once-in-a-lifetime timbre associated with the Sutherlands, Caballés and Milanovs of this world."

The editorial writer for the *Vancouver Sun* felt differently. "By the grace of God I was [at Bartoli's concert] and witnessed her phenomenal talent, an event I will cherish the rest of my life. . . . Make no mistake, this is one of the greatest voices of our century."

This is a world of considerable confusion, reminiscent of those great Rossini finales, when no one onstage can figure out what is happening.

E il cervello, poverello
già stordito, sbalordito
non ragiona, si confonde
si riduce ad imazzar.

And the brain, poor little thing,
already stunned, stupefied,
cannot reason, is confounded,
is reduced to madness.

The writer for *Opera News* felt that "she sounds like a soprano much of the time," and that when she does manage to sound like a mezzo, it is not "a mezzo of Horne's dark-hued variety."

The reviewer for the *New York Times* found Bartoli "an important and rarely found phenomenon [who] has joined the ranks of operatic singers, an authentic coloratura mezzo-soprano darkly beautiful in sound."

In this world nothing simply is; everything that might be taken for granted might immediately become something else. The evenness of registers, the seamless passage from one to the next, which most reviewers celebrate as Bartoli's outstanding characteristic, can also be put into question.

"Her low register, though hardly coarse," a reviewer observed, "seemed strained and not entirely connected to her upper voice."

Her expressivity, which would seem to speak for itself, can also be doubted. In the *American Opera Guide,* the reviewer says "she fails to touch the heartstrings in the way less technically accomplished singers, such as Conchita Supervia, De Gabarain, and Berganza did so admirably on earlier records." (Berganza, we may recall, had elsewhere been compared favorably to Bartoli for possessing the superior technical facility.)

The voice of this young singer is, it seems, simultaneously dark and bright, full-bodied and tiny, expressive and without feeling, pyrotechnically assured and technically lacking, made up of registers seamlessly united but with parts of the voice tacked on. The voice is young and old, unique yet not distinctive, simultaneously better than and less good technically than earlier mezzos, who are both more and less expressive than the young singer who certainly is a once-in-a-lifetime experience but not one of the great voices of the century.

If Bartoli were a prima donna we might not have to be concerned. But if she is also a young woman who might have become a tour guide instead of a singer, who studied trumpet at the conservatory before she discovered her voice, who in the early years of her career was wondering if she could have a career, we can wonder how she feels about all this. Identity involves recognition, and "recognition" for Bartoli has come to mean a madhouse of contradictory perceptions and responses. If I, a fan, reading these reviews, am forced to wonder how she endures it, when she does not receive the most elementary consistency of response, how can the singer herself feel?

When you ask her, she shrugs and seems about to laugh it off; then, she looks you in the eye and nods seriously with one of those speaking silences in which Bartoli says more than she is likely to say for print.

But sometimes even in print she is highly articulate. "I wish I could be 5 percent prima donna," she says to her interviewer from *Newsweek*. "Sometimes I think people can push a normal artist into a monster." (Katrine Ames, *Newsweek*, October 3, 1994)

*B*artoli's fifth Berkeley concert, in February of 1995, was the most highly anticipated event of the musical season, with all the familiar Bartoli elements firmly in place—the sold-out concert, the frenzy for tickets at any price, the presence of musical notables, the rapturous tension of anticipation in the plaza outside the theater, in the lobby, on the stairs, in the auditorium. For this fifth concert, Bartoli will sing (for the first time in Berkeley) with orchestra, a change that allows her to enter a purely operatic repertoire. She will sing Dorabella, Susanna, and Sesto, from Mozart's *Così fan tutte, Le Nozze di Figaro,* and *La Clemenza di Tito*; Zelmira from Rossini's opera of the same name; and Amina from Bellini's *La Sonnambula.*

Bartoli comes onstage in a simple black silk dress, as eager as ever, it seems, to give herself into the music. She moves with the old ebullience and high spirits, the same sense of radically focused concentration, but with a poise and bearing that refer, as she perhaps never would, to her conquest of the musical world. This is not the shy young singer of four years ago performing to a half-empty house.

The concert opens with Dorabella's exuberant, uninhibited aria, "*E'amore un ladroncello,*" in which she invites her more reticent sister, Fiordiligi, to surrender to love. As sung by Bartoli, there is a clear influence on Dorabella from the seductive, pandering, earthy maid Despina, a part Bartoli had sung in Europe and would sing for her debut at the Metropolitan Opera the following year. Had Bartoli caught this influence Mozart had made musically evident because she had sung both roles?

The singer leaves the stage. She returns as Susanna, who is, for this scene in the opera, dressed as the countess. Bartoli is dressed as herself. But with the first phrase the scene is set. Susanna is in the garden of the count's estate; Figaro, to whom she has just been married, sees through her disguise but believes Susanna is waiting for the count. Susanna, who knows Figaro is there watching, also knows what Figaro is thinking. There is, as Bartoli delivers it, the faintest, far-off touch of tender humor detectable in the exquisite siren call of "*Deh vieni, non tardar.*" Standing next to the piano, her arms at her side, Bartoli draws in the night, the scent of pines, the wandering erotic yearning that passes from character to character while Susanna calls Figaro to enduring marital happiness, in which the audience, however cynical, is also persuaded to believe.

This aria is followed by Mozart's Symphony in D Major, in which Bartoli of course has no part. She returns to the stage in her simple black silk dress as Sextus, the young Roman nobleman who has just been persuaded to join in a plot against the life of the emperor, Titus.

Bartoli has already moved easily from the happily seduced Dorabella to the sublimely seductive Susanna; it seems to require no effort for her to enter the role of the impassioned Sesto, who delivers his *"Parto, parto"* with the desperation and wildness of a young man hesitating no longer to revenge the woman the emperor has scorned.

As Zelmira, Bartoli delivers cascades of virtuoso joy to mark Zelmira's rejoicing when her father Polidoro, the King of Lesbos, is restored to his throne. She closes the program with the orphan Amina's splendid line of soaring gratitude to her friends—a choice for a final number that seemed particularly appropriate to me. Through Amina, I imagined, Bartoli was thanking her fans for our loyalty and devotion.

For this fifth Berkeley concert, Bartoli had brought a voice that had audibly changed since her appearance a year before; always reliable at the top, she seemed now to have opened paths of effortlessness as she soared up, pitched higher, rode the breath with the sustained power and grace of a vocal falcon. New colors had entered her always highly colored voice. The timbre was more sumptuous than ever, a pearly halo glowing at the outermost edge of the tone, surrounding the voice with its own dark luster. I had the impression that her voice might actually have grown since we had last heard it. The audience seemed conscious of this rare opportunity to participate in the suspenseful development of an artist who had seemed so good to begin with that one couldn't imagine what it would mean for her to get better. Yet now she had.

The performance had been so good that one scarcely noticed the singer had been onstage between orchestral numbers for little more than thirty minutes. But suddenly, when it was all over, the brief encores delivered, the stamping and whistling and clapping finally subdued, many people felt let down. We loved her, but there hadn't been enough of her; she'd gone full out for us, yet we left feeling deprived.

The conversations during the slow, reluctant walk up the aisle into the lobby were an odd chorus of complaint and admiration. The tickets had been expensive; they had been limited to series subscribers, many of whom had subscribed simply in order to hear Bartoli. People who had missed out on her the year before had been waiting a long time to hear her. The day had arrived to moody February sun and clear skies, the lobby had been packed with excited fans telling the newcomers what they were about to hear; now, after thirty minutes of song, Bartoli had left the stage.

I was thinking, as I walked out into the late afternoon, about Nietzsche's conviction that the only justification for human life was that the gods lived it. Was Bartoli indeed one of those who die young, as she herself had foretold? Would she be asked to pay for the perfection she had achieved? Was she—with cancellations, garlic poultices, short programs, and rigorous examination of the halls in which she appeared—guarding herself against this danger?

*I*n the late fall of 1995, Renate and I made our second trip to Houston. We were there on assignment by Amy Rennert for *San Francisco Focus* magazine, an affiliate of public television, to cover Bartoli's performance in Rossini's *La Cenerentola*. The opera, which gained new popularity in America largely through Bartoli, would be televised the following March. I also wanted to interview David Gockley, the director of the Houston Grand Opera, about the first time he had heard Bartoli sing. Had his introduction to Bartoli taken place through one of those irresistible siren tapes that had caught Mastroianni and Robert Cole? Had he too taken a risk in signing an unknown singer for the opera company he had built up over the last twenty years into one of the major companies in America? Christopher Raeburn, Bartoli's producer, would be in Houston supervising the recording. I wanted to talk with him about the changes I thought I had heard in Bartoli's voice during her fifth Berkeley concert, earlier that year.

We did a lot of work in Houston. We spent hours in the archive, watched the production video of *Il Barbiere* from two years earlier. We read old reviews, looked at photographs that might be useful in our article, talked at some length with David Gockley and Christopher Raeburn. Finally we attended Bartoli's performance in *La Cenerentola*. Renate, who had enjoyed Bartoli's comic ability two years earlier, now discovered Bartoli's flair for dramatic singing and acting. I too love opera and I love Rossini, but when Bartoli was present I found myself wishing that orchestra, sets, and other performers could be cleared away so that she could stand alone onstage to sing accompanied by a single instrument. I remained attached to my original impression of Bartoli in recital, while Renate was developing an enthusiasm for Bartoli the opera singer.

Bartoli had recently been awarded the 1995 Grammy Award for Best Classical Vocal Album for *The Impatient Lover,* her recording with András Schiff. She had received major critical awards in Germany, Italy, Belgium, France, and Japan. The Houston Grand Opera summed up her achievements for their press packet. "In 1993 Ms. Bartoli had the singular distinction of simultaneously having five of her solo albums among the top 15 best selling classical albums on the Billboard Charts in North America. Her latest recording of *Mozart Portraits* within the first six months of its release has sold over 200,000 copies in the United States alone. *Time* magazine named Ms. Bartoli the '1992 Top Recording Artist' in both classical and popular categories while *Musical America* named her 'Singer of the Year.' In 1993 she was recognized by the unique distinction of being named both Billboard's 'Artist of the Year' and 'Top Selling Classical Artist' as well as '1994 Female Classical Artist of the Year' at the Classical Musical Awards in London."

Bartoli had become, in the four years since we had first heard her, a unique phenomenon, breaking out of the restricted circles of classical music lovers into the largest musical and extramusical world. The directors of the Chunnel train linking France and England had named a locomotive "Cecilia Bartoli." She had her own Web site with hypertext links it would take hours to traverse. New dishes were named for her by famous chefs. She was, according to the *New York Times,* the only classical singer under forty-five to command a major following. Her albums sold in numbers large enough to compete with the Three Tenors. Yet, through all this, Bartoli the artist was quietly and steadily maturing, becoming more expressive, more refined and vocally exquisite, as if she had found the way to prosper within her protective circle while the public chattered away outside.

Perhaps Music itself was protecting her, I said to Renate as we walked into our hotel near the Wortham Theater in downtown Houston. Bartoli had arrived in the world in time to participate in the double bicentennials of Mozart's death and Rossini's birth; she had come in time to take the place of Horne and Berganza, the retiring mezzos, at a period of emergence of serious interest in serious Rossini. She brought a voice that was itself an original bel canto instrument, at a time when the period-instrument movement was moving on into dramatic Rossini and even Verdi—a direction in which Bartoli's dark, rich voice might one day conceivably move, although she continued to speak about her preference for the eighteenth-century repertoire.

She had been working with Harnoncourt in Vienna, performing Haydn's *Orfeo* with original instruments, experimenting with timbres and tonalities that were hard or dry and not always beautiful. There was talk of Bartoli recording *Orfeo* with Hogwood, in London, with original instruments. She was thinking about some roles from Vivaldi and Händel and was becoming interested in the castrato repertoire.

Bartoli had also been researching and performing songs by Pauline Viardot, the sister of Maria Malibran. They were both daughters of Manuel Garcia, a famous singer and teacher of singing whose methods have influenced generations of vocal teachers and students. Viardot herself had been one of the most celebrated divas of the last century, the lover of Turgenev, a close friend of the composer Saint-Saëns. She had also been a prolific composer, although she is remembered less for for her creative genius than for her Paris salon and the admiration she aroused in the famous men of her time, including the poet Alfred de Musset, whose poems she set to music. Bartoli had recently been searching through private collectins for scores of Viardot's work. The young singer was now eager to discover the work of women composers, an interest she had not yet developed at the time of our conversation two years earlier.

As a servant of music, a researcher, a discoverer, an explorer of an old, neglected repertoire that was waiting to be brought back to life, Bartoli stood for more than just good singing and performing. She was here, perhaps, on a historical mission. I said this to Renate, who smiled. This weighty purpose might cast its magic spell and protect her, I said. Renate reminded me that a similar accomplishment in the bel canto revival of the fifties had not done much to keep Callas safe.

*D*avid Gockley, the director of the Houston Grand Opera, had first heard of Cecilia Bartoli through her manager, Jack Mastroianni, who had worked for him for twelve years as a fund-raiser. In 1987 Mastroianni had joined Columbia Artists as an artist's manager. A few years later his friend, Christopher Raeburn, had played him the tape of Cecilia Bartoli. Mastroianni, in turn, had brought a tape of Bartoli for Gockley to hear.

I wanted Gockley to tell me about that first moment of hearing Bartoli.

"We played it right on that little boom box out there," Gockley said, adjusting his bow tie. "It sounded great. Other people had heard her and they said, 'Oh, well, you know, she's very young; a small voice, etc.' I heard a technical virtuosity that you don't ever hear. Coloration and expressivity. It was a dream combination. Of course, I wanted to hear her live. I went to a concert that was given in New York.

"That was very early on in her career, but we just went bingo, bingo for *Barber* and *Cenerentola*. It didn't matter to me whether she had sung them or not; it was just so clearly right that she would be appropriate for these roles. Her personality was very vivid, lovely, vixenish, dreamy at times. She had a very good range of acting expressivity as well as vocal expressivity. They were wedded together in this remarkable package. This was clearly somebody of extraordinary gifts."

Gockley had been sitting in a relaxed position, his hands folded around his knees. Now he leaned back and gazed at the ceiling.

"The first time you hear her," he says thoughtfully, "it is like a moment when God comes down with his hand and touches the earth. It's what Salieri thought of Mozart. I had not ever had this experience to that extent before. Not the voice as an instrument itself, but the voice as a medium. The voice becomes a medium of communication so profound that you're kind of taken aback."

Gockley had taken the risk of offering Cecilia her American opera debut. Did he, too, feel that some quality of her extraordinary presence was lost in operatic performance?

"Recently," he continued, "we asked Cecilia to give a private recital in a private home, as a perk to our major donors. When you see her in a salon environment and you get everything at close range, it is beyond description. I found myself with tears coming down my face, just because you know that you're in touch with something out of the ordinary.

"When she appears onstage, in the midst of scenery and costumes and other people interacting with her, the effect is diluted to some extent. It was as if I had been literally sitting in heaven in that intimate salon environment and now I was back in the real world.

"Onstage, there she is, she's doing her thing as Cenerentola in an opera production that is by definition imperfect. The orchestra balances are not perfect, the lighting doesn't catch her or others in exactly the right way, especially during the rehearsal process. The technical process went slowly with this production because we had imported it from Bologna. Then it had gone to Japan, then it was rented out without Cecilia to Reno, so we had to do a lot of fixing and it held us up.

"Cecilia knows about her gift. She knows that it has to be protected, husbanded, put in circumstances that are going to show it off. She is, I think increasingly, a perfectionist. She is a perfectionist in an inherently imperfect world of opera. She will do perhaps two opera productions in a year and those will be hand-picked circumstances. And even in hand-picked circumstances something's going to happen, something's going to go wrong because you are hand-picking them three to four years in advance. Somebody will get sick. A concept that looks good on paper sometimes doesn't come out right. She's going to have to be big enough to roll with the punches and hope that a few of these productions fulfill her expectations.

"She won't go into a project unless everything has been approved. Somebody such as myself takes the prerogative of putting something together. But if you want Cecilia you just say, 'Cecilia, here's a blank piece of paper. Write down what you want. We'll see if we can afford it.' The conductor is probably the core of any project with her. There are some theaters that want her and she has refused to perform because they are too big. The directors keep inviting her: 'Oh come, we can make it nice for you, keep the orchestra very low.' I know the artistic director of the Lyric Opera of Chicago was down here a couple of days ago, romancing Cecilia. What comes of it I don't know. I think those companies that are willing to offer the carte blanche, or have a music director like James Levine, or a handful of other extraordinary conductors associated with their house or accessible to their house will have a better chance with her. As for the smallness of the voice . . . that is not what matters, not if she has a sensitive conductor. If the voice has the right kind of focus and the right kind of articulation it can carry to the final row, and I think you'll find that with Cecilia also at the Met."

Cecilia had told us that she would use her diva status to make sure she could work with the best musicians in the world. Other than that (and the many shoes she could now buy), it didn't seem to interest her. Gockley had worked with Cecilia over several years. I wondered if he had found her changed by the pressures of an international career.

"Well, sometimes her tendency to choose what she's going to do comes perilously late, and sometimes it's almost too late to put together something. Cecilia has decided to perform in public six months a year. Maybe, of those six months, there will be two operas, the rest concerts and recitals. The average opera will take six weeks, so twelve weeks out of twenty-six would be opera. The rest would be concerts and recitals. The other six months would be learning, resting, and recording. So, if she follows through with that and only does two operas a year, you can imagine with what discretion they will be chosen. They will have all these perfect casts, probably a recording before or after; there will probably also be video involved. I think these are Cecilia's ideas, but it is very helpful that she has a manager who thinks strategically. In fact it is he, Mastroianni, who has formed the television production company that is producing this television video of *Cenerentola* for Public Television. Later it will come out on laser disc and VHS and whatever else develops."

Cecilia had been known as easygoing and perhaps compliant. Was she her own woman now? Had fame changed her, had it changed her relationship to her mother?

"When her mother is around Cecilia is constantly asking her opinion. How do I look? How's my costume? How's my hair? How does that sound? I can see her speak with her mother. Of course I don't hear everything they say. But Cecilia will look receptive, she listens as if she's going to follow the advice. During the rehearsal period for *Cenerentola* her mother has been here from the beginning. Christopher Raeburn has been here almost from the beginning. So she has had her two major mentors giving her feedback constantly.

"I was talking with Christopher the other day. I asked him about Cecilia's voice and he said her voice is right now the equivalent in size to Berganza's at her most mature. Remember, Teresa Berganza sang Carmen. If I could choose my next project with Cecilia that would be it. Cecilia is only twenty-nine. So I think there's no doubt that Carmen is in her future. But of course she is going to be very careful and take her time before she tries it.

"Cecilia knows what she wants. She's not afraid to say, 'This is not working and I'll go sit in my dressing room until it's fixed.' She knows how to be resolute. We have this situation here, on a day like this, with all

this heat, when Houstonians expect air conditioning. And Italians hate air
conditioning. They think it's the root of all evil. We had our dress
rehearsal the other night. We had quite a few people in the house. We
said, 'Well, at least a little bit of air conditioning or else it gets so hot in
the auditorium that people just can't take it.' But she let the stage management know that she would wait in her dressing room and when the air
conditioning was off she would continue. I think she's developed something of a crust. But not a nasty crust. Not prima donna. Just a resolute
crust: 'These are my needs and I'm protecting myself.'"

*C*hristopher Raeburn invited us to lunch. We found a table in a corner of a crowded restaurant, set up the tape recorder, pinned the microphone to Raeburn's tie. He seemed amused that we had taken over as
recording engineers and reassured us that he would not be drowned out
by the booming and clatter of the restaurant.

I told him my impression that Cecilia's voice had grown larger and was
in some way more mature.

"The voice," he said thoughtfully, "has become the voice of a woman
singing totally within her capacity. Perhaps it is very, very fractionally
darker, but I don't think so. It was always a dark voice. She has no trouble
at all with the top [highest register] now. The voice has extended so that
she can sing at either end of her voice with no difficulty at all. She is very
specifically mezzo-soprano. *Very* specifically. There are certain roles, even
by Rossini, she feels lie too low for her at present.

"Cecilia is not straining her voice. Her voice is in better condition now
than it has ever been. The top was always secure, but at the beginning it
sometimes sounded as though it was at a certain limit. I think now the
upper limit of the voice is even more comfortable, and you get the feeling
she could always go one note above."

I was curious to know what Raeburn thought of the contradictions in
the press's reactions to Bartoli.

"The press, who love sniping, like to say that she has a manufactured career. It isn't. It is completely her own. She is the one who decides what she will sing, what she wants to sing. She is her own promoter, by her presence. If there has been a buildup of excitement about a singer, the critics tend to feel a sense of personal insult. They're annoyed that they haven't been responsible for whatever reputation a singer has garnered. I believe it's pure egoism.

"Something happened in London recently. There's a magazine called *Gramophone*. They've always been very qualified with their praise of any record that Cecilia has made. If she's been nominated two or three times for a *Gramophone* Award she's never received one. This year there were some more *Gramophone* Awards and she was up for something. She didn't get it from the critics on the panel. But there is a classical radio station and they arranged with *Gramophone* to play the six or so records that had been nominated for *Gramophone* Awards. Six records, which they would be playing for weeks and weeks to their listeners. The listeners would then vote which was their favorite. They called it the Classic FM Award, but in effect it was the people's award. Cecilia won it by a huge percent, but it was never mentioned in *Gramophone*."

The conversation was going well; therefore, I confessed to Raeburn my various worries about Cecilia, who had in her keeping this remarkable, if perishable and perhaps fragile gift.

"I think Cecilia now is much less inclined to be bullied. When she was much younger, some people pushed her around. And she, being a good trouper and a very decent person, put up with far more than I think she needed to have done. But I think she realized that these people were taking advantage of her and now she's had enough of that sort of thing.

"I'll give you an example. When *Cenerentola* happened in Bologna, it was her first big opera there. She regarded herself as one of a team of singers. But she had it in her contract that the first night should not be broadcast because she didn't want to risk her very first Cenerentola onstage. But the people upstairs got all the other artists to sign a contract that they were willing to broadcast the first night, and then they browbeat Cecilia. 'Look here, you're letting everybody else down. You're letting down the theater. You're disappointing us.' Cecilia said, 'But look, I made this clear in a contract.' And they said, 'Well, we forgot to look at your contract and we signed for the rights for this broadcast.' So she was pushed around. She was treated just as a young girl who was lucky to get a break. But in fact this show was put on for her, there was a recording planned by her record company, and the whole venture was being put on entirely for Cecilia. Back then, she gave in and did the broadcast. Now she would be able to say no and absolutely not let that happen.

"She is very busy now and does not really like silly mistakes, which waste her time and give her extra trouble. From that point of view, I think she is no longer tolerant, but understandably so. People said Callas was so impossible. She basically was not. She was a professional. But when other people were not being professional, she would not just remain silent. She would protest. Cecilia has now developed an ability to protect herself because she needs to.

"Cecilia is, for me, absolutely, when *en forme*, at her very best now. Better than previously. You ask, have I noticed any difference in her voice? There are pieces of music that she has been doing longest, in recital or in the theater, which are her most developed characterizations. They belong to her more now. Not with the voice. There it's safe. I mean better in terms of interpretation."

I wanted to know who was responsible for the shape of Bartoli's artistic career and wondered if Raeburn helped her make decisions about roles, productions, repertoire.

"These are her own artistic decisions. We discuss projects in general, but she is the one who has a very, very firm idea of herself and where she is going. I mean, no Carmen before the turn of the century. She's quite clear. Why? Because of acts two, three, and four. Act two is becoming dramatic. Act three more dramatic. Act four is very dramatic indeed. You have to have a very strong physique for your voice. Your voice has to be physically very untiring for you to be able to cope with that. All this would tire her voice too much at present. Because her voice isn't made of steel. It needs treating with care and she has treated it with care.

"For these dramatic roles you have to sing over a heavy orchestra. There are certain parts that are written so dramatically, you can't take the orchestra down. The orchestral music is written for a voice that will carry over it. Furthermore, you have to sing so intensely that it's quite different from Rossini's Desdemona. After all, Carmen is involved in slanging matches. You've got to almost shout those. That means a voice has to take a lot of punishment. If it's naturally a loud and very strong indestructible Turandot sort of voice, fine. You can cope with this sort of business. When Cecilia is in her middle thirties I think her voice will be so settled she can do what she wants with it. But Cecilia has got a totally different kind of voice. In recital, she has about twenty shades between mezzo piano and pianissimo."

Espresso arrived, the restaurant emptied, we lingered over our discussion. I wanted to know about Cecilia's relationship to her mother. Raeburn assured us that it had not changed over the years. Cecilia's voice may have developed, her capacity to take care of herself may have grown, but her relationship to her mother had remained constant.

"They are totally close. Absolutely. If her mother is around, Cecilia will discuss anything vocal with her. Her mother will be at rehearsal and will make any necessary comments. It will be that way around. But the mother won't originate things. Cecilia prepares herself. There's not really tuition as such anymore; it is more overseeing. I feel that her mother is the most important person in her life. She's very close to her brother and sister also, but to her mother in particular. She depends upon her mother in the mother/daughter sense, even more than in the musical sense. Her father has lived elsewhere for maybe eight years. I think his career could have gone a very different way than it did. He could have become one of the big, dramatic tenors. I think Silvana could have had a much bigger career, too. Apparently she had the most beautiful voice. But the irony is, that was just before everybody had tape recorders and so virtually nothing of the mother's voice from back then exists. But both the parents were soloists and very good, and only made a decision to join the chorus because they couldn't rely on a soloist's life; they had to get salaried. It was a question of economics, not ability. He, as I said, could have been one of the very big tenors."

We look back as we are leaving the restaurant. Christopher Raeburn lifts his hand to wave to us. We have met the man responsible for Cecilia's career. He has followed it through every vocal and interpretive development; more than anyone in the world, apart from her mother, he is able to speak with authority about Cecilia's voice. And now there is also the story of the father's lost career and the tape of the mother's beautiful voice, which does not exist.

Houston is hot. I wouldn't mind some air conditioning as we walk back to our hotel. I feel a troubling sense of nostalgia for the days when Bartoli did not yet belong to the world, but could be heard in the intimate salon atmosphere of a half-filled hall. I would trade my attendance at all the operas she would ever perform for forty minutes at that private recital Gockley had described.

"The first time you hear her," he had said, with tears in his eyes, "it is like a moment when God comes down with his hand and touches the earth."

That had been my impression, exactly.

*R*enate and I have parted ways. I am for Cecilia the recitalist, in the smallest, most intimate settings, where one can take in the twenty shades between her mezzo piano and her pianissimo. I am nostalgic for the experience of the sacred breath passing through Bartoli to the unsuspecting members of her audience. I want the past, even if Bartoli's voice is growing more expressive and more daring. Renate is a champion of Cecilia on the stage. She can't wait to write about the essence of her comic ability and the way it shades over into a dramatic potential that will define her future career.

While we are still in Houston, Renate has become curious about Cecilia's early stage career and suggests we return to the archive to see if they have a record of her performances before she arrived in America, in 1990, to sing at the Mostly Mozart Festival in New York.

I think the hotel will be cooler than the archive, but we decide to go back to work, unaware that this decision to track down Bartoli's early operatic career is about to entangle us in a situation of true Rossinian comic perplexity. We thought we could gather in a few dates and theaters and roles, make a list of them for a sidebar to the article, show off a bit how thorough we had been in our research. We did not foresee that no one had a record of the early career, which had begun even before Raeburn or Mastroianni had discovered her. Raeburn remembered some of her early roles but was not sure of the dates or theaters; her manager's office did not have a complete list and could only provide the most impressionistic accounting. Her publicist promised to check with her manager, who promised to get the information to *San Francisco Focus* magazine, but after some ten calls it was not forthcoming. When it finally arrived it was more scattered and incomplete than our own fragmentary knowledge.

As we read through the articles I had collected over the years, we picked up here and there the date of a debut performance in a particular theater. That was a helpful beginning, but the various articles had different versions of these dates and places. Finally, in exasperation, we decided to make calls to the various theaters that had been mentioned in Rome, Bologna, Pesaro, Florence, Cologne, Paris. The time difference between California and Europe made it necessary to stay up late and make the calls after midnight. Renate was fluent in German and French, but her knowledge of Italian was limited. What little there was had been influenced by Metastasio librettos.

The Italian opera houses and press offices were enthusiastic and friendly, but Renate was not always certain that she had made herself clear. We got fax numbers, sent faxes, didn't get responses, made more calls, stayed up until two or three in the morning waiting for people to arrive at their desks, found that some houses had superb archival records, others weren't certain whether Cecilia had sung with them and, if so, in what role. Many places simply didn't answer us. Our tentative chronology, derived from reviews and articles, kept changing. Every morning I made a new list, which I revised in the evening, so that we could make calls and write letters and send faxes to places about which questions had arisen.

This calling and writing and gathering and sorting is the kind of task (quixotic, comic, heroic) only an outsider takes on. It belongs to the role of the unknown fan who worships from a distance, keeps a notebook of comments and impressions on the singer's various performances and recitals, gathers up every smallest bit of information that can be salvaged from the gliding of time and the quick fading of memory. But history, it seems, loves its chroniclers and provided us with abundant information.

The young singer had been in the business for a good ten years, from her first appearance on *Fantastico* in 1985 to her appearance as Cenerentola in Houston in the fall of 1995. In the winter of 1996 she would make her debut at the Metropolitan as Despina in Mozart's *Così fan tutte*. Bartoli had risen from obscurity, she had put in her apprenticeship years, she had set the highest possible artistic standard for herself. She was no longer a girl who could be treated with disrespect. She was a woman in charge of her career. She could choose her own conductor, casts, productions, perform whatever music fascinated her, work with the best musicians in the world. She had learned how to protect herself, knew now that she must.

With her debut at the Metropolitan, the first decade of her career would be over, her middle period about to begin. We had collected videos of Bartoli in some of her major early roles and were invited, by various opera houses, to visit their archives the next time we were in Europe to look at material that could not be copied or sent out of the house. Bartoli had a past, a history, her own developmental line, which we were now able to examine. "The historical record," I said to Renate one late night as we were looking over our material, "must have been brooding about its neglect. Now it has chosen us as its transcribers."

Renate smiled. "Lucky for us."

IV

The Master Class

MOTHER AND DAUGHTER IN BRAUNSCHWEIG,
1996

$\mathscr{B}$raunschweig is a small town between Frankfurt and Berlin. Its origins, in the ninth century, are attributed to the brothers Bruno and Dankward, who built the castle and the cathedral on the banks of the Oker River, which still runs through the stately town, with its thirteenth-century walls, old cloisters and churches. Braunschweig is resplendent with ponds and parks and old squares filled with outdoor cafés. Now, in early May, in a café built on terraces along the river, we are drinking strong coffee with whipped cream as we read up on the cultural history of this town. Here, in a few days, Cecilia Bartoli will hold her third local recital and give a master class in singing with Silvana Bazzoni, her mother.

There have been years when Bartoli's only German appearance took place in this small town. As she became famous, she has refused offers to larger, more prestigious places while faithfully appearing here. This may have something to do with the refined enthusiasms of Henry the Lionhearted and his wife Mathilde, in whose twelfth-century court the cultural traditions were established that have made Braunschweig the proud possessor of Europe's oldest museums, including the world's oldest Jewish museum. Lessing's *Emilia Galotti* and Goethe's *Faust* were first performed here, during the eighteenth century, perhaps beneath the same linden trees we have been admiring as we strolled through the town. Renate, who finds this possibility somewhat less exciting than I, observes that the blackbirds have a more ornate song than the California species. She is doubtful that Bartoli has come here because of Henry the Lionhearted and his wife Mathilde; she imagines that there are contemporary reasons that have brought Bartoli to this town.

Martin Becker, the press representative for the Kammermusikpodium festival, first heard Bartoli in Zürich before she became famous. He took the risk of persuading his chief to invite the unknown singer with the beautiful voice to perform at his prestigious festival. A man captivated by a voice takes a risk on a young singer, who remains loyal as she grows famous. It is by now the familiar Bartoli story.

The master class, however, is not familiar. At the time of my conversation with Bartoli several years ago her mother was reluctant to begin teaching other pupils. Bartoli, who felt strongly that her mother must have a life in music after her retirement as a singer, had hoped to persuade her to give a master class someday. Since then, Silvana Bazzoni has had private students in Rome. Tomorrow, when the class begins, Renate and I will attend the first master class Bartoli and her mother have ever given. The organizers of the Braunschweig festival are the first people in the world to have invited the two women to teach together.

Certainly, I am looking forward to meeting up with Bartoli again. There is an excitement I can scarcely contain, however. I will soon be able to witness the way Bartoli's teacher teaches singing. I have not forgotten my fantasies of the old bel canto schools, an ageless tradition that handed down, from teacher to pupil, mature singer to novice, arts and secrets of voice technique that most modern teachers of singing no longer know. Did mother and daughter have an approach to singing that was different from the teaching of voice in most conservatories? Were there secrets to be learned? If so, could they be transmitted? Years ago, I had imagined Bartoli and her mother teaching together someday. This obscure fantasy was about to come true. The master class would be held on the grounds of an old cloister some few kilometers outside of Braunschweig. There, I would be able to see how Cecilia herself had been taught to sing by her mother. I would find out how a bel canto voice was forged and refined through exacting technical and expressive training.

The cloister is surrounded by stone walls. Cars enter on a cobbled path and drive under the gnarled trees into an underground garage next to the modern building in which the class will be held. Outside the class-room, with its highly polished Grotrian-Steinweg grand, the trees tirelessly display new leaves to the ruined cloister across the pond. The six young women chosen for this class sit nervously in the front row. Silvana Bazzoni is sitting in a chair in front of the windows on our left. She is holding a small stack of music beneath her chin while she thumbs through a score. The young singers are watching her closely. She is very intense and focused, a small woman in her early sixties with short graying hair. She is wearing light-colored pants and a pink checked jacket, which she later tells me belongs to Cecilia. There is a rooted, earthy quality about her.

"The recital is more pure than opera," Bartoli says; "it is very exposed, you must show more states of the soul."

A connection had been
established between singer and
audience. Her nervousness
vanished, her dark eyes
flashed with a perceptible
gratitude, her voice opened
out beyond what seemed
possible.

Imagine a sensuous, embodied angel, standing quietly on a concert stage. . . reporting back to God about the mysterious joys and sorrows of human existence.

Bartoli applauds her audience after a performance because we have taken the risk of receiving what she has to give.

The interplay of risk and gratitude, gratitude and devotion, distinguishes Bartoli's relationship with her audience.

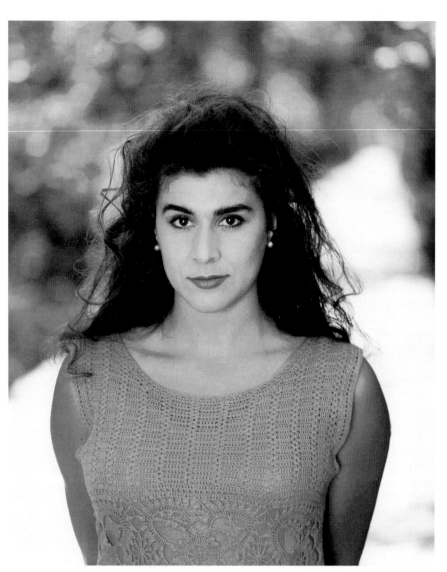

Who is Cecilia?

Who is she?

Her detractors claim that she is the product of clever publicity and media hype.

"I am like Rossini," Bartoli says, "earthy, spicy …"

"Many times my mother says to me, 'Cecilia, you have to find out for yourself. When you are at home, working with a pianist, you can try this role. . .'"

"When I studied with my mother it was not only two hours a day. If I was singing in the kitchen, singing for myself I heard her call out, 'Cecilia, non e giusto.' That's not correct."

"It's possible for my mother to help many young singers. She is reluctant; she says, 'Vediamo, vediamo,' We'll see, we'll see. But I tell her, 'Mommy, if you don't want to give individual lessons you can give a master class.'"

In the master class in Braunschweig it is possible to see how Cecilia herself has been taught to sing by her mother.

"*The Eternal Father gave me my voice. That is why I am here. To give people this joy, this beauty.*"

In person she is less glamorous, wearing no makeup or lipstick, her dark hair pulled back casually from her temples. But when she is excited, hands, arms, fingers, come to life.

They are a very close family. They are all very protective of one another. The bond comes from the mother, it goes back to the mother, it goes to the sister, it comes back to each sister.

Music, she seems to say, is a serious, practical business. We are here to learn, to work, and to master.

There have been forty-four applicants for this class. Each sent in a tape with six minutes of singing. Ten tapes were selected by the organizers of the music festival and sent to Bartoli and Bazzoni, who have chosen these six women. They come from Poland, Lithuania, and Germany, are between the ages of twenty and twenty-eight, and are all hoping for singing careers. Renate is surprised that there were so few applicants, as the class was announced internationally, from Tokyo to Australia. One of the singers, a German woman of Persian descent, suggests that most students were afraid to take the risk of singing before Cecilia and her mother and therefore didn't apply.

It is a risk comparable to the one that Cecilia herself faced when she decided to try out for *Fantastico*. The representatives of the show had come around to her conservatory looking for young singers, and Cecilia, who had never sung in public before, went for the audition. Here, in Braunschweig, the six women will have to sing for Cecilia Bartoli and Silvana Bazzoni, in front of some two dozen observers, most of them singers or singing teachers. They will be offered instruction, have their vocal problems named, analyzed, and corrected, be compelled to learn or fail to learn in public. After the three days of instruction there will be a concert sponsored by the festival. It will take place on the night following Cecilia's recital. She is close to them in age, shares a repertoire with some of them, is living the ideal future each must hope for herself. Silvana Bazzoni has insisted that the class consist only of women, a fact that does not seem to have pleased the festival organizers. Later, during the break, she tells me that women are easier to teach than men because they can learn through imitation.

Some of the students seem surprised that Bartoli is not present this afternoon, on the first day of class. Her mother will teach in Italian, her instructions will be translated into German. Everyone seems shy as the class begins: the students who come up to work with Cecilia Bartoli's teacher, the translator who practically whispers into the student's ear, perhaps also Silvana Bazzoni. Cecilia had talked to us about her mother's hesitations, her uncertainty that other students would be able to learn what she has to teach. Bazzoni herself has spoken about the courage it takes to face an audience. As she stands up to greet the first student we are witnessing her public debut as a teacher.

The first singer is a lanky young German, twenty years old, with her hair in a bun. She will sing *"Deh per questo,"* from Mozart's *La Clemenza di Tito.* As she takes a breath to begin singing, Bazzoni also takes a breath. The singer is interrupted after a few bars. Bazzoni is not satisfied with her pronunciation. She has immediately detected the singer's problem; she is unable to sing an "o." She sings "ah" instead, a very open vowel that she has to learn to close down. The singer's score falls, Silvana picks it up. The young woman sings a few more bars. Silvana stops her, to make the same comment. There is, she seems to say, no reason to go further when basic matters have not been addressed.

The next singer, also a German, is a few years older. Bazzoni listens to her with her legs spread, her right hand on her hip. She stops the singer after a few passages of *"Giunse alfin,"* Susanna's aria from Mozart's *Le Nozze di Figaro.* Here the problem is the movement of the breath, which Bazzoni illustrates with a gesture that will soon become the leitmotif of the class. She is on her toes, her hand moving upward in front of her face, the curved fingers describing the rounded peak the breath must learn to traverse. Then Bazzoni sings the passage the singer has been struggling with. We hear the voice of Cecilia Bartoli's mother, a rich, pearly soprano. The singer tries again: *"Un po' meglio,"* Bazzoni affirms ("That's a little better"), a statement so precisely factual it is received by the singer as encouragement.

The next singer delivers *"Parto, parto,"* from Mozart's *Clemenza di Tito.* It can't be easy to sing an aria Cecilia performs and has also studied with this teacher. The singer has a dark voice with a lovely timbre. Silvana smiles at moments, listens intently, shakes her finger. She shows the singer how the voice falling on a particular syllable or vowel is the secret of the aria's expressiveness. *"Passa,"* she says, and *"quasi"* when the singer tries again. She can get by with it. When she has trouble applying what Silvana wants her to learn, Silvana says consolingly, with a reassuring nod, *"Domani, domani."* We will try again tomorrow.

Bazzoni seems to have formed an immediate comradeship with the student's future ability. Therefore, she can be perfectly frank about what is not yet right in her delivery. There is an offhand, almost casual tone in the way she dismisses the impure note, the inadequate breath support, the poor pronunciation. She does not offer praise. She simply comments that a note or passage is not right, it is a little better, somewhat better, it needs work. There is a consistent acknowledgment in her relationship to the singer; yes, this work is hard, it may seem boring, but we are learning music and therefore it is worth it.

For the fourth singer, the young woman from a Persian background, Silvana interrupts to tell her not to force the voice. She offers a detailed explanation of what happens when the voice is forced and the sound becomes hard. But if you don't cramp, if you stay relaxed, she says, the sound comes as if by itself, the feeling is so pleasant it is like a massage, and the note you sing becomes so beautiful you may want to hold it for half an hour. Her face reflects this free and beautiful tone, evoking it, embodying it.

Bazzoni is by now absorbed in her task; she puts the singer's hand on the teacher's face, to feel the relaxation while she sings. She touches the singer's diaphragm firmly, to demonstrate the breath support. She talks about the portamento, the linking of one note to the next. The singer performs the passage again, her eyes very bright, her voice straining for a relaxation it cannot reach. But I have the impression she has been given a clue, for which she is grateful. She is radiant when she returns to her seat to exchange excited comments with the other singers.

There is a stark truthfulness in Bazzoni's method, a severity of precise naming that has, for most of the singers, a bracing effect. One of the singers whispers to us that her own teacher has been working with her on the very problem Silvana picked up after a few bars. It is possible that some of the women will find out over the next few days that they have to start all over again or give up if they do not have the discipline or patience. This recognition may lie in wait for each of them. Still, I have the impression that anyone who wants to know herself, be recognized for what she is and where she has to go, will thrive in this atmosphere.

To the Polish singer Bazzoni says, "Well, stay quite calm. You have a beautiful voice." Here the concentration is on remaining *"tranquilla,"* on concentrating and not letting the presence of the audience or the teacher affect the voice. Bazzoni uses the word *"spinto"* (pushed), in contrast to the free, relaxed voice she wants the singer to produce. She joins her in the recitative and aria from Bellini's *I Capuleti e i Montecchi.* Bazzoni's voice seems to catch hold of the singer, to coax, call up, and draw out her own latent potential. She touches the young woman's arm to relax her, and now the beautiful tone comes, the voice floating out on the breath, relaxed, free, and expressive. The small audience applauds, the singer is exhilarated.

Bazzoni's teaching reminds me of the comforting severity of a spiritual practice, with which the mastery of the technique of singing can clearly be compared, for it too is a voluptuous and ascetic discipline, more rigorous, detailed, and demanding than I had supposed.

To the last singer Bazzoni remarks, "If one pronounces correctly the voice adapts." The woman sings again, Bazzoni says, "Your throat is closed, this can't be learned in three days. Forcing is very dangerous." The singer asks what technical means she could use to open her throat. Bazzoni laughs, for the first time. She points her finger to her throat as if to vomit. "Well, you could use toothpicks," she says. "You could put them between your teeth to keep your mouth open." She points out that the muscles of the jaws and mouth don't want to give in and adapt to the tone—one has to constantly, relentlessly exercise them. She also adds that this is the one correct system of singing; there is no other that works, while this one always does. She demonstrates the sounds—"ooohwaah," like a roaring animal—and suggests that one must draw up the sound from the depth of the throat. There is nervous laughter about these examples, which may strike a German audience as somewhat earthy, animal, for such an ethereal art.

Bazzoni encourages the singer not to sing when she is tired, telling her, with a concerned frown, that this could be dangerous for the voice. The singer looks surprised, tries again, and then retires after a few bars, admitting with a relieved smile that she feels fatigue. I am reminded of Cecilia's comment that her mother knows more about Cecilia's voice than Cecilia herself.

The singers have introduced themselves, a central task has been defined for each, they will return the next day to work further. At the end of the class Bazzoni turns to the audience to apologize for concentrating on the singers. She explains that the most elementary foundation of singing is the breathing, the complete opening of the throat, as in yawning. This heightens the vault of the palate so the sound curves upward and forward all by itself. To practice this she proposes the vowel "oo." This exercise helps to lower the larynx and open the throat. She compares the palate to a cupola and repeats many times that the breath has to come as high up into this cupola as possible. Again, she makes the arching gesture with her hand. It is okay, she says, to exaggerate this in the beginning and then little by little gain control. But the exaggeration has to be without any pressure, or it could become dangerous. Yes, it is very boring to practice like this, but then music, she says, is so beautiful.

These simple words, spoken with a serene and radiant conviction, catch hold of the audience. I, who will never be able to sing, feel that it would be worth my while to spend the rest of my life practicing these basic techniques for music's sake. We have just met a master teacher who is direct, precise, and simple in her instructions. She emphasizes the most basic principles of singing but imparts to them an urgency and importance they do not often receive. If there is a secret to bel canto singing, she seems to say, it will be found in the relentless practice of an exacting technique. Nevertheless, a mystery remains. How will she be able to transmit the courage required to take on this seemingly impossible task of producing a beautiful sound?

*D*uring the second day of class I decide to introduce myself to Silvana Bazzoni, who is sitting by herself near the window. The translator, the singers, and some members of the audience have stepped out for coffee and cookies in the lobby. Bazzoni is thumbing through a score, but I have the impression she would welcome an interruption. Most people here do not speak Italian; I speak only a few words of her language, but it seems to me I should introduce myself as the person who is writing a book about Cecilia. I have regretted my failure to return to Houston to meet Cecilia's mother several years ago. I still want to ask her the same questions I wanted to ask her then. Bazzoni looks up expectantly when I start to walk toward her. I reach her chair, I say, somewhat too smoothly, because I have been rehearsing the words: *"Io non so parlare italiano. Io sono* Kim Chernin. *Io scrivo un libro su Cecilia."* ("I don't speak Italian. I am Kim Chernin. I am writing a book about Cecilia.")

She hesitates for a moment, seems to be considering something, then reaches out her hand and simultaneously pats the chair next to her. *"Piacere,"* she says, with that quality of stating what is true. The words are conventional, but she does indeed seem pleased to meet me.

I stumble on in my poor Italian, trying to tell her what I have understood about her teaching. It is a matter, I am trying to say, of making the basic, tedious practice somehow inspiring. Renate joins us. Her Italian is slightly better than mine, but only slightly. Still, it is very easy to talk with Silvana Bazzoni. She reads my face, takes in my expression, comes to meet me just where my sentence is about to fail. Then, promptly, she produces the word I have been looking for, and the faltering sentence gropes forward.

Cecilia, she says, was from the outset enormously musical. Absolutely, unusually musical. Music for her was a game; there were endless cadenzas and scherzi that she invented to amuse herself. When Mother explained something once, that was enough; Cecilia caught on, she had an easy time learning. Cecilia's older brother was a tenor; she had tried to teach him singing but he preferred the violin. Federica, her youngest daughter, is a stage designer. Singing did not catch on with her. Bazzoni likes to work with young singers, in whom the voice is not yet made. It is very difficult to unlearn the old mistakes, she says with a deep sigh. The age of seventeen or eighteen is a good age to start. Mediocrity, she says, is not good enough. It is very difficult to have a singing career. Very difficult. To let the voice come by itself is the key. There is not much that can be taught in three days. The discipline, the dedication cannot come from the teacher. The student must find out if she has them in herself. Singing is hard work, hard work. But when the voice comes, then you see it is worth it. Cecilia, she says, found everything easy, but even she had to work, to vocalize, to extend her range. Music, she says, narrowing her eyes, is never simple.

The second morning's session brings out a new quality in Bazzoni. She is perceptibly more relaxed and demonstrative, sings more often with the students or draws close to them, mouthing the words, her face miming the emotion she wants them to express. They seem to be gazing into her eyes as if they were catching glimpses of their own potential. She seems, even more than yesterday, so aligned with the singers' ability that she can take for granted their agreement with her judgment. We have not yet heard her say a word of praise. She says *"quasi"* (sort of), *"meglio"* (better), *"un poco meglio"* (a little better), *"va bene"* (okay).

"Non è pericoloso, prova" ("It's not dangerous; try it"), she says to the Persian woman, whose temperament pleases her. She has an obvious capacity to understand Bazzoni's instruction, can immediately apply the lesson, gets visibly excited as she learns. Bazzoni moves in close to her. *"E'*

stanca? E' stanca?" she asks repeatedly. "Are you tired? Are you tired?" She sings an aria to illustrate her point. A simple hand gesture, the expression in her eyes, the tilt of her chin, the inflection of her voice catch hold of the student's attention. No wonder; Bazzoni has just created a little *scèna.* The young woman imitates her, takes something in, gives something back with her own inflection. Bazzoni steps forward, very close to her, her knees bent, mouthing the words. It seems evident that the singer is being driven beyond her own capacity, given a taste of what she will own after years of work, if she has the courage and discipline to stick with it. For moments, it looks to me as if the singer were reading the score from Bazzoni's face, as if Bazzoni the teacher has disappeared and in her place stands music itself. She moves right up against the student in her eagerness to communicate, points to her nose, shakes her finger, nods when things are going well, throws her arms around her when she has finished.

Yesterday, we met Bazzoni the diagnostician, the severe instructor in the basic requirements of beautiful singing. Today we are meeting a woman who derives her capacity to teach from an intimate relationship to music itself. Merely to be in her presence brings one closer to an understanding of music. This is, I imagine, what Cecilia had tried to tell me three years ago, when she spoke of how thoroughly and completely she trusts her mother's musical knowledge. "Of course," she had said, "it is not always possible to do what a parent advises. But where music is concerned, my mother . . . well, my mother knows."

The student, also an expressive woman, returns to her seat with her eyes brimming. The next student gets slowly to her feet, drawn up in spite of herself. The audience is absolutely quiet; no one stirs, shifts, shuffles, or coughs, although there are more people present than yesterday. Word has spread that an unusual teacher is at hand and that something remarkable is taking place. For me, it is like being in an old, largely forgotten laboratory where essential experiments are taking place. The obvious, along with everything fundamental and basic, seems mixed in with what can scarcely be expressed, or can be expressed only in purely musical terms. I have reached what I have been trying to reach through all these years of studying Bartoli's voice. I have found the mother root.

*D*uring the lunch break Silvana comes up to shake hands vigorously with me. I imagine she knows how passionately I have been following the lessons. If I had a voice I would follow her to Rome and try to become her student. She has just told me she likes to work with people whose voice is not yet made. That, at least, applies to me.

It has been decided that the afternoon session will begin and end early, so that students and audience will have a chance to rest before Cecilia's recital. Silvana is on the way back to her hotel to change her shoes. She has to get going. She never takes coffee or cookies during the break; I now have the impression she will not have much time for lunch. She explains that the shoes are uncomfortable. If they interfere with her concentration they will be cast off in favor of something more practical.

We stay behind to speak with the students. One of them seems depressed, the others look highly satisfied, the best of them seem inspired. The Polish woman, who again today has produced a beautiful tone, has very red cheeks. Her somewhat plain, understated face has become exceptionally pretty. Her eyes seem startled in the suddenness of their initiation. She presses her limited German for sufficient language to talk to us. She has paid her own way to Braunschweig, but the rest of the expenses have been covered by the Kammermusikpodium festival. She has never heard Bartoli sing in a recital but loves what she has heard from recordings. She does not seem to think that she can ever become what Bartoli has become, neither as accomplished or as famous, but it is now clear that there is more to her than she imagined. It seems possible that while working with Cecilia's mother she has heard her own voice, really heard it, for the first time. Yet another singer tells us, with a sense of great bewilderment, that Bazzoni immediately recognized the very problems with which her own teacher had been working. She says she can take big risks with Frau Bazzoni because she immediately felt safe with her and knew she could trust her. The Persian woman can't wait to go back into class. The lunch break seems long to her, although the day is warm, the old cloister inviting. There are seeds drifting about overhead, the blackbirds are working at their coloratura. One singer is decidedly disgruntled. She feels that her confidence has been undermined. She is more worried than before about her concert tomorrow. Bazzoni, she insists, has been working on small problems while she has much bigger problems she thought would be addressed. Renate and I go in early, to be sure of securing our seats in the front row.

The afternoon session passes too quickly. I go up again to speak with Silvana, who is adept at guessing my meaning. I am trying to fit in all the words we might have spoken several years ago in Houston. I am curious to know about her own background as a singer. How did she get started? Was her mother a singer, too? She laughs at this, shakes her head, seems about to tell a good story, but the translator has returned. The break is over, I go back to my seat, the instruction begins.

I soon get the impression that Cecilia is present in the room in spite of her absence. She, the teacher's daughter and star pupil, sets the standard for perfection; it is her voice and expressiveness against which everyone else is implicitly measured. Silvana is wearing plain black walking shoes. She has changed into more comfortable pants and given up Cecilia's jacket. The weather has turned warm, it is beginning to affect her voice. The atmosphere in the room has also warmed up considerably, and now Silvana Bazzoni, who has shown herself as teacher and at times as music itself, becomes a mother to the young singers. By now we have heard *"Parto, parto"* and *"Voi che sapete"* and *"Cruda sorte!"* and *"Je veux vivre"* so many times I myself could almost sing them. She is preparing the singers for their recital, working with them on pronunciation, delivery, tranquillity. Some of them have picked up her familiar gesture, arm raised, hand overhead, fingers curved downward. By now we all know about the vault of resonance created by opening the glottis and lifting the palate so that the breath flows through naturally and the sound need not be forced. No one has mastered this, no one has been expected to master it, but I would guess the lesson has been indelibly imprinted. The young women come up eagerly to sing, the small audience is attentive and expectant. We know what the singers have been working on, we can follow their progress. Bazzoni has helped them withdraw the pressure and pushing they have applied to their voices. The singer who has found it hardest to learn still cannot manage the vocal arc, but Renate has observed that she no longer flattens her voice to the back of her mouth under the stress of producing a high note.

Silvana hugs the students, touches their arms, cheeks, sings along with them, silently mimes the characters they are struggling to bring to life. I imagine this is how she looked while working with Cecilia: stern, knowing, demanding, inspiring, protective. She has become a spirit of maternal encouragement whose love and affection are palpably transmitted through music itself. She reminds me of the ideal bel canto teacher described by

Giovanni Battista Lamperti, himself a singing master, taught by Francisco Lamperti, his own father, who had drawn much of his vocal wisdom from Rossini, Bellini and Donizetti. "There must be a reciprocal magnetic attraction between pupil and teacher, which helps to convey ideas from teacher to pupil. The teacher must have a profound knowledge of the aids to a properly cultivated mechanism, and ability to impart this knowledge to his pupils. The teacher should hypnotize the pupil with his knowledge." (*Vocal Wisdom,* Enlarged Edition, Maxims of Giovanni Battista Lamperti, New York: Taplinger Publishing Company, 1931, 1957, page 8)

Everyone seems reluctant to leave when the session is over. The students cluster around Silvana, who nods, pats, encourages, and reassures. "Will you be at Cecilia's concert tonight?" Silvana asks as we say good-bye. She tells us that she is always on edge when Cecilia sings. But Cecilia has already told us that she experiences her mother as a rock. There is an unshakable, grounded, deeply reassuring quality to Silvana Bazzoni. In her we have encountered a mingling of authority, wisdom, and tenderness, the rarely combined qualities of teacher, musician, and mother.

*O*n the third day of the master class most people arrive early, eager to talk about last night's concert. The young singer from Poland has the inexpressible in her eyes when she speaks about the perfection of Cecilia Bartoli. Herr Presse, the journalist from Switzerland who has been sitting behind us for the last couple of days, is severe and unexcited. He has been following Bartoli since the beginning of her career and now predicts that it will soon be over with her voice. He feels that its brightness is gone, she has lost her coloratura ease, she is no longer really a mezzo, the voice has become darker and deeper, the high notes are strained. Her own particular place in music, the mezzo coloratura voice for which she has become famous, is a niche she can no longer occupy. He feels that she should leave the arie antiche alone, she can't do them anymore, that there are ten singers in the world who are as good at them and even better.

He is a knowledgeable, thoughtful man with whom we have enjoyed several conversations. We are both shocked by our divergent response to last night's concert; we stand talking heatedly outside the classroom as our coffee grows cold. I mention Bartoli's majestic entrances and exits, which suit a woman who, entirely through her own merits, has conquered the musical world. All trace of shyness is gone; she carries herself with mature pride. She is larger, no longer in the least girlish; she holds herself with grace and assurance, as if she knows how well she deserves to have grown into this womanly body.

Herr Presse is troubled by Bartoli's conspicuous development from more slender girlishness to the statuesque figure amply revealed on the stage last night. He thinks her record company will no longer wish to present full-figure photos of Bartoli on her CDs, that she has literally outgrown the roles in which she had become famous. He is astonished, then perhaps disbelieving, when I say I like the way she looked.

A few months later, the same reservation about Bartoli would be expressed by the male reviewer of the *Cenerentola* laser disc for *Gramophone* magazine. "The camera emphasizes her now—shall we say—comfortable figure, unsuitable for a neglected Angelina." Various causes of this change, which most men seem to deplore, have been suggested to me in private conversations: the stress of public life, the ravaging performance schedule of the contemporary singer, the lonely life on the road away from home— food, it is implied, serving as comfort, consolation, and trustworthy companion. I have had the impression, when dining with Bartoli, that her love of food expresses the same vibrant enthusiasm with which she gives herself over to the pleasure of singing. When I spoke to Silvana Bazzoni about Cecilia's larger size, which I thought grandly suited her, Bazzoni shrugged. "She has matured," she said, as if the fact required little comment and no interpretation.

Certainly, Bartoli seems comfortable in her new "comfortable" figure; she had come onto the stage as if she were the proud figurehead of a splendid ship, her shoulders back, her head held high. Wearing a green taffeta dress with a tight embroidered midriff, a heart-shaped plunging bodice held by two scant strips of material on her upper arms, she carried her ample bosom as a veritable cornucopia, the skin of her chest, neck, and arms, with its mother-of-pearl shimmer, an entirely adequate substitute for jewelry. It is true that Bartoli's former beauty, full of incompletion and girlish promise, along with the coltish, heartwarming exuberance of the ingenue, has been outgrown. There are Bartoli admirers who may never forgive her this transformation that has set before us, in place of the seductive girl Bartoli has been, a woman of great personal and artistic power.

I hear in her singing more color and expression, a mastery and refinement that allow her to take incredible vocal risks. The characters she brings onstage emerge with a kind of sly and ironic vividness. She has no problem with the adolescent page Cherubino, although he has to make his way through this magnificent female with voluptuous breasts and shoulders.

Herr Presse is not moved by this tirade. He predicts that Bartoli is at the peak of her success, claims that the market has been glutted with her recordings, that sales will begin to drop. He grants that she had sung the Bellini well. He is dismissive of the rest of the program—the Beethoven and Schubert songs he too had heard her sing in Berkeley, along with the intricate arias from Gluck and Haydn, the unknown songs by Pauline Viardot. He is tired of her well-known and by now, he feels, mannered Rossini. Bartoli is clearly a passion for both of us, an enthusiasm still glowing for me, while darkening, losing its luster, for him. He disliked the forced smile with which she came out of her arias. These smiles demonstrated to him her emotional insincerity. I thought she had been making at times a perceptible effort to return to the audience from her own musical absorption.

We have trouble breaking off our conversation when the class begins. Cecilia will be present today; the room is nearly full. Renate had secured us good seats, but Herr Presse and I want to go on talking. "We must stay in touch with each other," he said, handing me his card. "We will follow this career over the next few years. It will be very interesting to see how it works out."

"But how is it possible," I ask, "that we have witnessed the same event and come away with such radically different responses?"

"Remember Callas," he remarks.

"Callas? Precisely. Perhaps every great artist creates this polarity in her listeners, because the voice is unique, unexpected, unpredictable in its development."

He is polite, but vehement; willing to listen, but sure of his own response. There were now more beautiful voices in the world than Bartoli's. It was all over for her.

Class is beginning. The doors will soon be shut; if we continue our debate we will not be allowed to enter until the first break. We take our seats next to Renate, who tells us that Silvana has lost her voice, she has to speak in a whisper. The sudden heat was always bad for her voice, she had said, and the room had been drafty. I think Silvana has given her voice to her students. Renate thinks that the master class may have been more of a strain for Silvana than one would guess from her sturdy demeanor and authoritative teaching.

She is now coaching the students for their recital, which will take place in a few hours. One of them, a tall, lean woman, will have to sing *"Voi che sapete"* the night after Cecilia had sung it. I have the feeling Cherubino will have more trouble embodying himself in her than in the womanly, voluptuous Cecilia.

Silvana looks exhausted; she is coming down with a cold, her students seem to be husbanding their voices, the small audience is enthusiastic, but I remain distracted. I have just been in conversation with the point of view I have been studying and privately fighting since I first began to follow Bartoli's career. From the beginning, certain reviewers heard strained high notes, an uneasy, aspirated coloratura; they had predicted an imminent decline for both voice and career. I had spent many years puzzling over this response to Bartoli, this seemingly irreconcilable difference in perception. But was it really a difference in perception? Both Herr Presse and I had noticed that Bartoli's voice had changed. It was the significance we assigned to this change that accounted for our disagreement. He heard the beginning of decline, a falling away from a former perfection. I saw a ripening, a growth, a movement into new dimensions.

Similarly, we both thought she was singing the arie antiche differently. He heard her inability to sing them in the old way and thought she should stop singing them. I felt that she was introducing a textural and emotional complexity that transfigured these seemingly simple songs. She had already, as Christopher Raeburn had pointed out, differentiated the coloratura of Mozart and Rossini. Now, I felt, she was discovering or inventing yet a third coloratura, with a marked and spicy differentiation of notes, letting her voice perform musical feats one did not expect of a coloratura mezzo. This could be seen, as Herr Presse saw it, as a failure to conform to the appropriate standard for the mezzo voice. Or one could experience it, as I had, as a playful and expressive extension of what coloratura means and does. She was experimenting with a slightly woody sound, like an oboe or bassoon, in the deeper registers of her voice. We both heard it; he objected to it, I found it fascinating. It seemed to me that Bartoli was about to introduce into her voice the individual colors of the woodwinds, to play with flat and sharp tonalities along with her lustrous, round tones. Was this a failing or a deliberate extension? Had she lost her beautiful coloratura voice or simply added to it another dozen voices?

*D*uring the break we speak with Silvana about last night's concert. She talks in a hoarse whisper, eager to discuss the event. I tell her it was, for me, Cecilia's most outstanding concert. I throw out something about expressivity, new tones and colors in the voice, the wonderful characterizations. What had she thought? It is impossible for her to judge, she says. She is the mother. She is so involved in the singing, aware of the choices her daughter makes, the risks she is taking. Suddenly, I understand that it cannot be easy to be teacher, musical guide, and mother all in one person, but this is a perception my exasperated Italian will not allow me to express.

There is loud applause when Cecilia Bartoli walks in briskly after the break. She is wearing a bright red jacket, black pants, and shoes with a small heel. She is carrying a purse just like her mother's. Silvana Bazzoni walks behind her with a quiet expression of shared accomplishment. This restrained, confident smile must have much to do with the mother as teacher. Or is she thinking what I am thinking? We are the first people in the world to see these two women, teacher-mother and famous daughter, teach together.

Bartoli, onstage, has a remarkable beauty; it is heightened whenever she is gripped by her own musical rapture. This beauty seems to arise from the harmonious presence of all those elements that have made Bartoli famous: her technical mastery, her emotionality, her dark eyes, abundant hair, low-cut gowns, full breasts, beautiful shoulders, perfect skin, mesmerizing voice. In person, on a working day, she is a handsome woman with strong features. It will take excitement, enthusiasm, or perhaps music itself to bring out the beauty we beheld last night.

Bartoli takes her place at the side of the room next to her mother. Both women lean forward, hands on their knees. One of the students comes up to perform for Cecilia Bartoli, who from the first moments is listening intently. Silvana stands up to share the performance with her student, moves with her into the role, takes part silently in the singing, drawing the music out, encouraging her. She smiles lightly when the singer has finished. Cecilia comes forward to take her mother's place.

Between Cecilia and the singer there is an immediate engagement. Cecilia is eager to talk, she has listened with concentration, she has something to say. There is none of the nervous laughter we have seen in her televised interviews. She explains that she will make general comments, not specific technical points as her mother has done. She talks about the imperative union between words and music. "You have a very pretty voice," she says to the singer, "but there are technical difficulties, as you must have heard from Mamma." She interrupts herself to urge her mother to sit down. Mamma sits, immediately gets up again. The other singers seem reluctant to come forward. Bazzoni goes back to confer with them. She is encouraging them to take the risk, assuring them they will not tire their voices, they will be fit for tonight's concert. She seems to sense that tonight's concert, before the festival audience, will be a good deal less intimidating than this miniature performance before Cecilia Bartoli. After much hushed and excited talk, Bazzoni, the mother-teacher, prevails; all but one of the women agree to sing.

Bazzoni stands up to approach her student, Bartoli leans on her knees, she and her mother both nodding, mouthing the words, caught up in the character of Cherubino, who now appears in triplicate in the lanky form of the young German singer, the mature face of the master teacher, the expressive, mobile, flashing eyes of the world's most famous coloratura mezzo. Occasionally, Cecilia glances with concern at her mother, worried about her cold and fatigue. When the singer has finished, Bartoli walks forward briskly. She says, in a comradely tone: "It's a beautiful role, isn't it? How many times have you seen the opera? Once? Have you studied the whole opera and role or only the aria?"

Silvana listens to Cecilia with her enormous, quiet pride. Cecilia is talking about the complexity of Cherubino; she goes to the piano, points to a place in the score, sings a few bars to demonstrate the confused passion of the page, interrupts herself, steps back to listen to the singer, imitates the way she has sung three identical phrases identically, whereas they offered the opportunity for careful differentiation, which she now demonstrates. "Cherubino is a very complex role," she says. "There is the youth and incertitude of his gender. What is he? Man? Woman? Something in between? Do you understand the text?" she asks the singer, who nods vigorously. "But one doesn't see that you do," Bartoli says gently. "Think of the emotional states he's in. He is walking and dreaming and falling about. This is what you must express."

Bartoli demonstrates the agitation, the *palpitar*. The singer can't take her eyes off her. "This is an aria following a recitative," Bartoli says. She describes the snatching of the ribbon, the running and chasing, heavy breathing, being out of breath even before the aria begins.

The singer tries the aria again; this time she produces a somewhat sleepy expression. "Don't keep to the strict rhythm," Bartoli instructs her. "You have freedom of improvisation. You must sing it every time as though it is the first time." Then Bartoli demonstrates a high note with the gesture—arm raised, hand lifted, fingers curved—that Bazzoni has made the signature gesture of the class. Everyone laughs, Bartoli catches on immediately. "You have heard this from Mamma," she says, touching the singer affectionately on the shoulder.

Bartoli speaks fast, her verbal speed communicating itself to the translator, who becomes charged up in turn. Bartoli talks about the greater freedom of the voice in the eighteenth century, when the vocal categories were not fixed by gender and the voice was allowed to be freer, more androgynous. Where Silvana Bazzoni has been grounded and rooted, Cecilia Bartoli is temperamental and excited. The room begins to crackle with her energy. When Bartoli wants urgently to communicate with the singer, who does not understand her rapid Italian, she switches into English, stops herself, waits for the translator to catch up with her. In Houston, when I first spoke with her, she used to switch spontaneously into French.

For the next singer, both mother and daughter stand with arms folded on their breasts, their legs spread. For a moment, both faces show an identical expression in response to the music, then mother coughs lightly, Cecilia glances at her with a worried frown, mother sits down, puts her hands between her knees, her head bent in concentration.

Cecilia is getting more and more beautiful as the afternoon passes. Sometimes she goes over to sit next to her mother, leans back against the wall, her knees spread, her finger over her lips, as she sinks into an attentive listening. Next to her, Silvana Bazzoni repeats the singer's words, sits at the edge of her chair, her breast lifted, her head back, her mouth opening for the high notes.

"You have a *voce carina*," Cecilia comments to the next singer, "you have a dear voice and a lovely timbre, your technique allows you to sing well. But I won't go into that, as Mamma has done all that already. But one senses that you think of the notes. Nobody should sing only because she has a nice voice, but because one wants to express something. It is necessary to use the face, the body, the eyes, the hands, everything. Only with the unity of music and text does the song become perfect. Tell me," she says, with a comradely, curious tone, "how do you understand what you are singing?"

A discussion of the aria from *I Capuleti e i Montecchi* follows; the translator has trouble keeping up, the singer is trying to soak up every word. Cecilia has a lot to say; arms, hands, eyes join in the communication, which comes, it seems, in part from Cecilia Bartoli, in part from the tragic young daughter of the Montagues.

Teacher Bazzoni seems pleased to rest, to let go of the reins, confident of her daughter's ability, curious about what she will say to the singers. The connection between the two teachers, mother and daughter, is maintained by occasional whispered conferences, their shared response to the music, a brief gesture or touch, a quick glance of concern, acknowledgment, or recognition.

To the next singer Bartoli says, "The text is more assured in you than your voice." When the singer tries again, she manages for a moment or two to bring the music and text together in a precarious balance that is already lost in the next moment. The knowledge of this fugitive accomplishment remains in the singer's face when she goes back to her seat, darkening very slightly the expression of her eyes.

Bartoli is, it seems, as quick where interpretation and expression are concerned as her mother is technically perceptive. What we have observed over several days, Bartoli immediately grasps, with temperament, ebullience, and drama. She shakes hands with the young mezzo who has just sung *"Parto, parto."* "I am a singer," she says to her, "with the same problems as you. You have a beautiful, dark voice; it is an old voice [suitable for baroque music]. You can have a career if you believe in what you do. Why did you choose *'Parto, parto'*? Tell me, what mood is Sesto in?"

Bazzoni looks up with interest when Bartoli tells the singer that pronunciation is not as essential as correct understanding and interpretation.

Bazzoni has worked with her extensively on her pronunciation. The singer glances at Bazzoni, who raises her eyebrows, then glances at her daughter, who looks back and forth from one to the other, laughing as she takes in the significance of the exchange. "I am sure you have worked extensively with Mamma on pronunciation," Bartoli says, in the tone of one who knows this extensive work only too well.

Bartoli has by now become as radiant and vibrant as she is onstage. She tells the Persian woman that she is highly expressive, perhaps even a bit too much. She mentions that she occasionally masks with her beautiful smile the technical difficulties she still has. The voice, she says, is a bit nasal at times. But then she grasps the singer by the shoulders and says warmly, "Keep your joyous desire to sing. Keep it, never lose it."

There is applause for the singers as they go back to their seats. Bartoli sits down next to her mother. The class is over. But the audience cannot be kept silent. Everyone has a question to ask Cecilia Bartoli. One of the observers, a Spanish singer who has been studying in Germany, asks why Bartoli does not teach more often. "I am very young," Bartoli explains, seriously. "I am still learning. I am not a master. Mamma is the master. What kind of impression does it give if I hold a master class?"

The singer assures her that none of this matters. She points out how much everyone has learned; she herself has learned so much just sitting in the audience. "Why can't you go on doing what you have just done?" she asks reasonably.

Someone asks how it is possible to get the score for an obscure work of Rossini; she has been looking all over for it. Bartoli says that the scores are in a private collection and one needs permission to sing them.

There is a great moment of stir and anguish when Bartoli mentions that she herself, when she began singing, worked for days and weeks on producing a single sound. She worked for seven weeks on only one note, she says, when she was studying with her mother.

The singers and observers register an audible astonishment. I myself have heard Bartoli speak about this strenuous exercise before. It is consistent with what I have heard about the old bel canto teaching methods. "It is a pity," says old Lamperti, "that young singers who are studying voice immediately sing songs and arias, literally before they know how to open their mouths, instead of earnestly studying the real support of the voice (the mechanism of the breath) in order to develop the voice and to make it smooth and flexible." Bartoli explains that the voice is like any other instrument: if you want to play a violin you won't begin with Paganini. *Si, si,* she repeats, how can you begin to study the voice by singing arias or songs?

We are now in the middle of a heated discussion of the methods taught in the conservatories. Most singers begin their training by studying a song. At Bartoli's *conservatorio* they studied arie antiche, because they were considered simple. This is crazy, Bartoli says; they are extremely complicated in phrasing and expression. Vocalizing is the only way to mastery, she says again. The repetition of a single sound. Especially the vowels, u (ooh), o (oh), a (ah). But it is necessary to work with all the vowels, to make the muscles of the mouth strong by teaching them to produce the correct mouth positions. That is building the house from the foundation, stone by stone, even if it takes a long time.

A few days later I discussed conservatory training in Italy with Luca Logi, the archivist at the Teatro Comunale in Florence. He had sat on the panel for his theater's choir auditions and had heard a lot of young singers. Musical education, he told me, and especially the teaching of singing, had undergone a rapid decline during the last decades, although Italian conservatories had been schools of a very high level, especially the historic schools like Milan, Rome, Pesaro, Parma, Naples, Florence, Bologna, Venice. Since 1960, political pressures had doubled the number of existing conservatories; in many cases teaching positions had been offered to unqualified or incapable teachers. In order to obtain a degree, which in Italy has a legal value, students still pass state examinations but very commonly study with private teachers. Good ones, he felt, were becoming rarer and rarer. He agreed that Cecilia's training, with her mother, had been exceptional.

There is, however, great exasperation on the part of the singers and participants in the master class when Bartoli talks about the continual repetition of a single sound.

Somebody asks, And then?

"Then?" Bartoli repeats, laughing. "Vocalizing never ends." She says that she practices all the time. When the voice is secure in its range then you can begin singing arias.

A member of the audience asks, "But how do you not lose your joy of singing with all this?"

"It depends on your will and your desire," Bartoli responds, with authority. "If you're strong enough you will survive. It's the same with any instrument, as with any artwork, you have to hammer and hammer if you want to get a plate. And anyway, it's very rich to do vocalizing. Maybe it is tiring, but it is also exciting and fun because one discovers one's voice. I had a *voce bianca* when I was sixteen and started singing. I had no idea whatever about my voice. Vocalizing is the discovery of one's own body."

A singer says, "Well if you do the vocalizing as you say, for years and years on end, which opera house will then want a thirty-six-year-old singer?"

"That depends upon your individual speed," Bartoli responds. "At the usual conservatories you practice one hour or two per week, that's all they put aside for singing. That's nothing. I practiced with Mamma two hours a day. But there is also often a refusal in young singers to study and sacrifice for their art. The will is often lacking."

An observer, who has been visibly growing restless during this discussion, now protests. "You have tempted these six young singers to come to the master class and now they are all told they are not ready," he says.

"Frau Bartoli is only expressing her own opinion," the translator immediately responds.

Bartoli, who has seemed surprised by the excitement in the room, looks curiously at the man who has just spoken. No one has translated his words into Italian. Someone says, in German, "But no one said they were not ready."

"Frau Bartoli is only expressing her own opinion," the translator repeats.

"That's not the point," I say, as excited as everyone else and therefore willing to risk my German. "Cecilia is explaining that this is the way she studied. She is telling us how she herself learned to sing with her mother."

The translator, irritated at the interruptions, does not translate what I am saying. Many people are talking at the same time. Bartoli asks me to speak in English; the translator calls for order, she says we are offending Frau Bartoli, who immediately responds, "Certainly not, certainly not."

Silvana Bazzoni has been sitting quietly, observing the excitement in the room. She has the expression of a woman who has seen it all and knows what to expect. She has brought the art of singing down to its fundamentals, which are practiced relentlessly until each is mastered in turn. If there is a secret to her approach, it is the ability to make this practice seem worthwhile because of the way it reveals and develops the self as it reveals to the singer the intrinsic value of music. Her daughter is voluble, intelligent, quick, clever, fiery, intense, authoritative, gracious. For the last ten years she has been the living proof of the soundness of her mother's teaching methods; now she has become their articulate champion.

A master class is not for teaching, Bartoli concludes. It is only to give some advice. Then it is up to the participants to use it or not, take it or leave it, do with it what they like.

"So, if the arie antiche are not easy, what music is easy?" someone asks.

"No music is easy," Bartoli responds. "But Vivaldi helps you to discover the secret of recital singing. Sound must be unified with the words, melted together, words and music a perfect harmony. Some arias of Mozart, like Cherubino or Zerlina, are considered easy at music schools, also Scarlatti . . ."

At this she laughs a hearty, dismissive laugh, in which the audience now joins, uneasily.

"So how does one choose the right music for oneself if nothing is easy?" someone asks.

"One has to find the music one loves. The music that fits one's temperament and personality and speaks most to one's heart. But that music," she says, with a quick catch of her breath, "is not necessarily the easiest music to sing."

*T*he three days of the master class have passed.

People are milling about, getting programs signed, talking to Bartoli and Bazzoni, discussing the class among themselves.

A woman tells me she came to the master class because her daughter had just started to study singing and she, the mother, wanted to know what it was all about. She shakes her head as if to say, How can she make it?

Renate is talking with Cecilia Bartoli. I have not left my seat. Perhaps I am sitting here because I have not finished taking notes. Therefore, I write energetically.

Renate interrupts me. "You will be interested in what Cecilia is saying."

Cecilia shakes my hand warmly. "I am very glad to see you here," she says. We talk about the Bartoli research Renate and I have been doing. She smiles somewhat grimly when we mention *Fantastico*. Renate has been curious to know why Cecilia performed "Summertime" on the show. Was it her own choice?

"They advised me to sing a very popular song," she says. "But if I had to do it all over again I might not do it."

Bartoli's English is much easier than it was three years earlier. She speaks with some of the same speed and heightened intensity that accompanies her Italian. We are talking about her performances of Zerlina and Despina. They were written for the middle range of the voice, she points out, not for the high register. But high sopranos feel most secure with the high notes. Therefore, Mozart must have had something different in mind for these roles, something like the mezzo voice, although of course this voice had not been named as such in his time. Dorabella, she points out, has the same voice register as Despina, except that it lies sometimes a little higher. It doesn't really make sense that Despina is mostly given to a light soprano, because her part is written for the middle voice.

"It is interesting to sing both roles, although of course it is not exactly common. When you perform Dorabella you learn about Despina. Then, when you sing Despina, you see Dorabella in another way."

A German singer from the audience comes up to join the conversation. She asks whether Bartoli sings in German. "There are all these lieder," Bartoli says, somewhat wistfully, "all that wonderful music. I am studying German, but you not only have to speak the language, you have to feel it."

Renate wants to talk about the choice of Despina for her Met debut. "It was crazy in a way," Bartoli agrees. "I was trying to send a message that I'm not a diva, I won't behave like people expect a diva to behave. Everyone was waiting for a big title role and I said, well, I have sung in New York at Avery Fisher Hall, at Carnegie Hall, and now I am making my debut at the Met. It seemed very important to think only of music for the debut, not about stardom. Music and voice always happen in an ensemble. It seemed important to me to do it that way, to be part of the ensemble. Anyway, I love the part of Despina, I don't think she is a soubrette, I want to perform her as a woman who knows something. Despina is the first feminist in opera."

Our little group forms and reforms around Bartoli. Sometimes Renate and I speak to her alone, with some of the same engagement we felt in the guesthouse in Houston. Most of the time we are joined by other admirers, who listen in, ask questions, drift on, talk with Silvana, come back again.

"*Così* may not be ideal for the Met anyway," Cecilia says. "It would be much better in a European eighteenth-century concert hall. There is something about these old halls, a certain atmosphere. You know, you understand? It is very, very inspiring."

She mentions, with great affection, the Theater an der Wien and speaks about a recent concert in the Concertgebouw in Amsterdam, where the audience was very knowledgeable. "The small theaters have a particular spirit they give to Mozart," she says. "Mozart wrote for the small theaters."

Someone asks if she ever feels that Mozart wrote for her voice. He asks if she thinks of herself as a great singer.

"That is a claim I could not make for myself. That is for someone else to decide. For myself I say it is always possible to get better."

A young woman asks if her mother was a strict teacher. "Very strict, very strict," Bartoli answers soberly. "She taught me an important secret. To exercise the notes of passage, mi, fa, sol, which move the voice from mezzo to soprano, from one register to another. These give stability to the voice. To master them takes much work, very much repetition."

The young singer still hopes to learn secrets that make her work less arduous. Bartoli holds her ground. The secrets are hard work, the complete mastery of the fundamentals, the will and discipline to practice.

The mysterious laboratory of the bel canto school amounts to no more than this.

But the ability to persevere in this, I say, is in its own right a great mystery.

Bartoli flashes me that sharp, encompassing glance she shares with Bazzoni. "When Mamma teaches singing," she says, "she teaches also more than singing."

This "more" remains the irreducible mystery of the master class. It has been present, in its palpable vagueness, from the moment Silvana Bazzoni strode forward to instruct her first student. It has something to do with the hidden resources of the singer, as these are detected, then called up by a master who knows what the best is and accepts nothing less.

This teacher, it occurs to me, would have had her own history, her own perseverance, struggles that have been overcome, difficulties that have been mastered. As yet, we know nothing of these where Silvana Bazzoni is concerned.

For the last three days I have been satisfied that I had reached the origins for which I have been seeking. Down there, in the workshop where the ethereal is broken down into the concrete, I have been at peace. I have been to the workshop where Cecilia Bartoli's voice was made. Now, however, I have glimpsed origins that are deeper, darker, farther off. I am as fascinated now by Silvana Bazzoni as I have been for all these years by her daughter.

We are sitting quietly in the empty restaurant above the room where the master class was held. Bazzoni and Bartoli are drinking mineral water. Renate and I, the translator, and two journalists have been served coffee. Bazzoni cannot talk above a whisper. Bartoli takes up her mother's lost voice to make it audible.

I have asked Cecilia to translate my questions to Silvana, so that I could speak to her in English. I wanted to know how Silvana's mother felt about Silvana's singing career.

"Oh yes," Cecilia exclaims, "that is a very good story."

She leans over to speak with Silvana, who repeats the familiar story patiently so that Cecilia can translate it for me. I am caught in the endless drift backward of origins. I have traced Bartoli's voice to Bazzoni, I am about to place Bazzoni's voice in relation to her own mother. I have the distinct sensation of a theme biting its own tail. Was Bazzoni's mother also a singer, a teacher of singing, who shaped her daughter's life and career?

"Nonna, my grandmother," says Cecilia, "did not want Mamma to sing. She wanted Mamma to have a practical life, to marry, work on the farm. Mamma sang in the church choir. The priest heard her; he thought she had a beautiful voice. So he worked with her, he gave her private lessons, he taught her to make the voice. It was the priest who helped her go to the *conservatorio* in Parma against her mother's wishes. But Mamma was determined to sing. So Mamma left home, she went to study, she began her career. Her life is in music, that is how it had to be. But perhaps there is always someone to help. In this case, well, it was the priest."

A single generation back and the mother-daughter line is already broken. There is no direct lineage from her own mother through which Silvana Bazzoni derives her musicality or the secrets of the old bel canto inspiration. On the other hand, she studied in Parma, one of the best conservatories in Italy, where there has been a considerable interest in opera singers since Verdi's time.

Before we leave, Bazzoni tells us, in her hoarse whisper, that she will not be going to Paris for Cecilia's recital. Cecilia's sister will travel with her. Bazzoni is going back to Rome to care for her parents, she says. Two days later, however, when we arrive at the Théâtre des Champs-Elysées, we find ourselves seated two rows behind Silvana. After the concert, Renate asks Silvana if her cold is better. *"Un po' meglio,"* she says, with the quiet emphasis that has characterized these same words throughout the master class. Cecilia has just performed the same recital she sang in Braunschweig. The same, but in no way the same, Renate says to Silvana, who had been sitting in the first row of the balcony, leaning forward on the railing with rapt concentration throughout the entire recital.

We stroll back to our hotel, along the Seine, past the Louvre and the Gare d'Orsay, across the bridge to the Ile de la Cité, where we eat pistachio ice cream and talk about the mother and daughter sopranos, Cecilia Bartoli and Silvana Bazzoni, and the old bel canto schools and Bartoli's wish to explore the castrato repertoire and the ravishing music of Pauline Viardot, which no one but Bartoli has sung (I like to think) since Viardot wrote it some hundred years ago, and the possibility that Bartoli is about to discover a new repertoire of music written by women, to which, in a gesture of voluptuous surrender, as she leans against the piano, she hands herself over, we think, with even more than her usual dedication.

The first decade of Bartoli's career is over, the apprenticeship years have passed, a mature artist has emerged who is about to challenge the established vocal categories as she explores the mysteries of the coloratura voice. There is a sense of suspense, the certainty of following an arresting vocal development whose direction and precise form cannot be known.

Over the years, Bartoli has consistently said that there has been, for her, no time for a great love. More recently, she has acknowledged the presence of a man in her life and now speaks affectionately about a friend whom she visits at Lake Garda. His farm produces wine and olive oil and offers Bartoli a romantic return to the family's rural roots. He loves classical music, admires her voice, and talks to her about the planting of grapes and other "very simple things" that remind her that there is more to life than a career. "Music is important," she says, "but there are other things in life." Does this mean she is thinking of family life? Children of her own? All things considered, "it is better," she has said, "to be a happy mother than an unhappy diva."

A Bartoli fan, attentive to every hint about the singer's future development, would be likely to sense in these words an unspoken reference to her mother's career, which was given up when she began to have children. Will the land claim Bartoli? Will the Bartoli voice someday be heard only in the privacy of her vineyards and olive groves above Lake Garda, calling up for a stranger walking in the hills the mysterious joys and sorrows of existence? Is she, in spite of her great accomplishments as an artist, evoking herself as the "unhappy diva"?

Fortunately for music lovers, Bartoli has ambitious musical plans. She hopes to revive neglected operas by Paisiello and Vivaldi, and talks about the remote possibility of *Carmen* staged along the lines of its original score and production at the Opéra Comique, in a small house, with a small orchestra.

This fall Bartoli's first recording of French songs will be released. Renate and I have heard some of them in her recent concerts. For the intimacy of her interpretation she makes use of extremely subtle piano shadings, frequently carried on an audible breath, a technique likely to arouse criticism from those who wish Bartoli to remain the coloratura perfectionist the world has come to love. Bartoli, however, is slipping past categories and conventional standards; she has proved herself, she can afford to go in new directions. As fans and critics we will have to decide for ourselves whether she deserves our respect for her interpretive subtlety and vocal daring. Bartoli, the Italian coloratura specialist in Mozart and Rossini, will be heard singing, on this recording, in Greek and French and Hebrew, as a small boy speaking Yiddish, and yes, even with the voice of a ladybug.

By the end of this year, she is planning to perform (with Claudio Abbado), Debussy's *Martyrdom of Saint Sebastian,* a composition originally written for Gabriele D'Annunzio's play about the Roman guard killed by his own archers when he revealed his sympathy for the early Christians. Debussy has commented on the "mystical heights reached by the poet's drama," which inspired his music for the play. He produced for it a suitably ecstatic, violent, erotic, and tortured music, a ritual sound-world of magical and cathartic elements. When Bartoli steps into this haunting world, she will once again make clear her own alliance with the sacred and mystical elements in music.

It is a warm night after rain; the past moves in close to us, bringing back the intuitions I have entertained since those far-off nights of solitary listening when I first began to study Bartoli's voice, wondering, even then, if the listener's infatuation with a beautiful voice might be a hidden form of spiritual awakening.

Performance Guide

1985–1996

By Renate Stendhal

$\mathcal{C}$ecilia Bartoli has often been called "the opera singer who almost never sings opera." Audiences, especially American audiences, who know her as a recitalist, are frequently unaware that Bartoli has had a ten-year stage career as well. At the time this book is being written, in 1996, thirty-year-old Bartoli has sung three fully staged operas in the States (Houston, 1993 and 1995; New York, 1996) and two semistaged operas (Chicago, 1992). In Europe, however, she has sung twelve different roles in fully staged productions. She has worked in major European opera houses, with world-famous conductors and directors.

Opera is an ephemeral art. Singers often study a role extensively, rehearse it for weeks or even months, then perform it for a few nights. Apart from newspaper reviews, there is often no lasting record of a performance. Budget restrictions and copyright complications prevent most productions from being professionally recorded. Thus the stellar moments in the career of a singer vanish from one day to the next, preserved only in the memory of music lovers. But memory is unreliable when it comes to establishing a historical record of an artist's career. The artist herself may be uncertain about details; her representatives may have forgotten entire performances (the less prestigious ones?); press releases tend to get rewritten and come to be filled with errors.

In Bartoli's case, it is difficult to establish the precise chronology of her roles and performances during her early years. In the beginning, before she had become famous, some opera archives did not keep records of her performances. Others, when pressed, were able to produce an original program of a production, or perhaps a date and a list of the cast. Sometimes a photo could be found or traced back to a newspaper article. In a few cases, a production video turned up in the archive but, when viewed, rendered only white shadows on a black background. Sometimes, although a performance had been professionally filmed, the archival record contained only a snippet of the production from a TV report.

The movements and gestures we see Bartoli make in a particular role, at a particular moment of an opera, have been gathered, shaped, and refined by her in numerous practice sessions, rehearsals, productions. What seems new, fresh, spontaneous is also the sum of the work Bartoli has done until that moment. It is too easy to say, "She is a natural" or "She is simply a genius." To understand her art it is crucial to observe her development as an artist.

Bartoli has developed step by step. She has worked her way through the complex challenges of becoming a performer, raising her own stakes as she went along. Certainly, her development moved at an uncanny speed. But her mastery is the fruit of ten years of intense work in a great variety of performances. The development of Bartoli as a recitalist can easily be followed through her recordings, but her opera work remains elusive. Ten years into her career only two full operas, a 1988 *Barber of Seville* and a 1996 *Cenerentola*, are available on video or laser disc.

The aim of this performance guide is to establish a written record of Bartoli's first ten years of stage performances, to describe her step-by-step maturation, and to render her stage appearances as visible as possible for anyone who has not been able to follow her in live performances or piece together the fragmentary record preserved in obscure archives around the world.

CECILIA BARTOLI'S FIRST PUBLIC APPEARANCE AS A SINGER

The Italian TV Show Fantastico, Rome

1985

Fantastico was a widely watched Saturday night show hosted by Italian TV star Pippo Baudo, featuring guests from a wide range of performing arts. Unknown talents competed with one another for the favors of the audience and, with the help of celebrities in their field, got their first chance to become stars.

Cecilia had performed as a flamenco dancer in her earlier teens and, at the age of eight, had sung the offstage shepherd in *Tosca*, at the Rome Opera. She heard about the TV competition at the Conservatorio Santa Cecilia, in Rome, where she was studying music. *Fantastico* accepted her and gave her two opera celebrities as her TV *"padrones"*: soprano Katia Ricciarelli and baritone Leo Nucci. She was nineteen years old. This was the first time she sang in public.

The camera zooms in on a small, frightfully thin young woman in a short black skirt with a patent leather belt and a simple red satin blouse. She wears a choker of thick black beads. Her hair is pulled straight back from her face with a clip and falls over her shoulders with few waves. The serious face with its pointed chin and sharp nose comes as a shock. This is not the beautiful face one would have expected to see in its teenage version. Her teeth are pointed and a bit crooked. This awkward, gaunt, perhaps even anorexic young student of music bears painfully little resemblance to the gorgeous, full-bodied singer the world has come to love for her vivacity, her joie de vivre, her sparkling, spontaneous charm.

This young woman seems nervous and very shy. She clearly is not used to the spotlight. She hardly moves from her position at the microphone even though in that position she has to strain to see the conductor. She has only studied singing for about two years. She has perhaps never before sung with an orchestra. The song, not chosen by herself but by *Fantastico*, is Gershwin's "Summertime." Throughout the song, she does not turn her face to get the conductor comfortably into her field of vision. She seems frozen into place.

But her voice reveals, although in miniature, what is soon to come. There is already some color, some velvet, a beautiful, natural phrasing even though the Gershwin song is a bit too high for her voice. Her English pronunciation is surprisingly good. But the emphasis is careful, the feeling controlled and contained as though closed in a glass box. Her face shows tight concentration. Perhaps sensing the eyes of thousands of people inhibits her from "singing out" and revealing anything as intimate as an emotion. She sings but does not seem to address anyone with her song. Consequently, one gets the impression that the song does not reach much beyond the singer. The last long, high note gets somewhat stuck in her throat; her voice flutters, gets very thin, and yet she manages to slide down the cadenza on the same breath to a delicate pianissimo close. Nothing in her face or attitude lets on that there was a problem. She stumbles but does not fall. It is a touching moment. We witness a surprising determination, already a decidedly professional attitude, and at the same time a strange indifference, as though all this didn't have all that much to do with her.

Perhaps, indeed, singing Gershwin for a television audience did not have much to do with the serious young bel canto student. Perhaps in these circumstances all that could be accomplished was to hold out against the stage fright and get through the song with dignity. Afterward, she does not express either relief or contentment. Her arms hang down without energy. She looks up to host Pippo Baudo with the shy, almost pleading eyes of a child as he hands her a record with a large picture of himself on the cover. He directs her to her audience and the cameras, and for a second she can't help breaking into a sweet, vulnerable smile. Her parents—Mummie and Daddy are indeed "standing by"—clap and smile from the audience. Already the fanfare announces the next guest on the show, director Franco Zeffirelli.

Cecilia's appearance in the first round of the competition shows an unmistakable move toward more audience appeal. She wears a pretty sleeveless evening dress in royal blue with a sequined skirt and a simple V neckline. Already there is a note of her future style of presenting herself: she wears no jewelry, except for earrings. Her essential "jewel" is her hair. She wears it in light curls that frame her face but are held back from her forehead with a rhinestone clip on one side.

She sits in the front row of the audience with Katia Ricciarelli and her rival competitor, sixteen-year-old tenor Roberto Scaltriti. This time she knows she has to smile at the camera, but little jerks of her feet betray her nervousness. Pippo Baudo takes her by the hand and leads her to the microphone. She is going to present the aria that will quickly become her signature concert piece: Rosina's first aria in *Il Barbiere di Siviglia*, *"Una voce poco fa."*

Rosina has just heard the courting song of her clandestine suitor, Lindoro, under her window, has fallen in love, and has decided to get this man. But she is sequestered in the house of her jealous old guardian Bartolo, who has his own designs on her. The aria professes Rosina's determination to use "a thousand tricks" before giving in. She will pretend to an exemplary docility, but if she is pushed, she will be as cunning as a snake to win in the end.

Technically speaking, Bartoli's earliest public rendition of "*Una voce*" proves her extraordinary natural ease with Rossini's coloratura scales. Her voice is young, a bit green and thin, especially in the upper register, but the rendition is pretty enough, she makes no mistake, and her technique is very impressive. In the balcony, the camera again shows her parents, both voicing the words of the aria along with her, her father round and smiling, her mother slender, visibly moved, leaning forward and conducting with her chin. At the end, both parents clap enthusiastically and shout "Brava!" again and again.

The applause is well deserved. Young Cecilia accomplishes a lot in this performance. She has clearly been taught to make more of herself in front of an audience, to address her listeners, to try to act the part, to be charming. What is striking in these earliest documents of a career is that these elements of opera performance apparently did not come naturally to Cecilia Bartoli. She did not jump onto a TV stage and captivate the audience. On the contrary, engaging an audience seemed to pose a formidable challenge at first.

She does not yet know how to use her beautiful, expressive eyes. She seems to remind herself not to glue them to the conductor, who again is positioned at an awkward angle, but also to look at her audience and the camera. In her attempts to act she suddenly rolls her eyes without apparent dramatic reason, perhaps trying to convey Rosina's scheming. The effect is of a crazed bird looking for an exit from a cage. When she sings the line "*Io sono docile*," she nods a lot, probably in order to indicate that this is only a pretense. She tries occasional "seductive" glances and makes heavy use of her hands in a flamenco dancer's poses to convey Rosina's feminine charm. At the same time, she struggles to rein in her all-too-unruly dancer's gestures: her calmer right hand repeatedly catches hold of the naughtier left one and immobilizes it for a moment. When she gets to Rosina's threat of turning into a snake, a few royal head thrusts indicate that she won't give in. Every now and then, she drops entirely out of the role, perhaps from sheer nervous exhaustion.

The next round in the show provides us a record of the first duet Bartoli ever sang in public. In "*Dunque io son*," from *Il Barbiere di Siviglia*, Cecilia is once again Rosina, Leo Nucci is Figaro. (Three years later, in 1988, the two of them will sing in the Bologna recording of *Il Barbiere* under Giuseppe Patane.)

This time, Cecilia is dressed up in Spanish style: a dark burgundy dress with black lace sleeves and flounces, flamenco shoes, her hair pulled behind her head in slightly lacquered waves. But there is nothing sexy about her outfit, nothing that anticipates the later glamorous, racy album covers that will help spread her fame. Her dress is rather tame, and her heavier "Spanish" makeup makes her look older and oddly matronly.

Her singing technique with easy, quick roulades, leaps, and trills is again astonishing, but her performance is lifeless. There is no emotion in her exclaiming, *"Dunque io son la fortunata!"* ("So I am the lucky one!"), nor in the later passages of happy relief, *"Fortunati affetti miei! Io comincio a respirar"* ("How lucky I am to be so happy! I begin to breathe again"). There also is no anxious, teasing, excited play between this Rosina and her Figaro. Cecilia remains rigid and serious, and her efforts at charm are restricted to a bit of mincing and throwing glances from the corners of her eyes. Once or twice, she turns to Nucci with one hand lifted in a coquettish gesture of surprise that comes across as old-fashioned feminine wiles rather than youthful charm. Once again, one gets the impression that she tries hard to follow someone's stage directions, and this obedience ironically places her in square opposition to Rosina's rebellious, indomitable spirit. Very soon, however, Bartoli will make this spirit her very own. Rosina will become her first important stage role. She will make her operatic debut with it in Rome, only one year after *Fantastico,* perform it across Europe, record it on CD and laser disc, and successfully take it abroad.

The most fascinating glance *Fantastico* provides us into the laboratory where a great singer was made comes in Cecilia's third round. The show starts with a brief interview of both Cecilia and her rival. She wears the same blue dress and a slightly more fashionable hairdo, with more curls coming down closer to her face. She answers questions about her age, her date of birth, her singing practice—she practices two and a half hours a day aside from studying music at the *conservatorio.* Pippo Baudo asks her what her dream role would be. *"La Carmen,"* she says with a shy smile. She still seems uncertain whether or not to look at the camera. She sometimes does, then looks away as though caught doing something forbidden. But then, where to look instead? She turns her head and stares at the audience. She appears restless; her body betrays her nervousness with little sways and jiggles. When Katia Ricciarelli joins her and Baudo for a moment of reminiscences about auditions and competitions in her own career, Cecilia still manages to be distracted and peek about the room.

Finally, Ricciarelli leads her to the microphone for their duet, the barcarolle from *The Tales of Hoffmann.* She conveys a few words of encouragement in private, Baudo joins in, puts an arm around Cecilia, concerned about the young singer's stage fright. The orchestra starts the famous melody of the scene placed at a courtesan's palace in Venice. Ricciarelli is the courtesan, Giulietta, Cecilia the young student, Niklausse. Cecilia's mezzo voice begins:

Belle nuit, O nuit d'amour
Souris à nos ivresses,
Nuit plus douce que le jour,
Oh belle nuit d'amour!

Night divine, O night of love,
O smile on our caresses:
Moon and stars keep watch above
This radiant night of love!

There it is, for the first time, the Bartoli voice that will soon ravish the world with its dark velvets and honey sheens. Perfectly placed in a low mezzo range, this duet allows her true voice to appear: rich and sensuously radiant. There is not the least timidity or hesitation in her attack. She instantly brings the aroma of a voluptuous summer night into her lines. The effect is so striking that Katia Ricciarelli turns her head to look at her in silent amazement. Has she ever heard this voice before, in the rehearsals? Or is this the very first time that Cecilia, in her contact with an audience, is transported by the music and free of certain more earthly constraints? From today's vantage point, now that we know Bartoli was taught by her mother, one could wonder if singing with an older woman, a professional like her mother, gave her the confidence she needed to be herself. Whatever the reason, it is like witnessing a real-life Cinderella transformed by the presence of her fairy godmother. Until this moment, there hasn't been much movement in Ricciarelli's perfect porcelain face. But now, as she turns to the audience again to join Cecilia for the second stanza, her face reveals that she is pleased.

It is a gorgeous sight, the two very different singers joined by the song: the mature, statuesque blond beauty in a glistening silver gown, all cool and smooth perfection, and the young singer with her dark hair and anxious eyes, her dark, erotic voice and the slim body and nervous tension of a racehorse. It is clear that the diva is helping the young one by holding back: the lead soprano voice is letting the mezzo voice take center stage and shine. It is also clear that for the diva, all this is easy: she knows how to reach her audience, how to carry herself so that her eyes, her facial expression, her body are a unified, effective support for her voice and the song. Her gaze is aimed at her audience, but she seems to contemplate a misty horizon of eternal pleasures; her body is perfectly still as though under the spell of the Venetian night.

For the novice, none of it is easy. Her left arm, her dancer's arm, keeps trying to accompany her. Her hand wants to grab at her dress. Her eyes search for the camera, but there are several cameras at work. As a result, half the time Cecilia's gaze is fixed in a corner, and it's often the wrong one. The mismatch between Ricciarelli's inspired gazing at her imaginary horizon and Cecilia's staring into corners has its comical effects. At the more ecstatic moments of the barcarolle, Ricciarelli goes inside and closes her eyes with a smile while Cecilia looks decidedly past her. She does not seem to notice, when she has another solo passage, that Ricciarelli turns to her as though to engage her. It clearly would be one thing too much to cope with.

Almost nine years later, Cecilia Bartoli could be seen on the American TV show *60 Minutes* (January 1994) in an extract from a concert duet she sang in Zürich, together with her mother. The contrast between these two televised duets could not be more arresting. In the Zürich concert, mother and daughter sing *"Io sono felice,"* from *Così fan tutte*. Silvana Bazzoni, a lyric soprano, sings Fiordiligi; her mezzo-soprano daughter sings Dorabella. Every line of the duet is an address, an exchange of looks, spontaneous smiles, embraces. This *"Io sono felice"* ("I am so happy") is a seemingly "natural" heart-to-heart dialogue. The attention each singer focuses on the other does not distract them from the musical-technical task, nor from the purpose of performing for an audience. On the contrary, the deeper shades and colors of Mozart's music are heightened by this intimate, emotional rendition.

If *Fantastico* demonstrates the difficult path of a novice singer to mastery and artistic freedom, Cecilia Bartoli's appearance on the show inspires admiration for her courage. The glance at the past proves that the "God-given voice" that is often evoked by Bartoli's mother is only one part in the equation. So many different qualities have to be perfected, so many personal, psychological challenges have to be met. There is the technical virtuosity, the emotional expressivity not only of the voice, but also of the face and the entire body. Everything has to be learned. How to use one's face and body as crucial instruments in the dialogue with an audience. How to use and not use one's hands, where to look, how to sing with one's eyes. How to enter a stage, how to position oneself in front of a microphone. How to keep one's concentration, how to appear calm, how to convey the mood of a song. How to enter a role, how to embody a character, how to engage through a character with another singer onstage. How to end, how to take the applause, how to exit. These are only a few of the elements a singer has to master.

We recently asked Bartoli how she mustered the courage to participate in the talent show. "Television is a double-edged sword," she replied. "It can make you or destroy you. If I had to do it all over, I am not sure now that I would take that risk." She looked doubtful, then she laughed. "But I like to take risks!" The risk paid off, even though nineteen-year-old Cecilia lost the competition. As a result of *Fantastico,* she was invited to sing Rosina at the Rome Opera. Two years later she participated in another televised event, the gala for Maria Callas in Paris. Here the young singer caught the attention of Herbert von Karajan and Daniel Barenboim.

$\mathcal{D}$ONNA ABBANDONATA (PASTICCIO DI OPERA BAROCCA)

Opéra de Nancy et de Lorraine, Nancy

1986

CAST: Conductor: Ivan Anguelov/Orchestre Symphonique et Lyrique de Nancy/Choeurs de l'Opéra de Nancy et de Lorraine. Production: Antoine Bourseiller. Queen of Sweden, Dido, Ariane: Nella Anfuso; Juno, Alminera: Cecilia Bartoli; Mary Stuart, Selene, Alcina: Jill Feldman; The Virgin Mary, Penelope: Nathalie Stutzmann; The Wounded Knight, Aeneas: Mark Tucker.

No recording exists of Bartoli's first operatic appearance in France. Her participation in *Donna Abbandonata* is never mentioned in any press release or account of her career. Bartoli happened to mention the performance in a very early interview on French television. Our research in Nancy turned up a helpful press representative, program notes, newspaper clippings, and a press photo of Bartoli onstage.

With *Donna Abbandonata*, the well-known French theater and opera director Antoine Bourseiller re-created the popular eighteenth-century "*pasticcio*," translated as "literally a pie," by the late music historian W. S. Rockstro. The pasticcio, he wrote, is "a species of Lyric Drama composed of airs, duets and other movements, selected from different operas and grouped together not in accordance with their original intention, but in such a manner as to provide a mixed audience with the greatest possible number of favourite airs in succession."

Bourseiller created his pasticcio on the theme of the abandoned woman, a cultural archetype that was the most popular theme of baroque opera, beginning with Metastasio's *Didone abbandonata*. The "favourite airs" in Bourseiller's pasticcio are lamentos, arias, masses, and hymns from the works of a dozen known and unknown composers, among them Handel, J. S. Bach, Lulli, Monteverdi, and Rameau. The women in question are the abandoned women of mythology, religion, and history. The central figure, Queen Marie-Eleonore of Sweden, goes insane over the death of her husband, Gustav II ("*Lamento de la reine de Suède*" by Luigi Rossi). In her delirium, the queen evokes the figures of other tragic operatic heroines abandoned by lovers or separated from loved ones. The loosely connected dramatic scenes touch the present in the brief appearance of a young woman, played by Cecilia Bartoli, whose husband was taken hostage by Lebanese terrorists.

Bartoli also appears as Juno, Jupiter's betrayed spouse, in extracts from Händel's *Semele*, and as Almirena, the virgin abducted by Armida, evil queen of Damascus, in Händel's crusade opera *Rinaldo*. In a pasticcio characterized by lamentos and other airs of despair, the press nevertheless singled out Bartoli for the emotionality of her singing. According to one critic, the "twenty-one-year-old mezzo soprano Cecilia Bartoli from Rome" is "the true discovery of this production" (*Luxemburger Wort*). Another newspaper wrote that singing Juno ("Hence Iris, hence away" from the second act of Händel's *Semele*), she stood out for her "lovely vehemence and lots of ease" (*Est Républicain*). As Almirena she "created one of the most powerfully moving moments of the show" (*Nouvelles de France*). *Opéra International* reported that "young Cecilia Bartoli turns Almirena's aria, another extract from *Rinaldo*, into an extremely strong moment of the production, and this impression is underlined by her appearance as a woman of the twentieth century, linking the destiny of the abandoned women of yesterday with the solitary ones of today."

$\mathcal{T}$HE GALA *CALLAS À PARIS*

Opéra National de Paris, Paris

1987

Television once again played a major role in Cecilia Bartoli's life. This time, in 1987, her participation in a televised event opened the doors for her international career. The French were commemorating the ten-year anniversary of Maria Callas's death with a "grand gala," televised live from the Paris Opera on September 16, 1987. Maria Callas had made her French debut at the Paris Opera, in 1958, under the baton of Georges Prêtre. Now, almost thirty years later, Prêtre conducted the Orchestre de l'Opéra de Paris once again, and three young singers—among them Cecilia Bartoli—each presented one famous aria from Callas's repertoire.

Bartoli had sung in France shortly before, at the Opéra de Nancy, in *Donna Abbandonata*. At the Paris gala, she sang Angelina's final recitative and aria *"Nacqui all'affanno . . . Non più mesta"* from Rossini's *La Cenerentola*. She created a sensation. Herbert von Karajan and Daniel Barenboim were among the millions of viewers of the TV program *"Musiques au Coeur—Callas à Paris."* Both called Bartoli the following day and invited the young singer to audition for them. Both auditions led to instant close collaborations. What was it the two great masters saw and heard in the young mezzo-soprano?

The moment Bartoli appears on camera, one thing is clear: the nervous stiffness and strangeness of her first television appearance on *Fantastico* has vanished. There is a mellow, more mature unity in her looks, demeanor, facial expressions, and her singing. She already conveys the harmony that comes with the mastery of artistic skills.

The young woman walks out, her hair gathered into a single, sober braid down her back. Her walk is modest, her hands held at her side, fingers curled up, the way a graceful young girl would walk up to receive her college diploma. She wears a scintillating blue dress with a high heart-shaped neckline and bouffant sleeves. A bracelet and her earrings, simple triangles, match the glitter of the dress. It is an elegantly understated outfit with a small romantic touch, perfect for a debutante on the grand Paris stage.

She turns to the camera, acknowledges her audience and her conductor with a little smile, then gets into position and folds her hands, very contained, erect, and *comme il faut*. Her face stays calm and doesn't show any trace of nervousness as she begins. Now that there are no curls, no visible makeup to distract the eye, her simple allure is charming. One notices her youth, her beauty, her expressive eyes. Most charming of all, she now sings with those eyes.

She has learned how to address an audience with her singing, how to communicate beyond the words and sounds she emits. There is for the first time a visible pleasure in her face. After a phrase of virtuoso roulades, a natural, winning smile appears in perfect harmony with Angelina's state of joy over a happy ending. She shows considerable emotion in her pleading offer of forgiveness to her sisters, *"Figlia, sorella, amica/tutto trovate in me"* ("Daughter, sister, friend/you will find all in me"). She dares to abandon herself to the romantic lines *"Padre, sposo, amico, O istante!"* ("Father, husband, friend, oh what a moment!"). There is a hint of impishness before she begins the second part: *"Non più mesta accanto al fuoco"* ("No longer shall I sadly sit by the fire").

Only two years after her difficult start on *Fantastico*, Bartoli has begun to express the music she sings, to live that music onstage. She even manages to play up to the camera at moments, without any break in her character. Her diction is remarkable, of an almost exaggerated precision that betrays, by comparison with her later Cenerentolas, the precocious youth of the singer. But then it is precisely her youth that sets off her accomplishments, making it that much harder to believe that Angelina's bravura aria could be delivered with such technical sophistication and ease. It seems almost reassuring that there are a few flaws. She still changes expression in the moments when she doesn't sing—the energy is turned off, then turned on again. A few shy, sideward glances make their appearance while she is waiting for her next *Einsatz*. Then she seems to remind herself to be exuberant, and she goes into it with something like an attack. Toward the end, lines on her forehead and tightness in her face betray the sheer muscular effort of her singing. A slight look of fear appears in her eyes right before the high final notes. But then she is radiant, she has made it, her smile is victorious. She soaks up the applause, her hands crossed over her chest; she takes it in with deep, sensuous breaths as old Georges Prêtre nods his approval.

It is easy to imagine von Karajan and Barenboim nodding their approval as well—in the foreknowledge that the slight imperfections of this young singer's delivery are not so much flaws as a promise: the necessary developmental baggage of a woman on the way to becoming a major artist.

Meanwhile, television catches on just as fast, noting that this talented and expressive singer *"ne cache rien"*: she doesn't hide anything. Bartoli will be the musical darling of French TV, with ten appearances and interviews over the next five years. If one studies these documents of a beginning career, it is evident that Bartoli had on nights as well as off nights on camera. On the whole, however, she had learned how to perform for a camera, once and for all. Two years after *Fantastico*, millions of viewers, musicians, and music lovers could witness on their TV screens the birth of a new opera star.

BERTOLDO, BERTOLDINO E CACASENNO

VICENZO LEGRENZIO CIAMPI

Teatro Filarmonico, Verona

1987

CAST: Conductor: Giorgio Croci/Orchestra e coro dell'Arena di Verona. Production: Marco Messeri/Fiorenzo Giorgi. Ipsicratea Regina: Patrizia Orciani; Alboino Re: Cecilia Bartoli; Aurelia: Francesca Franci; Erminio: Nuccia Focile; Menghina: Lucetta Bizzi; Bertoldo: Giancarlo Tosi; Bertoldino: Bruno Praticò; Cacasenno: Maurizio Comencini; Lisaura: Cristina Pastorello.

It can be a mixed blessing to find traces of an early performance by Bartoli. They offer us hints about first operatic choices and challenges in her career, but they also make us aware of accomplishments vanished forever from the historical record. In the case of her performance in *Bertoldo, Bertoldino e Cacasenno*, all that remains is a program with the mention of her name. The loss seems particularly regrettable as the contralto role of King Alboino was Bartoli's first principal trouser role.

The production at the Teatro Filarmonico in Verona was the first revival of this once extremely successful and influential opera in about two hundred years. The dramma giocoso that is better known under the later title *Bertoldo alla corte* is one of several comedies by Goldoni

that Ciampi composed in Venice around 1748, the year *Bertoldo* opened. Goldoni seems to have amused himself by giving the two principal noble roles of the king and his brother-in-law, Erminio, to two women. A woman thus pursues Menghina, Bertoldino's wife, and her aide de camp in these amorous escapades is another woman (Erminio). According to the late music historian O. G. Sonneck, Goldoni devised this plot in order to make fun of the fact that castrati were predominantly singing the roles of women in the heroic operas of his time. Nearly 250 years later, we can imagine the Verona audience enjoying the gender-bending revival of an opera that was so successful in Paris in its time that it inspired numerous parodies (most prominently Favart's *Ninette à la Cour*, 1755), spurring the development of the French *opéra comique*.

The text of the Verona revival is a modernized version of Goldoni's libretto, but the story remains the same: The amorous King Alboino invites Bertoldo and his family to exchange their village life for the court. While trying to appear innocent to his royal spouse, he showers the villagers with rich clothes, gifts, and all kinds of amusements in order to seduce Menghina and make her leave Bertoldino for him. As in all commedia dell'arte plots (and with interesting parallels to Mozart's *Don Giovanni* and *The Marriage of Figaro*) the designs of the powerful villain are frustrated and "the unpardonable sin" is not committed. Most of the comic ammunition derives from the fact that the villagers are not impressed by the king's efforts. Bertoldino, his father Bertoldo, and his son Cacasenno prefer their meager country life. The king has to renounce his adulterous appetites, be pardoned by his wife, and send the villagers home.

What Bartoli did with the libertine role of Alboino Re, his pursuit of the village woman, his hide-and-seek games with his wife and court is left to speculation. It may have been unusual enough to raise the ire of some Italian critics. *La Repubblica* from Rome named Bartoli as one of the "worst singers" of that opera (which is hard to imagine), and *Il Giornale* from Milan reported that "Alboino, by C. Bartoli, was a complete disaster." When I asked her about it many years later, I was not surprised that she sided with the critics. Knowing Bartoli's drive for perfection and her readiness to criticize herself, it would have been impossible for the young singer to contradict such a verdict. "It was a bad decision," she assured me. "I prefer not to think about it."

La Pietra di Paragone

Gioacchino Rossini

Teatro Massimo Bellini, Catania

1988

CAST: Conductor: Marcello Viotti/Orchestra e coro del Teatro Massimo Bellini di Catania. Production: Eduardo De Filippo/Italo Nunziata. Clarice: Cecilia Bartoli; Aspasia: Gloria Scalchi; Fulvia: Patrizia Orciani; Asdrubale: Natale De Carolis; Giocondo: Luca Canonici; Macrobio: Bruno Praticò; Pacuvio: Alfonso Antoniozzi; Fabrizio: Fabio Tartari.

Shortly after the adventure of *Bertoldo, Bertoldino e Cacasenno*, young Bartoli launched into another contralto role. (Rossini gave the principal roles of this opera to a bass and a contralto.) *La Pietra di paragone* (originally *La Pietra del paragone*, "The Touchstone") was Rossini's seventh opera, written at the age of twenty, in 1812. The "melodrama giocoso" has been compared to *Così fan tutte* because of its theme, the question of women's constancy. But in this case, the fidelity test launched by Count Asdrubale is won by his love interest, Marchesa Clarice (Bartoli's part). The heroine outwits the disguised count with a successful disguise as her own brother, proves her faithfulness (the touchstone of the story), and wins the count's hand in marriage.

Bartoli received praise ("a beautiful dark timbre," *Giornale di Sicilia*) as well as criticism ("a not particularly pleasant timbre," *Catania Sera*) for her Clarice. A look at Bartoli's early biographic notes and press releases reveals that by 1992 (and in the hands of a new management), *La Pietra di paragone*, together with most of her early operatic experiments, has vanished from the record. These experiments are, however, an essential part of Bartoli's operatic formation, reminding us that even a fast-rising star is rarely born overnight.

The early roles like that of Clarice, a both witty and virtuous woman—with an androgynous disguise thrown in for good measure—, give us an idea of Bartoli's first theatrical inclinations. They show her appetite for comedy and disguise. It is easy to imagine the part of Clarice as a training ground for both her upcoming witty heroines, Rosina and Dorabella, as well as for tackling the role of Cherubino.

IL BARBIERE DI SIVIGLIA

GIOACCHINO ROSSINI

Teatro dell'Opera di Roma, Rome
1987

Rokokotheater der Schwetzinger Festspiele, Schwetzingen
1988

CASTS

Opera di Roma
Conductor: Maximiano Valdes/Orchestra e coro del Teatro dell'Opera di Roma. Production: Antonello Madau Diaz/Silvia Cassini. Rosina: Cecilia Bartoli; Figaro: Angdo Romero; Almaviva: Maurizio Comencini; Bartolo: Mario Bertolini; Basilio: Silvano Pagliuca; Berta: Laura Zannini.

Schwetzingen
Conductor: Gabriele Ferro/Radio-Symfonieorchester Stuttgart. Production: Michael Hampe/Ezio Frigerio, Mauro Pagano. Rosina: Cecilia Bartoli; Figaro: Gino Quilico; Almaviva: David Kuebler; Bartolo: Carlos Feller; Basilio: David Lloyd; Berta: Edith Kertesz-Gabry. Released on video and laser disc in 1993.

Bartoli remembers her operatic debut as Rosina at the Rome Opera in 1986, but the records of the Rome Opera maintain it was 1987. (The Rome newspaper *Il Messaggero* notes the fact that "apart from Bartoli, the performance was like last year: almost good, not very colorful.") The outcome was an invitation to sing Rosina one year later, at the Schwetzinger Festspiele, in a coproduction with the Bühnen der Stadt Köln. The production was videotaped. Released five years later on video and laser disc, this performance constitutes the earliest existing documentation of Bartoli on stage.

By 1988, Bartoli had frequently sung Rosina's aria "*Una voce poco fa*" in concert and was getting attention in Europe as a Rossini recitalist. She would soon record her first Rossini album and a sound recording of the Barber under Giuseppe Patanè would follow a year later.

Her earliest existing performance recording offers a surprise. In the few years of her career, Bartoli has made a major leap both in her singing and her acting. She commands enough stage presence and vocal and acting skill to carry off the female lead of an entire opera. Her performance in this 1988 *Barbiere* defines a magical moment in the career of a young artist: the moment when, in the difficulties she has not yet mastered, one catches the promise of what she will soon become.

Rosina is not exactly a beginner's role. Even though she only has two major arias and two duets, her part is technically demanding. Rosina has plenty of stage time, with numerous recitativi and ensemble pieces. She is the center of this typical opera buffa plot, which turns its merry carousel around the question of how the innocent, young *innamorata* can get her *innamorato*. In classical commedia dell'arte fashion, the odds are against her. She lives under the suspicious tutelage of a jealous old guardian, Dr. Bartolo, the traditional *dottore* of commedia dell'arte: the miserly pedant. Bartolo has his own designs on Rosina, and his ally is Rosina's singing teacher Don Basilio, another stock character: the greedy old scandal-monger. Rosina's connection to the world, apart from the balcony that allows her to listen to her lover's serenades, is the barber, Figaro. Figaro, the archetypal servant clever enough to outwit his masters, devises the plot that will get the two lovers together. Naturally, the plot provides for numerous opera buffa disguises: first, Rosina's lover, the powerful Count Almaviva, pretends to be "Lindoro," a poor student, in order to test her heart. Then he enters the house where Rosina is sequestered, in the disguise of a drunken soldier billeted to those quarters. Next, he masquerades as a singing teacher, a dead-ringer for Don Basilio. These comic devices, together with Figaro's meddling, advance the love plot and heighten Dr. Bartolo's haste to marry Rosina himself. Everything culminates in a big Rossinian confusion of mistaken identities and botched solutions before the happy ending can occur.

If Rossini wasn't made for Bartoli, this early *Barber* suggests that Bartoli was made for Rossini. She is not yet a master of the role or of the stage, but the "bubbling animality" that Nietzsche attributed to Rossini finds a surprising match in Bartoli's stage presence. The nervous awkwardness of her first public rendition of

Rosina's aria and duet on television are only a faint memory. She not only negotiates the tricky coloratura of the part with bravura, she also cavorts across the stage, laughs, pouts, scolds, bangs doors, and flirts with such agility that she appears to be a natural embodiment of Rosina. One suddenly realizes that Cecilia Bartoli is indeed Italian. A few days before her twenty-third birthday (on June 4), she is almost as young as the story suggests. (Geltrude Righetti-Giorgi, who created the role in 1816, was twenty-three, while Rossini himself was twenty-four.)

How did Bartoli accomplish such a transformation in this short time? She is barely recognizable. What was rigid, shy, inhibited is now fluid, ebullient, and expansive. Her almost anorexic frailty has turned into a solid roundness that gives her an air of maturity beyond her years. We see her wearing a wig for the first time, a head of tight little curls with a corkscrew pigtail. Her costume—a cream satin dress with little black dots and an apronlike black lace application on the crinoline skirt—also gives her stature. Black lace and ruffles border the neck-line —the first of the many low-cut necklines in Bartoli's career, which point to an erotic sensuousness as one of her trademarks. A light blue sash with a large bow in the back seems to have been added to the "adult" dress as an afterthought.

The youthful temperament of this Rosina erupts instantly in her first appearance, on the barred balcony of her house. She has just dropped a love note for her suitor in the street, and Dr. Bartolo threatens to have that balcony bricked up. With a hot temper, she hisses, "*Ah che vita de crepare!*" ("What an unbearable life!") before she is locked in again. In one instant, the spectator knows that this Rosina is to be reckoned with. She is not going to be one of the traditional kittenlike Rosinas raising a dainty claw against her condition. For Bartoli, being very pretty and very charming is only one part of the "hundred tricks" her Rosina will pull out of her sleeve. She won't hesitate to show the entire spectrum of her "bubbly animality," from temper tantrums to sensuous ecstasy. And, with a few difficulties, the young singer carries it off. She stakes her claim on Rosina, a role she will slowly come to perfect. At this point, in 1988, her gifts are already obvious, as the French critic André Tubeuf notes in *Diapason* (November 1989): "The physical appearance and voice of a winner, plus the one thing that is paramount if one wants to make it in Rossini: the energy....She has what cannot be learned: vivacity, quicksilver speed, cockiness."

And she has the lightness and fluidity of movement that make her stage appearance instantly appealing. When her first big scene opens she is just finishing another love letter to her "Lindoro." She walks back to the balcony with her letter, scans the room for danger. Her scanning turns her whole body to and fro with the graceful, swaying steps of a dancer. Her first aria ends with her vow, "I'll play a hundred tricks before I yield," and she seals her determination by launching into one of her beautiful gallops: with one swift turn, she lifts her skirts and gambols to the balcony. The joyful movement comes to an abrupt halt when she meets the bars of the window. All energy drops from her body. She just hangs there in a touching pose of resignation, a bird in a cage.

As this is a live performance and Bartoli has to once again negotiate a camera, she shows understandable nervousness at the start. In Rosina's first aria, *"Una voce poco fa,"* in act 1, she anxiously stares in turn at the conductor and at the love letter she has just written as though she were in dire need of an anchor. Her first lines are "A voice, a little while ago,/echoes in my heart;/already my heart has been pierced/and it was Lindoro who inflicted the wound." Staring at the letter makes no psychological or dramatic sense and therefore gives the odd impression that she is singing from sheet music. Then she loosens up and manages to give the aria appropriate emotional colors. At moments, the stage direction is in her way: when she threatens to use her "one hundred tricks," for example, she is made to sit down with her embroidery frame. Obviously, a young singer doesn't yet command the authority to replace a stage director's absurd idea with a better suggestion of her own. At the same time, there are original interpretive moves that could not have come from any other source than Bartoli herself. One such original touch occurs at the line *"Mi fo guidar"* ("I let myself be guided"): while she sings the long fioritura of the last word, she lifts one hand in a slow, accusing arc as though the musical rise toward the expected *"Ma . . ."* ("But . . .") rouses rebellion in her whole body. She doesn't, however, sing the *"Ma."* She only mouths the syllable like a curse, while her balled fist does the talking and delivers the punch.

Nervousness and stress also show at times in her singing. Her voice does not yet hold a perfectly consistent line. It wavers during *"Una voce,"* apparently the result of the amount of moving around she has to do. Certain words in a phrase are overexposed, whereas others lack breath support. She visibly prepares for high notes: her facial expression suddenly turns serious, and instead of Rosina we see Cecilia concentrating and making an extra effort to take sufficient breath. Later, in the duet with Figaro *"Dunque io son,"* the highest register of her voice still reveals a trace of comparative thinness and strain, and in the repetition of *"Fortunati affetti miei!/Io comincio a respirar,"* the vocal demands cause her to look tense instead of happy with relief, as the words would suggest. At the end of the duet, as in some parts of the ensembles, she is barely audible.

Another difficulty shows in the recitativi, when Bartoli has to create Rosina's character by merely acting. When Rosina is interrogated by Bartolo about her secret letter, for example, the character splits apart. In one moment, her Rosina is extremely fiery and feisty; in the next, she is extremely intimidated, even crushed; and at the end, when Bartolo threatens to lock her up, she goes into hysterics. The exaggeration may simply be a "bubbling over" of temperament. Or it may be an attempt at comedy, pushing the character toward the farcical realm. But the numerous more subtle, psychological moments in Bartoli's acting stylistically contradict the farce and render these attempts ineffective. There is a fine line between a caricature and a character, and this early Rosina proves that the "natural comedian" and "born Rossini heroine" praised by the critics of the world was not quite born that way.

The recorded live performance gives us an idea of how an audience reacted, in 1988, to an almost unknown singer. There is friendly applause at first, nothing exuberant like the clapping and shouting her partners, Gino Quilico (Figaro) or David Kuebler (Almaviva/"Lindoro"), receive during the first act. But as the opera takes its course, the audience warms up to the young mezzo-soprano. And while Bartoli herself seems to warm up to the fun of the task, it may grow on her audience that Rosina's struggle against the odds is paralleled by that of the singer herself. In the end, enthusiastic applause suggests that Rosina's determined *"Io vincero!"* ("I shall win!") has won her audience, too. She gets her bouquet of flowers and Gino Quilico's as well. She runs out alone for her curtain call, throws up her arms, then holds them open at her sides as though to say, What can I do, I was just lucky. Finally she brings her folded hands to her chest and lips to show her gratitude. Gabriele Ferro comes out and doesn't notice the bouquet thrown at his feet. When the ensemble joins him, someone hands it to Cecilia, who presents the flowers to her conductor.

*L*A SCALA DI SETA

GIOACCHINO ROSSINI

Auditorium Pedrotti del Conservatorio Rossini, Rossini Opera Festival, Pesaro

1988

CAST: Conductor: Gabriele Ferro/Orchestra del Teatro Comunale di Bologna. Production: Maurizio Scaparro/Emanuele Luzzatti. Dormont: Oslavio Di Credico; Giulia: Luciana Serra; Lucilla: Cecilia Bartoli; Dorvil: William Matteuzzi; Blansac: Natale De Carolis; Germano: Roberto Coviello. Released on CD in 1989.

Only a few months after singing Rosina in Germany, Bartoli appeared at the prestigious Rossini Opera Festival in Pesaro. The performance was taped (and recorded on CD). *La Sala di seta* is an early Rossini opera, a comical one-acter that shows the young composer solidly established in the genre of farce. The story is a variation of the archetypal theme of the secret marriage, derived from a French opera libretto by Pierre Gaveaux, *L'Echelle de Soie*. As in the original, the "silken ladder" of the title allows a young woman, Giulia, to lead her secret married life with her beloved Dorvil in the house of her guardian. The comical plot is set in motion when Giulia's guardian presents her with the husband of his choice. She is to marry Blansac, a flirtatious young army officer, within a day. Giulia's way out of the dilemma is to tempt Blansac's appetite for her pretty cousin Lucilla (Cecilia Bartoli), who has fallen in love with him at first sight. Giulia's not-too-witty servant Germano is supposed to spy on Blansac and Lucilla for her. A predictable night of intrigues ensues, with overheard conversations, mixed and missed messages, and a typical Rossinian moment of chaos: Giulia's, Dorvil's, Blansac's, and Germano's heads are spinning in the quartet *"Ah, la testa in confusione traballare or qui mi fa."* At the expected climax both husband and would-be husband climb up the silken ladder to Giulia's room. Dorvil hides in a closet while Giulia confronts Blansac. Lucilla spies from behind a door, the servant Germano from under a table. Awakened by the noise, Giulia's guardian enters the scene. The truth comes out, Lucilla gets Blansac, and the farce ends with two happy couples.

Seeing Bartoli at the Rossini festival in Pesaro (Rossini's birth town) in 1988 gives the odd impression of a time warp. She looks about ten years younger than in the German *Barber* production. She has the same extremely slender look, with an occasional touch of shy fragility, as she did at the Paris gala for Maria Callas, a year earlier. If it weren't for the performance dates, one would swear that *La Scala di seta* was the earlier performance and that her much more solid, mature appearance as Rosina at the Schwetzinger Festspiele came quite a bit later.

Lucilla is a tiny role with several brief recitativi and one short aria, but Bartoli makes her mark on the Pesaro stage. She looks enticing enough to make the advances of Blansac (elegant-looking baritone Natale De Carolis) believable, even inevitable. Her pretty dark head of hair (no curls; her hair is loosely piled up in turn-of-the-century fashion) strikes an attractive contrast with the mass of red curls of cousin Giulia (soprano Luciana Serra). Bartoli wears a simple light-blue muslin dress with a bow in the small of the back, a ruffled seam, and a collar that plunges into a deep V. The eager youthfulness of Lucilla, the nubile cousin, is conveyed both in Bartoli's voice (her little sighs, an occasional giggle) and in her swift, slender body. Throughout the opera, Bartoli's entrances and especially her exits stir the air with a trill of little steps that are as much dancing as running.

She gathers up her skirt with both hands and bends her upper body as though launching into a wild polka. Her shoulders turned, her head leading with the willful grace of a colt, she bolts across the stage. In an otherwise static stage production, Bartoli's Lucilla embodies movement. Her small part in this musically inventive and high-spirited Rossini one-act leaves the impression of a shooting star.

Bartoli also enacts the sexual undertones of the plot in a moment of comical pantomime. During Blansac's brazen flirtation with her, she is at first embarrassed. But when he falls on his knees before her and Giulia secretly signals her to go ahead and do with him as she pleases, Bartoli's Lucilla literally leaps on the occasion. With a sudden turn, she eyes him with teasing menace, ready to attack. She grabs her skirt and chases him to a half-transparent screen that signals a bedroom. What follows is acted in the syncopated speed of silent movies: she clasps him and while they spin in a passionate embrace, she begins to pull his clothes off his body. His jacket flies through the air, he wants to run after it, she catches hold of him again and clutches him, they kiss, she sets his tie flying. The next moment she staggers out from behind the screen in a swoon, one hand groping for balance, the other at her forehead as though to say, "Phew!"

The whole scene, which lasts no more than a few measures, is a perfect evocation of the music Rossini composed for this passage, its provocative pipes sounding very much like a representation of lovers cavorting. A moment later, Lucilla has managed to steady herself, her hands on her heart, for her aria of sudden enlightenment: this is clearly the ideal husband for her. *"Lo sento! Lo sento!"* She knows it with all the charming certitude of youth, the wishful thinking, the unabashed adoration. She steals starry-eyed glances at the object of her intuition, who meanwhile is getting dressed again.

In this short, but significant scene, Bartoli's comic timing is picture perfect. She moves with ease and grace. And here again is the element that first showed up at the Callas gala and made Bartoli's Rosina so appealing: her singing with her eyes. In Lucilla's aria, between peeks at her lover, Bartoli looks straight at her audience, inviting us to be her witness. We are called into her confidence as she confesses her appetites, bites her lip with desire, shares her surprise in her own delight.

La Scala di seta is another proof of the tremendous leap the young singer has made since her *Fantastico* debut. Her top range still appears a bit thin, a bit strained at moments; every now and then a gesture sneaks in that seems motivated by nervousness (like straightening her hair) rather than by her role. But we witness for the first time Bartoli's capacity to make a genuine erotic impact from the stage. Even then, in her very slender youthful frame, she is embodied in a wholesome, harmonious way and her joie de vivre has irresistible erotic appeal.

As her career develops, she will bring this rare, essentially "Bartolian" quality to every single role.

Critics singled her out. *American Record Guide* reviewer Michael Mark, for example, wrote, "She steals the show whenever she is around," and calls her Pesaro performance on CD "the best thing to happen to Rossini since Marilyn Horne."

Le Lucio Silla

Wolfgang Amadeus Mozart

Wiener Festwochen Konzerthaus Wien

1989

CAST: Conductor: Nikolaus Harnoncourt/Concentus musicus Wien/Arnold Schönberg Chor. Giunia: Edita Gruberova; Lucio Silla: Peter Schreier; Cecilio: Cecilia Bartoli; Cella: Yvonne Kenny; Cinna: Dawn Upshaw.

Lucio Silla does not truly belong in this performance guide. It was a concert version, not a fully staged performance of Mozart's third opera (1772). The two performances were recorded live in Vienna, in June 1989, and issued as a CD in 1990. I only marginally include *Lucio Silla* here because Bartoli's participation marks an important step in her career: the beginning of her fruitful collaboration with Harnoncourt.

Bartoli took on another gender-bending part with Cecilio, the heroic lover who risks losing his life and his beloved to the tyrant Lucio Silla. The recording documents that Bartoli sang the role extremely beautifully without, however, the heroic vocal power that the role of Cecilio (at Mozart's time usually sung by a castrato) might call for. The Vienna audience was enchanted by the beauty of her voice. "Mozart would have thought himself lucky if at the Milan opening in 1772, he had been provided with vocal phenomena like Edita Gruberova or the only twenty-three-year-old Cecilia Bartoli," speculated the *Salzburger Nachrichten*. The *Vienna Kurier* wrote: "The twenty-three-year-old Cecilia Bartoli, with a precious and already 'mature' mezzo voice, made her enthusiastically celebrated Vienna debut as Cecilio."

$\mathcal{L}$E NOZZE DI FIGARO

WOLFGANG AMADEUS MOZART

Opernhaus Zürich, Zürich

1989

Opéra National de Paris Bastille, Paris

1990

CASTS

Opernhaus Zürich—Zürcher Mozart-Zyklus

Conductor: Nikolaus Harnoncourt/Ochester der Oper Zürich. Production: Jean-Pierre Ponnelle. Count Almaviva: Haakan Hagegaard; Countess: Roberta Alexander; Susanna: Barbara Bonney; Cherubino: Cecilia Bartoli; Figaro: Anton Scharinger.

Opéra National de Paris Bastille

Conductor: Gabriele Ferro/Orchestre de l'Opéra de Paris. Production
assistant: Marina Bianchi. Count Almaviva: Sergei Leiferkus; Countess:
Lucia Popp; Susanna: Joan Rodgers; Cherubino: Cecilia Bartoli; Figaro:
Ferruccio Furlanetto.

Bartoli's next trouser role was
Cherubino in Mozart's *Le Nozze di
Figaro*. She performed this role first
in 1989, in Zürich, with the
conductor Nikolaus Harnoncourt,
then, in 1990, in Paris with
Gabriele Ferro. The comparison is
interesting; it demonstrates that in
opera, in contrast to concerts and
recitals, the performance of a singer
stands and falls with the quality of
the direction. In my discussion, I
will go back and forth between the
two productions.

Bartoli's debut in the role took
place under the fortunate guidance,
once again, of Nikolaus Harnoncourt, in a production created by
another outstanding theater creator,
the late Jean-Pierre Ponnelle. The
Zürich *Figaro* was an unmitigated
success, both for Bartoli in this new
role and for the whole production.

By contrast, the Paris *Figaro* fell victim to an operatic scandal: the new Opéra
Bastille had just opened its troubled career with labor strikes and a first
production flop. *The Marriage of Figaro* was supposed to be a safe bet for the new
company; it was the reopening of a celebrated production from the past. In 1973,
the Italian theater director Giorgio Strehler and his decorator Ezio Frigerio had
created this *Marriage of Figaro* for a small, historically suitable theater in the
Versailles palace. The production, arranged by Rolf Liebermann, had signaled the
start of a grand opera period in Paris, the so-called Era Liebermann. The success
of this "ultimate" *Marriage of Figaro* had continued over the years with great casts
of singers (among them Teresa Berganza and Frederica von Stade in the role of
Cherubino) after Strehler and Frigerio had adapted it for the nineteenth-century

stage of the Opéra National de Paris, in the Palais Garnier. Now, in 1990, it was supposed to lend the brand-new Opéra Bastille its seal of quality. But Strehler and Frigerio refused to have anything to do with a project that appeared to them as a misconception, an error that the French press called "placing a *bonbonnière* into an airplane hangar." The creators threatened a suit against the Opéra Bastille, and the orchestra threatened to go on strike. In the end, the Opéra Bastille prevailed and adapted the famous *Marriage of Figaro* with a helping hand from Strehler's assistant Marina Bianchi, but the opera opened without a mention of a director or set designer. According to the press, the conductor, Gabriele Ferro, was also more absent than present. Ferro complained that he didn't have enough rehearsal time because of the strikes. With all these absences, the singers were left to themselves and to the ghosts of the original Versailles creation.

"The marriage of Figaro?" the renowned music magazine *Diapason* asked. "His golden marriage perhaps—with the action and spectacle dragging to such a degree." The majority of the press agreed that the captainless ship was a wreck, another disaster for the Opéra Bastille.

The impact can be felt in the depressed, forlorn mood of the singers. Not even Cecilia Bartoli can muster the exuberant energy she is already known for. Her energy seems constricted in a costume that is ill-fitting and ill-suited to her rounder body. The tightness of her hip-long brocaded vests over knee pants makes her look stuffy and heavy; the high hat with a large bush of ostrich feathers gives her an air of foppishness rather than charm. Her movements, too, apart from some nice moments of running, are surprisingly heavy and sometimes even clumsy.

"*J'aime me travestir*" ("I love to dress up as a man"), Bartoli told *Le Figaro;* she seems to have decided to leave no doubt about Cherubino's gender. She uses the edgy roughness and clonk-clonk stride that she will soon adapt into a successfully comical caricature as Isolier, her next trouser role, in *Le Comte Ory.* There is no comical or ironic touch, however, in her characterization of the aristocratic page.

Bartoli's Cherubino is a young ruffian who slumps down in a chair with his legs spread and one fist under his chin, his face betraying his frustrated boredom with all the fuss the women (and men) are making around him. Bartoli hardly shows any reaction when Cherubino is sent away to become a soldier and Figaro teases him about the loss of his gay life with "ribbons and laces . . . , frills and feathers and favors." The military life, for this impassive Cherubino, oddly doesn't seem much of a stretch. He doesn't plead or fight against his destiny; on the contrary, without a single look back, he walks out in stiff military step.

In the scene with the Countess, Bartoli delivers Cherubino's love tribute, the aria *"Voi che sapete"* ("You, my fair ladies, who know what love is"), with the immobility of a concert recital. The romance of the adoration scene is bungled when Bartoli misjudges the distance to the sofa in front of the Countess's bed and has to awkwardly adjust her kneeling position. The final misfortune for this Cherubino strikes when Susanna dresses him up as a girl: when Bartoli reappears in something like a huge white nightgown pulled over her page outfit, the last chance for a playful, erotic tinge in this production is lost.

Orphaned by the absence of a director, the twenty-three-year-old Bartoli played the role as she understood it. She revealed in an interview with *Le Quotidien* that she saw Cherubino as a "real little macho guy, who is certainly still marked by childhood, but also by the very macho influence of the Count." This interpretation of Cherubino might have been an interesting concept if it had been supported and fine-tuned by a coherent production of the entire opera. Unfortunately, it was not.

Few critics liked Bartoli's "savage" Cherubino, as the *Tribune de Genève* put it. Most critics praised her voice; *Valeurs Actuelles*, for example, wrote that the "hotly awaited 'revelation,' Cecilia Bartoli, does not disappoint even though the costume of Cherubino doesn't suit her plumpness. Her voice fulfills the promise of her reputation, full-fleshed, caressing, of an extraordinary musicality."

L'Express, by contrast, found that she "has an easier time with Rossinian roulades than with Mozart's delicacy. Her Cherubino has the brains of a stuffed bear."

Le Monde found her "clumsy and belabored, like in a singing competition," and *Le Nouvel Observateur* concluded: "Cecilia Bartoli is as seductive as a policeman."

An entirely different Cherubino comes through in the spirit of Jean-Pierre Ponnelle's production. Here, Bartoli as the young page has all the androgynous qualities of charm and grace that are an indispensable part of eighteenth-century court life, of Beaumarchais's original play, and, of course, of Mozart's music. According to Beaumarchais, Cherubino is thirteen years old and so delicately beautiful that Susanna envies his looks and predicts that with all his seductive charms, in three or four years he will be "a real good-for-nothing." Bartoli's Zürich Cherubino proves Susanna's predictions right. "He" pirouettes and gambols with quicksilver speed, radiant smiles, irresistible childlike faces and pleading glances. Clowning about in one moment, impatient to play the romantic lover in the next, he has the innocent naughtiness of a boy who knows he can't do wrong because he has been doted upon all his life. He jumps onto the bed where Susanna is lying, eager to steal a kiss, snatches the ribbon of the Countess, chases around with it, leaps back onto the bed with his trophy, triumphant, throws off his courtly wig and, breathless with excitement, launches into his aria: "*Non so più cosa son*" ("I don't know any more who I am"). The delightful energy of these outbursts, mixing childish pranks with the sweet and painful confusions of puberty, finds a perfectly natural outlet in Bartoli's ebullient temperament.

By contrast to the Paris production, when this Cherubino is teased by Figaro, he rebels, tries to argue, pleads with Susanna, is torn between anger, shame, despair. In everything he does, Cherubino is allowed to be graceful and seductive instead of a "little macho guy" who pouts and stomps about. But Jean-Pierre Ponnelle also allows him the full erotic impact of his age, his nature, and his social class. In the second act, when Susanna dresses him as a girl in front of the Countess, Bartoli acts out delightful confusions and is appropriately spellbound by the Countess. Singing "*Voi che sapete*," she kneels before the Countess, kisses her hand, and stays in this romantic pose during the long applause. Finally, with a clearing of her throat, Susanna breaks the spell and separates them. Shortly after, when Cherubino is alone with the Countess and cries in her lap about being sent away, his pleading ardor provides highly convincing reasons for the Countess's fascination with him—and for the Count's jealousy. All of a sudden, playwright Beaumarchais's intentions come to mind: after writing *The Marriage of Figaro* as the second part of *The Barber of Seville*, Beaumarchais devised a third part, *La Mère Coupable* (*The Guilty Mother*), where he provides the Countess with an illegitimate son . . . fathered by Cherubino.

When *The Marriage of Figaro* opened in Paris in 1784, the sexual undercurrent between the Countess and the page created a scandal. In Zürich, in 1990, the mutual attraction between Roberta Alexander's beautiful Countess and Bartoli's Cherubino is given free rein, allowing the spectators' imaginations to play with any possible outcome.

In a discussion of the role during her first master class some six years later, Cecilia Bartoli described Cherubino as a mixed-gendered character: "He doesn't know yet if he's a boy or a girl."

That is how she played the character for the first time, in Ponnelle's production. That is how she sings him today in concert performances. Hearing today her more developed rendition of Cherubino's arias, one can only regret that Bartoli, as she matures physically, has begun to shy away from trouser roles. With Bartoli performing, a plump Cherubino would be far more desirable than no Bartoli/Cherubino at all.

$\mathscr{L}$E CANTATRICI VILLANE

VALENTINO FIORAVANTI

Teatro Mercadante, Naples

1990

CAST: Conductor: Umberto Benedetti Michelangeli/Orchestra del Teatro San Carlo di Napoli. Production: Roberto De Simone/Mauro Carosi. Rosa: Cecilia Gasdia; Agata: Lucetta Bizzi; Giannetta: Cecilia Bartoli; Don Bucefalo Zibaldone: Bruno De Simone; Don Marco Mbomma: Giulio Liguori; Carlino: Bruno Lazzaretti; Nunziello: Giovanni Lamagna; Don Fastidio: Vigilio Villani; Giansimone: Antonio Coletti.

Our research into the Teatro San Carlo production of *Le Cantatrici villane* remained fruitless. Apart from the cast list, Bartoli's participation in this enticing musical venture seems to have left no trace. Most likely the version performed at the Teatro Mercadante in Naples was the one that has been traditionally used in the last fifty years, a version with large cuts and secco recitativi. The opera by the young Roman composer Fioravanti premiered in Naples, the city of his choice, in 1798. In its extremely successful first fifty-year run, fifteen versions of the libretto (by Giuseppe Palomba) circulated across Europe, all of them different, with all kinds of musical pasticcio additions, some of them by Rossini and even Donizetti.

Shortly after the Naples production in which Bartoli appeared, the original version of *Le Cantatrici villane* turned up. Conductor Roberto Tigani discovered it in the library of the Santa Cecilia Conservatory, where Bartoli had studied music. In 1992, Tigani conducted and recorded the reconstructed original version (CD Bongiovanni, Bologna, 1992), which had not been performed for almost two hundred years.

A simple cast comparison shows that the Naples production is missing the character of Nunzietta: originally four country women competed with one another for the honor of turning into a prima donna in this buffa parody of the world of bel canto opera. Eighteenth-century comic opera loved the topic of naïve village singers fired to entertain dreams of diva stardom by an incompetent *maestro di cappella* and a would-be impresario. Comic rivalries and the true motivations behind "*tante smorfie*," namely love interests and jealousies, set to delightful music, assured the instant and long-lasting success of this opera.

Frontespizio del libretto dell'opera (1798).

In the foreword to the libretto for the CD, Alessandra Doria writes about the composition: "All the elements of the Neapolitan school are combined in it with rare inventive freshness: affectionate, spontaneous portrayal of the characters, smooth, light rhythm and above all natural melodic invention embellished by bright, transparent orchestral structures. ... The entire opera continues to astound for the large amount of constantly new, lively ideas, the perfect combination of musical impulse and character description, to which even the genius of Rossini was by no means indifferent."

It seems easy to imagine what attracted Bartoli to this enterprise, apart from the bonus of working under the subtle direction of Roberto De Simone. Giannetta is not the principal role and does not carry the principal love interest.

Her realm is that of jealous dreams and doubts, which she expresses with a lot of common sense in her first act recitative and aria: "The profession of singing is fascinating/But it is not without traps;/We had better be very cautious." The aria, *"Un cor mi predice,"* with its beautifully hesitant melodic modulations and broken-up words, transposes Zerlina's *"Vorrei e non vorrei"* into a dilemma about an opera career:

> One voice is foretelling me
> Wealth and glory
> But another is saying
> "No, Giannetta, don't!"
> So I am between two fires,
> I am caught in a tangle,
> I hesitate,
> I want to, but I do not as well.
> I know that "singer"
> Means "artist"
> But the singing is also . . .
> Stop this now,
> I am a simple-hearted
> Country girl,
> And this new life
> May trouble me.

Bartoli has often commented on the importance of choosing roles that correspond to her own character. Playing a more naïve, comic version of herself would have its obvious appeal, as would the fact, one imagines, of performing in an opera about opera, an eighteenth-century village precursor of Strauss's *Capriccio*.

$\mathcal{L}$E COMTE ORY

GIOACCHINO ROSSINI

Teatro alla Scala, Milan,

1991

CAST: Conductor: Bruno Campanella/Orchestra e coro del Teatro alla Scala. Production: Pier Luigi Pizzi. Comtesse Adèle: Mariella Devia; Comte Ory: William Matteuzzi; Ragonde: E. Podles; Isolier: Cecilia Bartoli; Raimbaud: Claudio Desderi; Le Gouverneur: P. Spagnoli.

The role of Comte Ory's page Isolier was another trouser role for Bartoli—and her last one, to date. This role, with which Bartoli made her debut at La Scala, pushes her comic acting abilities further than perhaps any other role she had taken on in the first years of her career. She gives the trouser role a decidedly masculine bend and she does it with astonishing aplomb. A debut at La Scala with its particularly demanding and partisan audience is never an easy affair. Bartoli confessed in Italian interviews that it was an excruciating experience and that she felt "like an ant" on the La Scala stage. But Bartoli's debut performance was received with enthusiastic applause.

Interestingly, the critical voices of concern about Bartoli's "small" voice were not predominant in Europe. The anxious question as to whether Bartoli could be heard in any but the smallest opera houses was raised in the United States when her European fame had crossed the Atlantic and when most American critics had only heard her in recital.

Rossini's *Le Comte Ory* is a little-known opera of great charm, wit, and musical beauty that is likely to see a revival in the course of the present Rossini renaissance. This opera (first performed in 1828), written in Rossini's Paris period, was his third opera in French. A good part of his 1825 opera-cantata *Il Viaggio a Reims* was recycled into this new "*opéra comique*" that was, however, not written for the Opéra Comique but for the Opéra; as a result, complex elements of both opera buffa and opera seria were brought together in a new form. "In Rossini's world of disguises and masquerades, the 'true' meaning of his music is as difficult to pin down as are his characters," writes Philip Gossett in his introduction to the CD of *Le Comte Ory*. "In what other opera does the confusion of identity and the resulting erotic vortex extend so far as to present a tenor disguised as a woman who thinks he is making love to a soprano, when in fact he is making love to a contralto in the role of a man who takes the place of the soprano?"

The opera is based on a vaudeville by the French writer Eugène Scribe and his collaborator Charles-Gaspard Delestre-Poirson, who had based their one-act play of the same name on a bawdy troubadour *chanson*, changing the story in order to accommodate the moral sensibilities of the early nineteenth century. The Rabelaisian elements of nuns giving birth to little knights was abandoned and replaced with a more Mozartian touch. The story now places a noble young widow, Comtesse Adèle, and her women at the center of Comte Ory's intentions. Like another Cherubino, the page Isolier is seriously in love with the Countess and, like Figaro or Masetto, he has to defend his love interest against the powerful manipulations of a Count with the traits of both a Don Giovanni and a Count Almaviva. The role of Isolier could be played for its buffo elements, or explored for its deeper psychological and social implications. Characteristically, Bartoli chooses the latter approach.

The Countess Adèle has secluded herself in her castle of Formoutiers while her brother and the rest of the men are on a crusade. Unbeknownst to his page, Count Ory is pretending to be a hermit in order to get access to the ladies of the court (and the village girls). Meanwhile the lovelorn Isolier has devised a plan to sneak into the castle disguised as a nun, but he naïvely enlists the support of the "hermit," who immediately turns the Countess against Isolier. At the end of the first act, just before Count Ory can arrange a tête-à-tête with Adèle, he is unmasked but not discouraged.

In the second act, he adopts his page's plan. Under the cover of a dark night and a thunderstorm, he and his men dress up as nuns and plead with the Countess to be "saved" from the terrible Count Ory. The men enjoy a night at the castle drinking—and mock-praying whenever the Countess or her women appear.

Isolier is invited into the castle and warns Adèle. He has discovered the "nuns'" secret, and he informs her that the crusaders are going to return at any moment, to find the castle occupied by a group of men. In order to save Adèle from the Count's amorous attack Isolier conceals her and takes her place in bed, dressed as a woman. When Ory approaches disguised as a nun, Adèle lends her voice to the dialogue; the false nun soon shows "her" true colors. Isolier encourages Adèle's verbal love play in tender ways while he offers himself to the caresses of the nun, a.k.a. the Count. The Count realizes his fatal attraction when the lights come on and the victorious crusaders have returned. He admits his defeat in this round of the game, pointing to his page as the culprit: *"C'est lui qui nous a joué tous"* ("He made a fool of us all").

The page who has fooled them all: this is precisely the character Bartoli creates, a cocky, witty, rash young man with some bad manners and a good heart. Under the obviously excellent guidance of director Pier Luigi Pizzi, Bartoli develops masculine behavior along the lines she had tried out, unsuccessfully and without guidance, in her Paris incarnation as Cherubino. Here, it makes perfect sense to think that the master's "macho" habits would rub off on his page. It is Isolier, after all, who has come up with the naughty plan to sneak into the castle disguised as a nun. Isolier proves that he is Count Ory's best pupil by outwitting his master in the end.

The modernized setting of the Scala production transports us from the Middle Ages into the early twentieth century. Bartoli sports a conventional man's suit, a buttoned vest, a large silk tie, and a droll little straw hat with a visor that gives her the air of an adventurer. The modernization provides her a good reason to use the more contemporary, edgy body language that wasn't suitable for a decadent eighteenth-century page. She pushes her movements toward a comically exaggerated nonchalance. Her walk is a large, cocky stride with a certain flat-footed male stiffness. She stands with her legs aggressively apart. Her arms are brusque and flailing, indicating a readiness to punch. At the same time, she makes comically clear that this young man can't quite afford the rough male image he likes to project. In his weak moments, when he spies on the Countess and the "hermit," his jealous longing reveals him as a little boy who trembles in the presence of his beloved. He is naïve enough to need the "hermit's" helping hand for his amorous plans—a trait in charming contrast to the "macho" crust of his persona. In

Bartoli's modernized rendition, it is precisely this androgynous quality of her Isolier that provides a rationale for his willingness to take on the role of a woman with his master.

The frivolous love triangle is of course the high point of the opera. The La Scala production introduces some changes in the stage directions of the original libretto. Isolier, in the La Scala version, does not dress up as a woman and does not immediately take Adèle's place in bed. Here, Isolier first hides behind the head of a Récamier sofa on which Adèle reclines. The "nun" approaching in the dark of night to seek the Countess's comfort from the thunderstorm is simply the Count, without any disguise. While this simplification of the whole masquerade flattens the erotic purpose, the principal relations stand out: the Count presses and kisses Adèle's one hand, Isolier presses and kisses the other. The Countess in the middle is the love object of two rivals, one of them a merciless Don Juan, the other a cavalier who trembles with her as he encourages her to keep up the pretense. The ambiguous, floating waltz rhythm of the orchestra seems to envelop Adèle and Isolier and carry them away in spite of themselves. The soprano and mezzo-soprano voices, rising with the clarinets, melt together in an enchanted harmony of thirds while the tenor's voice encircles and entices them. The trio culminates in an intoxication of "terror, error, and bliss" (Marie-Aude Roux, in *L'Avant-Scène Opéra*). Finally, the Count declares his true intentions. The foretaste of victory makes him lose his head for a moment: the Countess escapes and Isolier takes her place. The roles are changed: now the Countess hides and holds Isolier's hand, encouraging his endurance. The spellbinding chromaticism of the trio (according to Gossett, Berlioz considered it Rossini's masterpiece) shifts to a belligerent agitato passage as the Count struggles with his victim, then the brass and a progressive crescendo of the whole orchestra announce the arrival of the crusaders. The Count throws himself on top of Isolier. He is ready to reap his harvest, but gets distracted enough to inquire: "Heavens, what is that noise?" The lights come on. In the cocky fashion of a victor, Isolier informs the Count: "It's the hour of your *retraite.*/For you have to leave, monseigneur."

When a trouser role is played convincingly, the fluctuating images of male and female overlap, become interchangeable, a Rorschach test to our fantasies as spectators. The woman within the man in the mezzo-soprano playing a male character provides the perfect erotic pleasure of role-playing within the role: Bartoli lends her Isolier a naïve, delicate side that makes his masquerading as a woman a "natural" success, while she convinces us at the same time that he is enough of a guy to profit from the ambiguous erotic situation.

While Count Ory has to leave the castle, furious at his page, Bartoli's Isolier leans against a wall, his arms crossed, and looks on with the arrogant "coolness" of a young man who has outplayed a dangerous rival and is sure of his lady's reward.

Così fan Tutte

Wolfgang Amadeus Mozart

Teatro alla Pergola, Florence

1991

CAST: Conductor: Zubin Mehta/Orchestra e Coro del Maggio Musicale Fiorentino. Production: Jonathan Miller/Sue Blane. Fiordiligi: Lella Cuberli; Dorabella: Cecilia Bartoli; Despina: Joan Rodgers; Ferrando: Frank Lopardo; Guglielmo: Natale De Carolis; Don Alfonso: Michele Pertusi.

Dorabella was the role American audiences wanted to see Bartoli perform when she made her Met debut in *Cosi fan tutte* in 1995. To the surprise and disappointment of many critics and fans she did not sing Dorabella, one of the female leads of the opera; she chose to sing the role of the servant, Despina, which is usually regarded as a secondary role. (We will get to her reasons in our discussion of that role.) The surprise was partly founded on the fact that Bartoli had already sung Dorabella, and she had done so with considerable success in 1992, in a semistaged version of the opera in Chicago, under Barenboim. The disappointment was partly based on an expectation created by Bartoli's CDs: the glossy, sexy covers and the abundance of sensuous, tender, romantic arias (Dorabella's included) had made her audience eager to see the young star in a more romantic, feminine, erotic role. Indeed, in a role just like Dorabella, the young lady who is seduced by her sister's disguised fiancé, while her own fiancé seduces her sister.

The Maggio Musicale Fiorentino production of *Così fan tutte* at the Teatro della Pergola was Bartoli's second Dorabella (she debuted in the role in January 1990, in Toulouse, at the Théâtre du Capitole, the same year she recorded the opera with Barenboim). Her second *Così fan tutte* was a particular highlight in her early career. According to record producer Christopher Raeburn, it was a "quite exceptional event" with a "very, very romantic" Dorabella. Bartoli here worked for the first time with director Jonathan Miller, one of the great masters of the stage. When one has seen one of Miller's productions (or even the TV documentary about his work produced by *The South Bank Show*) it is clear that a superb psychologist is at work. He is known for shedding new light on the evergreens of the operatic repertory and for eliciting subtle and surprising interpretations from his singers. Consequently there was a particular suspense about the meeting of the young mezzo-soprano, who had already proved herself to be an astonishing actress, with the wizard of stage psychology.

The main setting of the Florence *Così fan tutte* is a stately room with huge doors leading to a balcony or roof terrace with potted trees, some bric-a-brac of antique statues and bas-reliefs, bathed in southern Italian light. In the distance, the roofs and churches of Naples are visible beside the silhouette of Mount Vesuvius. Fiordiligi and Dorabella, the two sisters who inhabit this luxurious mansion, are shown as high-bred young women. They appear in very decent white dresses, with long sleeves and moderate necklines. Large satin sashes with bows in the back are the only sensuous element in their appearance, reminding us at the same time of the innocent, girl-like status of the two. Fiordiligi's sash is blue, Dorabella's dark pink and matched by a pink hair bow. The manners of the sisters are extremely *comme il faut*: the proper behavior of the two upper-class sisters is the pivotal stratagem in Miller's approach to the opera. He takes the opposite approach to Jean-Pierre Ponnelle, whose licentious *Così* on video/laser disc (conducted by Nikolaus Harnoncourt, with Dolores Ziegler as Dorabella, London/Decca 1994) offers a fascinating contrast. In Miller's interpretation, the challenge as to whether the sisters can be seduced is less a question of their faithfulness than a question of their sexuality. Faithfulness, in Miller's reading, is a function of the strict sexual inhibition of a certain class of women, requiring matching restraint from the gentlemen of their class. In order to make these women "do what all women do" ("*così fan tutte*") a whole set of social structures and meanings has to come undone—not only for the women, Miller points out, but for the men as well.

To communicate this radical interpretation of Mozart's opera, Miller requires an ensemble, and perhaps especially a Dorabella, with a capacity for comic, ironic, vibrant, and expressive acting. Bartoli proves herself equal to the task.

We get a first impression of Fiordiligi and Dorabella as they go about watering their potted trees in a leisurely, dreamlike way, with Dorabella breathing in the scent of the flowers. We can imagine their peaceful, protected life as quite similar to the life of well-tended potted plants. The fact that each sister has a sweetheart for whom she swears undying devotion fits perfectly with the blissful domestic monotony of their lives. This is now going to change. The sisters' fiancés, Guglielmo and Ferrando, having made a secret bet on the women's faithfulness, are going to do everything they can to uproot them.

The friend who bets against them, the old philosopher Don Alfonso, presents Fiordiligi and Dorabella with a lie: their lovers, he says, have been called to arms and have to take leave of them. The long scene of separation at the seashore, in Miller's direction, doesn't allow the couples more than restrained hugs, little kisses on hands and cheeks, and couth, controlled glances. The parting pains of the women are interior: the emotions that must not be shown on the surface are expressed in the intensity of their singing. Don Alfonso's sniggering in the background reminds us that for the men, this is nothing but a game, a masquerade. In the languid exchanges of the quintet and in the following *terzettino* of Fiordiligi, Dorabella, and Don Alfonso, "*Soave sia il vento*" ("Let the wind blow gently"), Bartoli's voice does not have the slightest problem with audibility. On the contrary, in this and other ensembles, her voice is notable for its dark radiance, vibrant emotion, and sensuousness.

Bartoli's Dorabella is quickly established as the younger, less fearful, and more sexually curious of the sisters. She goes so far as to lean her face against Ferrando's, creating erotic tension by moving her mouth tantalizingly close to his. By subtle contrast to Fiordiligi, Dorabella manages to steal a furtive good-bye kiss from her fiancé, as the two lovers depart for "war."

Dorabella, the sister with the hotter temperament, has the first open outburst of feelings after the separation. In her accompanied recitative "*Ah! scostati!*" ("Out of my way!"), everything that had to be held back for the sake of good behavior now pours out with full force. With fiery indignation, Bartoli launches the line "*Deh, fuggi, per pietà!*" ("Get away from me, for heaven's sake!") at Despina, who has just brought in the sisters' breakfast chocolate. A somber agitato aria follows, "*Smanie implacabili*" ("Relentless frenzies"). In Bartoli's rendition of the aria, the inexperienced Dorabella seems to discover misery and despair for the first time in her life. The sudden reality of loss, with the possibility of death for her beloved, literally knocks her down. Her knees give in, she ends up doubled over on the floor, her hands at her temples, her face the mask of Greek tragedy. There is not a trace of hysteria or irony, however, in Bartoli's singing and acting. She seems to demonstrate that under the spell of such a discovery, any romantic young woman endowed with a vivid imagination would enter a "state." Any such state, of course, with its high-colored drama, would seem funny and incongruous to a world-wise observer like Despina, or to an audience who knows what the stakes are and thus has the advantage of a comical perspective. Fiordiligi, who doesn't have that perspective, feels compelled to comfort Dorabella like a child in the throes of a serious tantrum. Dorabella, after all, is the little sister, who has the right to lean her head on the older one's lap, hold on to her dress, and receive caresses. Bartoli childishly sulks at the picture of Ferrando that she wears in her locket. Like a good girl, she then accepts her chocolate from Despina but marks her act of obedience by drinking it with amusing expressions of martyrdom. Then she hands the cup back to Despina as though her arm can hardly muster the effort.

In these few scenes of the first act, Bartoli designs a richly textured portrait of a young woman with a passionate nature who makes a contemporary audience smile with recognition—not just because her contradictions make for delightful comedy, but because we realize that in Dorabella's time, social class, and setting, there was not much appropriate outlet for such a nature.

In the next scene, when Guglielmo and Ferrando barge into the house in their exotic disguise, Miller's staging leaves no doubt that this invasion of the women's privacy is both a hilarious prank and a breach of the most sacred rules of the propriety the couples have followed so far. The moral chaos that threatens in its wake is perfectly expressed in Dorabella's exclamation, *"Uomini in casa nostra!"* ("Men in our house!"). Bartoli's whole body takes on the proud indignation of a battleship, and she charges the word "men" with the full social disapproval the fact calls for. But now a different kind of social guilt is laid upon the sisters by Don Alfonso. The old cynic implies that it would be rude to be unkind to the foreign "gentlemen," whom he presents as his "best friends." Well-bred women, we are reminded, have a moral obligation to be polite to any gentleman. They are trained to please. Thus Guglielmo and Ferrando can begin to launch the slings and arrows of seduction at each other's fiancée.

Modern audiences tend to have difficulties suspending disbelief in this comic plot: two intelligent young women unable to fend off two opportunist strangers or recognize their fiancés in disguise. In Jonathan Miller's staging, however, the story gains plausibility. In the small, domestic existence of Fiordiligi and Dorabella, any element of the foreign—not to speak of the outright exotic— would have a powerfully confusing and enticing effect. The usual rules would be upset; "appropriateness" might have to be redefined, and any event so far from the ordinary would create a potentially extraordinary spin of permissiveness. But there is another psychological element at play: whether or not the sisters deny the similarities of those foreigners with their fiancés, the fact that the intruders are "familiar strangers" must provide an illusion of safety within the adventure. Consequently, Don Alfonso's "moral" pressure, together with Despina's earthy ideology of pleasure, would make the sisters vulnerable to their exotic suitors—to their unabashed masculinity, their sexual flair.

In Miller's staging, the two men use the fool's freedom of their disguise to break all the habitual rules of courtship; the women are confused and aroused by such a physical approach. Guglielmo and Ferrando invite the women to inspect them, touch them: *"Toccate, bel naso!"* ("Feel it, a beautiful nose!"). They brag about their masculine attributes, calling their mustaches "the real triumph of men." And indeed, the naughty Bartoli/Dorabella goes for Guglielmo's mustache, much to her older sister's dismay.

Jonathan Miller clearly implies that the sisters were never truly sexually aroused by their conventional fiancés, and that their awakening has the shocking sweetness of a response to a drug they cannot refuse. At first, of course, they try. The defensive postures Fiordiligi takes in her aria of abstinence, *"Come scoglio"* ("Like a rock"), are imitated by Dorabella with great comical timing, always one beat too late. After the men's fake suicide attempt Bartoli liberates her leg and dress from Guglielmo's grip, but her movement is so voluptuous that a message of invitation is conveyed. The same ambiguity is conveyed by Bartoli when Guglielmo finally demands a kiss from her. She cries out, *"Un bacio!,"* pushes him back, and, as though furious that she can't grab him, pursues him like a vengeful goddess who threatens never to let him get away.

In subtle gradation, Bartoli escalates Dorabella's ambivalence toward more serious temptation. During Despina's diatribe on women's powers and pleasures Dorabella plays with her dress, pretending she is superior to her servant's lower-class appetites, but her secretly wistful looks and the treacherous smiles forming at the corners of her mouth tell a different story. The sisters conclude that some pleasure might be allowed if nobody knows about it. This is a considerable step away from the proper rules. It can perhaps best be understood as a response to Despina's implicit charge that women who don't take their pleasure aren't real women. This new pressure tips the scales. Once again, it is Dorabella who first crosses the line: with the beautiful movement of a dancer, Bartoli pretends to walk on a tightrope toward her sister and asks the crucial question: "Which of the two . . . do you want?"

"You choose," Fiordiligi holds back.

"I have already made up my mind," Dorabella confesses and announces her choice of Guglielmo, her sister's fiancé.

Fiordiligi, in fact, couldn't agree more. She, too, finds her own fiancé less "amusing" than her sister's.

In a small erotic gem Miller now lets the sisters open up to their desire for life, for experience. In their next duet, *"Scherzosetta ai dolci detti"* ("Playfully I'll answer"), they practice how to flirt, joke, provoke, sigh, how to cast telling glances and apply sensuous touches. Then, encouraged by their little role play, they decide: *"Que diletto"* ("What a delight").

When the flirtation game becomes reality, however, Miller lets them revert to the awkwardness and inhibition of young women of their class. They giggle and puff like schoolgirls, trying to hide behind each other. They run away in sudden fear of being left alone with a man, then return, shy and tongue-tied. Miller also makes the most of the men's nervousness: open seduction is clearly an unfamiliar task for everyone involved.

Finally alone with Guglielmo, Bartoli's Dorabella is not forthcoming and doesn't immediately know what to do. Guglielmo has to be coached by Don Alfonso to use as bait for her a jewel in the shape of a heart. Dorabella warms up to the game of flirtation and declares she can't return this gift because she has already given her heart away. Guglielmo, perhaps drawing courage from his exotic disguise, responds with a somewhat barbaric move: he grabs Dorabella's breast and rudely squeezes it in the staccato rhythm of his repeated question, *"Perchè batte, batte, batte qui?"* ("Why then is it beating here?"). Dorabella's eyes open wide with shock, then she enters the experience, asking in turn, *"Che mai balza, balza, balza lì?"* ("What is pounding, pounding, pounding there?"). Slowly the erotic recognition warms up her voice and face. With superbly velvet, throaty emotion she admits she feels "Vesuvius in my bosom." She and Guglielmo come to an excited agreement about the pleasure they share: *"Che nuovi diletti, che dolce penar!"* ("What new delights, what sweet pain!").

In the opening performance, Bartoli seemed overtaxed in this scene, having to clear her throat before singing, peeking at the conductor, going in and out of character with an anxiety that didn't belong only to Dorabella. But already on the third night, she was able to give a convincing performance of Dorabella's seduction.

We are not told, of course, what else happens that night between Dorabella and her lover, but Mozart and his librettist, Da Ponte, present Dorabella as suspiciously different when she tells Despina about the "artifice" of "that little devil" whom she "tried in vain to resist." Dorabella argues very much like Despina when she urges her reluctant sister to give in as well and not to worry that their fiancés might come back from the front: "We shall be wives by then, and a thousand miles away!" Bartoli's acting in this scene and in her following aria, *"È amore un ladroncello"* ("Love is a little thief"), lacks conviction. Her attempts to seduce her sister's mind, tickling and making fun of her, seem forced; she sings with an exaggerated gaiety that doesn't convey the authority of real change. A number of Italian critics found her "a little immature" for the role. One could argue, however, that a naïve young woman could not possibly mature so fast as to be convincing in this new role she tries out on her sister. Perhaps Dorabella—whom Mozart and Da Ponte may have imagined even younger than the barely twenty-four-year-old Bartoli—has to remain somewhat immature. One could argue that no matter how sexually awakened she now is, she would not be as much at ease as she pretends. There would have to be a false note in her bragging, a shrillness in her claim of superiority, now that she is "a proper woman," as Despina puts it.

For their marriage to the strangers, the sisters appear as seriously adult women, in elegant dresses and elaborate turban-like headdresses with veils and flowers. Their behavior is once again grave and stately, *comme il faut*. But when the military chorus from act 1 announces the reappearance of the sisters' fiancés, Bartoli's face mirrors the comically slow breakdown of matrimonial hopes and marriage pomp: she freezes, shows no emotion, only her eyes betray that she is listening intently, then her face falls, worry appears in her eyes. She turns her gaze to Fiordiligi, and it's all over: she is the little sister again, in need of a "firm rock" to hold on to.

Miller introduces a sly Freudian comment on the reappearance of the fiancés; he makes them invalids who come limping back on crutches, as though announcing their state of impotence. And he gives us hints that the happy ending with the reunion of the couples is highly questionable. The Pandora's box of women's sexuality has been opened, Guglielmo and Ferrando have lost much more than their bet, and the rest is left to the audience's imagination. Dorabella walks over to her sulking Ferrando and gets him to respond reluctantly to her touch. Guglielmo keeps staring after her, unable to go back to Fiordiligi. Dorabella holds hands with Ferrando, but turns to Guglielmo with a long, regretful glance before they all walk out.

This thought-provoking *Così fan tutte* offered audiences the rarity of a staging that is faithful to the social mores of the time depicted in the story, while yet illuminating the story from a very contemporary viewpoint. Sexuality, Miller seems to say, was absent in the courtship of the two couples; its sudden unrestrained presence overwhelmed the women as well as the men. His point comes beautifully across in the entire ensemble, and it was the ensemble that the critics unanimously praised. Bartoli's "witty" and "flighty" Dorabella was very much appreciated for her "musical results" and "vocal features," but she was not particularly noticed. This certainly proves her unusual capacity to melt in with an ensemble (an artistic ideal she often talks about), but it fails to appreciate her accomplishments sufficiently. She once again, as in *La Scala di seta,* carried the erotic charge of the opera. Her natural voluptuousness and her highly romantic expressiveness made Bartoli's Dorabella the point of erotic gravity around which the men revolve, precisely because she embodies the irrational qualities of life, without which the men, the ensemble, the opera itself would have lost meaning.

We can only imagine how Bartoli would have played Dorabella in the Metropolitan's more conventional production four years later. But we can also imagine that her earlier performance as Dorabella influenced her interpretation of Despina. For her Metropolitan debut, Bartoli did what American critics called "stepping down" from the coloratura role of the aristocratic young woman to the role of her maid. But was it really a step down for Bartoli to choose Despina?

$\mathscr{I}$L Barbiere di Siviglia

GIOACCHINO ROSSINI

Houston Grand Opera, Houston

1993

CAST: Conductor: Ian Marin/Houston Grand Opera Orchestra and Chorus. Production: Willy Decker/Anthony Pilavachi/Wolfgang Gussman. Count Almaviva: Ernesto Palacio; Figaro: Paolo Gavanelli; Rosina: Cecilia Bartoli; Dr. Bartolo: Enzo Dara; Basilio: Joszef Gregor; Berta: Elizabeth Jones.

In 1993, Bartoli was already world famous as a Rossini specialist, but American audiences had only heard and seen glimpses of her Rosina in concert halls. Echoes about her powerful stage presence had spread not only from Europe but from the semistaged Mozart operas under Daniel Barenboim a year earlier in

Chicago. There was particular excitement about this first fully staged *Barber,* imported from Europe, which was considered Bartoli's stage debut in the States. American audiences and critics were impatient to see the young mezzo's temperament in unrestrained action, onstage.

The Houston *Barber,* a production from the Bonn Opera, supplied evidence that Rosina had become Bartoli's signature role. It is a comparatively undemanding role, but its dramatic essence, as critic Willard Spiegelman (*Wall Street Journal*) pointed out, has "often eluded experienced singers, Maria Callas among them." Rosina's character had already puzzled Rossini's contemporaries. The French author Stendhal, for example, complains in his biography *The Life of Rossini* that Rosina is not believable. In his eyes, a woman with such clarity of purpose, such determination to get what she wants, can't possibly be a young girl. She can be at best a "young widow." He clearly bases his argument on the slightly different character of Rosina in Beaumarchais's play *Le Marriage de Figaro,* Rossini's model for his opera. Stendhal explains that a girl on the edge of womanhood would be more romantic, passive, and weak. She would swoon. The last thing she could do was act like such a cold, calculating cynic.

Singers of the past have tried to take care of this questionable character by sugar-coating Rosina with "charm." The general rule of interpretation has been to avoid anything that could be perceived as "unfeminine." The result was a kitten-like character, regularly described as a "cunning, but charming vixen." Bartoli, in an interview with the *Dallas Morning News,* simply called Rosina *"cattiva,"* or "naughty," and admitted that she understands and likes her, even though she saw herself as "a more reflective version of Rosina."

Contemporary audiences, of course, have fewer problems with the character of a rebellious, sexually precocious teenager. Enlightened by postmodern and feminist views, our late twentieth century might perceive the traditional interpretations of Rosina, from Callas to Teresa Berganza to Jennifer Larmore, as conventional and therefore psychologically limited. Berganza, as she can be observed on laser disc/video in Jean-Pierre Ponnelle's *Barber* production (with Claudio Abbado, Deutsche Grammophon, 1972), has the astonishing ease of always sounding and seeming natural, but with her imperturbable smiling self-assurance she does come across as much too mature. She is the perfect incarnation of Stendhal's young widow.

But even a recent Rosina like Kathleen Battle's rendition on laser disc/video in John Cox's Met production (with Ralf Weikert, Deutsche Grammophon, 1990) falls into the old one-dimensional trap. She, too, is "charm at any cost." Battle's Rosina seems young and graceful, full of laughter and giggles; she is pretty and seductive from beginning to end. There is no emotion, no dramatic development. This Rosina has nothing at stake. She has won the minute she enters the stage. All Battle's Rosina has to worry about is her vocal virtuosity, which takes center stage. Battle's extended fioritura variations are constantly pushed into the high soprano range, and, surprisingly, the top notes cost her visible effort.

After all these coquettish, sweet, but flat Rosinas, along comes Cecilia Bartoli and reminds us that the heroine of one of the most popular repertory operas is a child-woman whose complex character can strike our interest and whose story can evoke unsuspected, powerful feelings. In the process, she proves Stendhal's misgivings wrong.

Interest in Rosina's character? Powerful feelings? Stendhal wrong? How on earth does Bartoli do it?

She doesn't do it single-handedly. Willy Decker's unconventional conception of the opera, directed in Houston by Anthony Pilavachi, provides the platform for her new, surprising interpretation. In our talk with Bartoli in Houston, she admitted to us that she wasn't sure what to think about this modernized version of the *Barber* (which most American critics also found puzzling and questionable). But a singer, shortly after the opening of a production, cannot have the distance needed to evaluate the overall effect of the production she is part of. From the outside, the artistic match between singer and director seems striking: Decker's concept of the *Barber* gives free range to Bartoli's acting and stage intelligence, as though he had conceived it with her in mind (which he had not). With this support, Bartoli does the seemingly impossible: she creates a portrait of

Rosina that is archetypal and contemporary at the same time. She uses the body language of slapstick comedy, dance, and pantomime, squarely placing her Rosina in the Italian commedia dell'arte tradition. At the same time, the emotional truth and intensity of Bartoli's singing and acting lets us see the opera buffa character through the magnifying glass of modern psychology. We discover Rosina for the first time as a young woman in three dimensions, a person of flesh and blood.

The stage by Wolfgang Gussmann has Rosina imprisoned in the proverbial dollhouse. The doors are huge; she doesn't reach the windows. The room in its entirety is tipped forward toward the spectators: the audience is in the position of a child on the floor, peeping up into the dollhouse. Most of the back wall of the room is covered by an etching of Rossini, who towers over his characters with the ambiguous smile of a parent or voyeur. The stage and all the costumes are in black and white, reminiscent of the time before color movies were invented. The black and white also evokes and heightens the nightmare of Rosina's being trapped in what might be called a girl's destiny. Bartoli wears a modest black schoolgirl's dress with white collar and cuffs and a large white hair bow. The ends of her bow cover the entire length of her dark hair; seen in profile, their largeness occasionally alludes to a nun's wimple or a bridal veil. Bartoli is less chubby than in the videotaped *Barber* from 1988, and she looks just the way one would imagine young Cecilia (who still likes to wear bows on her head) as a girl. The only element of the erotic smoldering under' this Alice in Wonderland air are her shoes. With their little raised heels they belie the childlike innocence of her white bobby socks and signal Rosina's readiness to leap into sexual adulthood.

Bartoli's first appearance builds on her talent for pantomime that she had already displayed, five years earlier, in the comic seduction scene of *La Scala di seta*. She slides into view behind the barred window, signaling with a simple movement that Rosina is acting on the sly. Her hand is half raised in a gesture of eager anticipation and, at the same time, caution: she might get caught. While she listens to her admirer in the street, her neck takes on a delicate curve of longing. Her hands on the bars of her window seem to seek for an exit, but also for a hold from being swept away. Before even singing a line, Bartoli conveys the basic colors of Rosina's situation: she is a bird in a cage, with a romantic as well as erotic longing (the swoon Stendhal thought the character lacked) and a fierce determination to get out.

A little later, when she begins to sing, Bartoli delivers what her audience expects. She is by now known for the extraordinary technical prowess of her singing and for her emotional expressiveness and character shading through song. What is not yet known and expected is her equally important skill with movement, gesture, and facial expression. Nobody would expect an opera singer to be a dancer, but Bartoli started out as one and she draws on the body's potential for expressive language to a degree highly unusual on the opera stage.

Bartoli tells us through her body language that Rosina is a truly naughty girl who knows that she is always in danger. She moves fast as a flash of lightning to pursue or conceal her interests. When she walks or runs she often lifts her feet just enough to give us the feeling that the ground is burning under her. The next moment, her stride is confident, even defiant. Small leaps of joy punctuate the end of her first aria, "*Una voce poco fa*," as though her determination not to give up is a physical instinct, a knowledge rooted in her body. She never leaves a doubt that her playing the good girl is a strategy for sheer survival. Her feet in the orderly "ready" position of a ballet dancer, her hands demurely on her back, she pretends to listen to her tormentor, Bartolo. But secretly she makes fun of him with little backward kicks of her feet as though to say, Go to hell, old goat! She pulls more Chaplinesque tricks when she is torn between what she is supposed to do and what she wants, her feet already running in one direction while the rest of her body is still turned to the opposite one. When she is caught in an act of disobedience, trying to exchange a word with her disguised "Lindoro," for example, she pretends comical innocence by skipping a few steps like a girl on the way to the playground. Or she turns from the spot of her crime with an insipid little pirouette that professes mere airheadedness.

Bartoli's comic timing in this physical downing is admirable, the more so as with every step she has to negotiate a steeply raked stage floor. Only a consummate dancer could master such a task.

The woman in the young girl comes out when Figaro gives Rosina a pair of silk stockings and she can't wait to try them on. This Rosina certainly won't wait until she is done with her coloratura singing. In a sensual as well as comical touch Bartoli rolls her roulades and her silk stocking in perfect synchronicity. She lets Figaro help her into a new pair of shoes and stick a red rose into her hair (the only color onstage). Now she is in ecstasy. Her singing takes on a decidedly erotic expression; Rosina sways with self-delight, and the coloratura elements turn into fireworks of sexual excitement.

Another thrilling moment occurs in Rosina's singing lesson in act 2. Running and tiptoeing back and forth between her guardian and her lover, Bartoli transforms herself into a snake charmer and the snake, using the undulation of her neck and the trills of her fioritura as a dangerously seductive way to put the old man to sleep. Bartoli has replaced the usual aria Rosina rehearses in her lesson with the much more difficult coloratura aria "*Tanti affetti*" from Rossini's *La Donna del lago*. This kind of substitution, which was common practice until some thirty years ago, today is a bold unconventionality. Bartoli may have wished to reinstate the custom of Rossini's time. She does so, however, with a contemporary sensibility that requires the words to support the scene's dramatic coherence. The words fit perfectly: "So many emotions crowd my heart that I cannot express to you . . ." or "Here with my father and lover, ah! what a blessed moment . . ." In Bartoli's vocal and physical interpretation, these words become in turn a burning love declaration, a mock pacification in the guise of seduction, and a passionate plea for liberation.

What makes Bartoli's portrait of Rosina special is the unusual richness of her interpretation. She establishes Rosina as a woman who, with all her cleverness and plotting, is still a child. Bartoli uses many subtle movements and expressions to convey Rosina's innocence and dependence. When she is scolded, she sits down at the front of the stage, her feet turned in, and pokes at her face with boredom. She pouts and cowers at the proscenium, all by herself, as though sent into the corner, her arms wrapped around herself. The huge doors and windows of the dollhouse towering over her remind us that the world holding her a prisoner could easily crush her. It is in moments like this that the soap bubble of the opera buffa bursts and allows us to experience a deeper insight into the heroine's character. Rosina's flirtatiousness and seductive determination, in this light, might be just another trick to escape pain and loneliness. All of a sudden, through a simple childlike gesture, one senses how much is at stake for Rosina, and how dire this girl's destiny would be if anything in the lovers' plot were to go wrong.

Traditionally the *Barber* is played and perceived in a superficial, farcical way. In the words of Rodney Milnes, "The whole joyous point is that all the characters are opportunist monsters; this is why, gazing into the proscenium mirror, we all love it so much." ("Barber Black Sheep," *Spectator,* March 1985) True as this may be, one could argue that there are always deeper and more subtle shadings to a great work of art, even to comedy or opera buffa. To bring some of those hidden shades to light—without losing the more obvious joyous ones—seems to be Bartoli's particular artistic gift. It shows for the first time in the Houston *Barber,* but one can already predict that she will bring this gift to every role she takes on.

$\mathscr{C}$OSÌ FAN TUTTE

WOLFGANG AMADEUS MOZART

Settimane Musicali Internazionali, Teatro Mercadante, Napoli

1990

The Metropolitan Opera, New York

1996

CASTS

Teatro Mercadante

Conductor: Salvatore Accardo/Orchestra dei Solisti delle Settimane Musicali Internazionali/Coro Ensemble Vocale di Napoli. Production: Giacomo Battiato/G. Agostinucci/N. Cecchi. Fiordiligi: Lynne Dawson; Dorabella: Monica Groop; Despina: Cecilia Bartoli; Ferrando: Raul Gimenez; Guglielmo: Roberto Frontali: Don Alfonso: Rolando Panerai.

The Metropolitan Opera

Conductor: James Levine/The Metropolitan Opera Orchestra. Production: Lesley Koenig/Michael Yeargan. Fiordiligi: Carol Vaness; Dorabella: Susanne Mentzer; Despina: Cecilia Bartoli; Ferrando: Jerry Hadley; Guglielmo: Dwayne Croft; Don Alfonso: Thomas Allen.

Strictly speaking, Cecilia Bartoli's Despina at the Met in January 1996 falls outside the frame of the first ten years of her career. A review of it here likewise falls outside a strict chronological sequence, but it is tempting to place the discussion within the time frame of Bartoli's first approaches to the role.

Bartoli sang her debut Despina as early as June 1990, at the Settimane Musicali Internazionali in Naples. Press research reveals that in this new role, Bartoli managed to stand out. *La Repubblica* of Rome lists her "first among the singers," calling her Despina "splendidly outlined . . . , full of verve and supported by her ultimate musicality." *L'Unità* agrees: this Despina is "truly living in her character's clothes." Only the Naples daily *Il Mattino* criticizes her two "ugly transvestite scenes," but instantly excuses her by holding the director and conductor solely responsible.

The next Despina (which Bartoli's press releases mistakenly present as her debut in the role) came in 1993 at Salzburg (under the baton of Christoph van Dohnanyi). The Wiener Festwochen offered her another stab at the role, a year later (with Riccardo Muti conducting). Now the reactions were more mixed. The *Neue Zürcher Zeitung* found that she "excessively delivered up her declamatory and comedic talent while she was strikingly miserly with her voice." And the *Süddeutsche Zeitung* wrote about her Vienna Despina: "Strangely, Cecilia Bartoli does not sing Dorabella but Despina—with beautiful legato lines, but the role of soubrette does not really suit her."

These earlier performances have vanished. Their presence, however, could be felt in Bartoli's comfort with the role at the Met. The same critical voices were not to be heard in the United States, and nobody mistook her for a soubrette. One

puzzle, however, remained: the question of why the celebrated singer who had sung both the soprano (Dorabella) and the mezzo-soprano part (Despina) in *Così* chose the less celebrated role for her Met debut. Bartoli thus added a contemporary ambiguity to Mozart's last and most ambiguous opera.

By 1996, Bartoli was the world's most famous opera star and biggest box-office draw since Luciano Pavarotti. Had she wanted to enter the Met as Dorabella, she would have been welcome. Instead, she chose to do what critics have called "backing into the Met" in a "low-flying role" (*The New York Times*). Suspicion circulated: was she afraid that her voice would not be large enough to sustain a Dorabella at the Met? It was noted, after the opening, that "contrary to fears about her Despina, Ms. Bartoli's small but ebulliently colored mezzo-soprano had no trouble filling the house" (*New York Observer*).

Whatever Bartoli does or does not do tends to be explained, by American music critics, with reference to the size of her voice. Her own reasons for the choices she makes are often disregarded. Yet Bartoli states her reasons clearly. They have much to do with her outspoken refusal to cater to stardom or play the role expected of a diva. Had she chosen to start at the top, with Dorabella as her Met debut, Despina would most likely never have been offered to her in America. It matters to her that opera is ensemble play. Why not start small, she asked when we discussed the matter, and then have something to look forward to?

As a strategist, she may also have known that after singing in Jonathan Miller's production of *Così fan tutte* in Florence, the very conventional Met production would not allow her any worthwhile exploration of Dorabella's character.

It is extremely rare to have a singer who can perform both the roles of Dorabella and Despina. By playing the two parts virtually back to back, Bartoli may have wished to demonstrate her virtuosity and flexibility.

Despina, in Bartoli's eyes, deserves more attention than she usually gets: "She is not a soubrette. She is much more than that: she is the first feminist in opera!"

A feminist in Mozart's *Così*? Bartoli offers this interpretation of Despina defiantly, with laughter, but the idea gives one pause. Certainly, *Così* is a battle between the sexes, with Despina as a radical commentator who consistently advances the cause of women. Despina's cross-dressing and her diatribes about equal power and pleasure for women were perhaps as shocking in the eighteenth century as they remain in ours. Despina, a woman of the people, is streetwise. Therefore, as a woman, she has more knowledge of the world than her well-bred mistresses, sexual knowledge included.

That is how Bartoli plays her, solidly rooted in the commedia dell'arte tradition of the servant who outwits her mistresses, whose clear-eyed skepticism is grounded in the reality of work. The Met production opens with a stunning symbolic image of Despina's function: a heavy rope over one shoulder, she drags the entire set behind her onto the stage. Despina's kitchen is at the center of the set; she is the solid foundation of her mistresses' life and her authority is not restricted to pots and pans.

Bartoli's Despina busies herself while she watches, comments on, and interferes with the goings-on in the house. When she isn't stirring chocolate over the stove or serving breakfast she takes stockings off the washline; she sweeps around Guglielmo and Ferrando, who are committing their fake suicide; with a look from the corner of her eyes at the audience, she exchanges the knife in desperate Fiordiligi's hand for a big wooden cooking spoon; she rids the sisters of their tokens of obsession by dunking the lockets of their fiancés into a bucket, then cools her feet in it. When she isn't busy dressing or undressing the sisters she hands out crude moral and sexual advice as another way of taking care of their needs.

Bartoli sings Despina with a raucous, earthy vibrance, which heightens the servant's mockery. In her recitativi, she occasionally shows a daringly vulgar tendency to perform the words as if they were plain speech. Her movements have the down-to-earth feistiness of a peasant; she sometimes stands and watches the lovers' antics with her arms folded or her hands on her hips, her glance suspicious, her head shaking. Then she calls the audience to witness with a wink or a roll of her eyes. Playing Despina as a one-person version of a Greek chorus, Bartoli's face and gestures deliver the wisdom of common sense, which heightens the hilarity of the drama.

The "feminist" touch in this running commentary can be found in the way Bartoli's Despina cares for her mistresses, no matter how naïve and misguided they may seem to her. She laughs at them with obvious tenderness, in good humor, and when she helps the male intruders with their seduction plot it is because she is convinced that a taste of virility and sexual experience can only be good for her innocent young ladies. With the same democratic belief in good-hearted fun for everyone, Bartoli's Despina launches into her commedia dell'arte cross-dressing. As the "doctor" she turns a pair of garden shears into the mesmerizing instrument of the cure; she sings in a Mickey Mouse voice and pipes the exaggerated last note of each line onto a magnifying glass that makes her mouth look hugely authoritarian. As the "notary" she uses the stereotypical nasal drawl of all Italian comedy notaries, but spices up the Italian with a hilarious American accent, while her mustache performs a little Chaplin dance.

Reactions to Bartoli's Despina have been mixed. Many critics remain frustrated with her choice of role and maintain a watchful reserve: "Let's wait and see," says the *New York Times*. Others see a meaningful symbol in her first appearance onstage, pulling the set along with her. "Bartoli did seem to be carrying the show single-handedly. Or at least much of the audience must have thought so—

Despina, the housemaid, seldom stops a performance of *Così* the moment she comes into sight, or finds herself covered with floral bouquets during curtain calls at the end."

Bartoli's earthy, working-class, witty, "feminist" interpretation certainly makes us rethink the character and role of Despina. We are either used to the soubrette stereotype (Adelina Scarabelli in Michael Hampe's La Scala production with Riccardo Muti, on HomeVision video) or the impish-clownish version (Teresa Stratas in Jean-Pierre Ponnelle's *Così* with Harnoncourt on London/Decca video). After all the annoyingly cute, catty, snooty, or otherwise irritating Despinas, Bartoli's portrait is a considerable relief. Indeed, the opportunity to heighten the colors in the character of Despina may best explain why Bartoli chose the role for her Met debut.

DON GIOVANNI

WOLFGANG AMADEUS MOZART

Teatro alla Scala, Milan

1993

Großes Festspielhaus, Salzburger Festspiele, Salzburg

1994

CASTS

Teatro alla Scala

Conductor: Riccardo Muti/Orchestra e coro del Teatro alla Scala.
Production: Giorgio Strehler/Ezio Frigerio. Don Giovanni: Thomas Allan;
Leporello: Alessandro Corbelli; Donna Anna: Carol Vaness; Donna Elvira:
Renee Fleming; Don Ottavio: Goesta Winbergh; Zerlina: Cecilia Bartoli;
Masetto: Pietro Spagnoli/Roberto Scaltriti; Il Commendatore: Alexander
Anisimov.

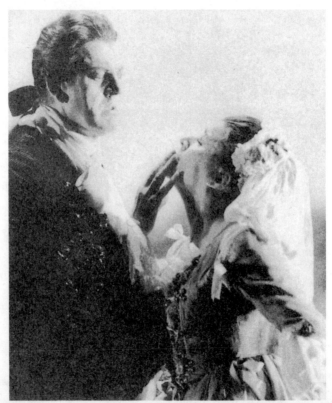

Salzburger Festspiele

Conductor: Daniel Barenboim/Wiener Philharmoniker/Wiener Staatsopernchor. Production: Patrice Chéreau/Richard Peduzzi. Don Giovanni: Ferruccio Furlanetto; Leporello: Bryn Terfel; Donna Anna: Lella Cuberli; Donna Elvira: Catherine Malfitano; Don Ottavio: Peter Seiffert; Zerlina: Cecilia Bartoli; Masetto: Andreas Kohn; Il Commendatore: Matti Salminen.
Live recording released on CD.

Zerlina was Bartoli's second role at La Scala, after Isolier in *Le Comte Ory* in 1991. The decision to give the part to Bartoli (who had already tried out the role in Zürich, in 1991) was both canny and obvious. Next to Carmen, Zerlina is one of the sexiest operatic roles in the repertoire. Although Zerlina is a secondary role with comparatively simple melodic lines (only the upper class sings coloratura in opera), it is a pivotal role in the drama. Zerlina is the only victim of Don Giovanni whose seduction we witness from start to almost finish. While Donna Elvira's accomplished and Donna Anna's botched seduction have happened offstage and made both women Don Giovanni's pursuers, with Zerlina we see Don Giovanni in his element as the hunter. We, the audience, are witnesses to and perhaps participants in a musical and psychological seduction that proves irresistible not only to Zerlina.

Mozart has defined *Don Giovanni* as a dramma giocoso, thus giving rise to numerous reflections by music historians, conductors, directors, and singers: How much drama? How much comedy? On the one hand, hellfire and the loss of a soul; on the other, the amusing and titillating attempt to seduce a peasant girl on her wedding day.

Endangered marriage is a favorite commedia dell'arte theme; most often, interpretations of *Don Giovanni* have moved in that direction, streamlining Zerlina as the charming but gullible Colombina and Masetto as the honest but dumb Arlecchino. For these productions, Zerlina's wedding day adventure provides a lot of fun and spice and not much drama. Even the great 1978 film version by Joseph Losey with its dark, driven Don Giovanni in the guise of an eighteenth-century Marquis de Sade offered largely erotic and comic relief with Teresa Berganza's Zerlina and José Van Dam's Masetto.

Berganza's calm, friendly seductiveness is never seriously disturbed. Her Zerlina is fascinated and flattered rather than attracted by her noble suitor, and their only passionate exchange comes right before Donna Elvira interrupts them: Don Giovanni takes off her modest cape, Zerlina lies back on a bed in a gentle swoon and lets him kiss her décolletage. Berganza's smiling maturity (she is not quite young enough for the character) lets the seduction scene play as a simple and charming mistake on Zerlina's part.

With Bartoli in the role, we have a different story. In the La Scala production, when Don Giovanni appears in the middle of the wedding preparations, Bartoli's face and body betray immediate interest in him, establishing Zerlina as a sexual young woman who doesn't need to be awakened. She is ready to pick up Don Giovanni's innuendos and respond with a good game of flirtation. But she gets caught when Don Giovanni employs the highly ambiguous language of a marriage proposal for his libertine intentions and, hiding the wolf behind the sheep's skin, clothes his proposal in the most seductive, insinuating music imaginable.

In *"Là ci darem la mano"* ("There you will give me your hand and consent") he suddenly abandons the formal address and uses the familiar *"tu."* Bartoli's eagerness and suspicion emerge in a voice charged with emotion and tremolo: *"Vorrei e non vorrei"* ("I want to and I don't"). She strains away from him while he firmly holds her by her hand. They remain fixed in this symbolically charged position that marks his determination and her indecision while she turns the proposition over. At *"Non so più forte"* ("My strength is failing"), she detaches herself and comes forward, as though needing to step aside from his overwhelming presence in order to continue her inner debate. His *"Vieni! Vieni!"* then rings with particular allure across the distance she has created, while Zerlina's impatience with her own contradictory desires makes her stamp her foot: "But he can still make a fool of me," she counsels herself.

He draws in on her, a hunter going after his prey; now his sly "I will change your fate" tips the balance. Her voice in the repeated *"Presto, non son più forte, non son più forte"* enlarges the vertigo in Mozart's musical line, adding a note of pleading, then a sense of breathlessly giving in. When he now steps up the pressure in the more imperative *"Andiam!"* ("Let's go!"), she lets him take off her veil. Her consent, *"Andiam!"* in which she addresses him for the first time, is both a cry and a sigh of surrender. She rushes into his arms for the excited, playful coda of their love pact. He sarcastically drops her veil to the floor; they walk out tightly enlaced.

A year later, in the Salzburg production by Patrice Chéreau, Bartoli's erotic stage presence is even more highlighted. Under Chéreau's direction, Bartoli's Zerlina is in torment over the elementary sexual attraction she experiences for the nobleman. The Salzburg Don does not immediately take her hand; he stays close by, shadowing her every move, ready to strike. Bartoli's voice and expression in her first *"Vorrei e non vorrei!"* is a supplication as much as a confession. She sings the words half to herself, turning away from him in anguish. He goes after her, takes hold of her arm; now she shows that his touch moves through her whole body. She is drawn back to him until he can press against her from behind. Her voluptuous response, in *"Presto, non son più forte,"* rings with a clear appeal for a larger embrace. She reaches behind to touch his body. That gesture, her hand pressing against his hip, seems to steady her while at the same time gluing her to him.

It would be hard to imagine a more embodied expression of Mozart's music in this duet of shared sexual attraction. Zerlina's desire (convincingly captured in the sound recording as well) is an erotic agony, with its mixture of danger and impatience, while his is a cold, calculating fire. She is feeling, her body curving into and away from his touch; he is watching, his detachment making him a voyeur to his own power and magnetism.

The usually light amorous game audiences are used to, in Chéreau's direction, unfolds its full power and potential drama through Bartoli's intensity, the daring way she lets herself feel, embody, and express desire. Bartoli's Zerlina transcends both her inferior condition as a woman and the class difference between noble and peasant. She seems to suggest that Zerlina chooses the erotic danger, not that she is about to be victimized by it. As the impatient, equally desiring partner, she becomes, in terms of erotic power, Don Giovanni's full equal.

The same fiery Zerlina comes across in both the La Scala and Salzburg productions in her scenes with her jealous Masetto. Here, Bartoli's Zerlina is highly volatile; when her pacifying maneuvers don't work immediately, she gets impatient and angry. In the La Scala production she kneels down so he can beat her, but does so with pronounced sexual overtones in her voice; she then peeks at him to check the success of her offer. When he is not seduced fast enough or sufficiently pacified by her *"Pace, pace, o vita mia!,"* she attacks him with playful slaps and provokes him by spinning him around until it is clear to everyone that she will have her way.

The happy ending between her and Masetto, however, has a different flavor in the two productions. At La Scala, Zerlina seems to settle for her husband without much excitement. Her singing and acting portray extremely tender emotion; she is more a sister or mother to him than a lover, and in this respect she reminds one of the matronly Berganza. The audience, as though experiencing this as a letdown, offers her only a polite applause.

Chéreau, by contrast, lets Zerlina act as passionately with Masetto as she did with Don Giovanni. Her passion, however, does not transform Masetto into a great lover; it simply underlines the impatience of a truly sexual woman to finally get what she desires.

By 1993, the singer had already proved her ability to turn comic characters into rich, multilayered characterizations that never missed out on the darker underpinnings of human personality. Having added romantic depth to her Dorabella and unexpected childhood drama to her commedia dell'arte Rosina, Bartoli now gave her Zerlina an unexpected and unusual quality—fully realized, full-powered female passion.

*L*A CENERENTOLA

GIOACCHINO ROSSINI

Houston Grand Opera, Houston

1995

CAST: Conductor: Bruno Campanella/Houston Symphony Orchestra
and Chorus. Production: Roberto De Simone/Mauro Carosi/Odette
Nicoletti. Angelina: Cecilia Bartoli; Clorinda: Laura Knoop; Tisbe: Jill
Grove; Don Magnifico: Enzo Dara; Don Ramiro: Raul Giménez; Dandini:
Alessandro Corbelli; Alidoro: Michele Pertusi.

Angelina, in Rossini's *Cenerentola,* has been Bartoli's most widely popular and
successful role to date. She recorded the opera right after her Bologna debut in
the role, in 1992, under the baton of Riccardo Chailly. The record was a runaway
success, winning the 1994 *Classic CD* awards in both the Opera and the Disc of
the Year categories. The Bologna production by Roberto De Simone was taken

on by the Houston Grand Opera (this time, Bruno Campanella was conducting), providing Bartoli with her American debut in the role. The performance was telecast and recorded on video and laser disc.

The enthusiastic audience response to Bartoli's Cenerentola is understandable. Her concert rendition of the famous showpiece *"Nacqui all'affanno ... Non più mesta,"* with its coloratura acrobatics, had been the highlight of many of her earlier recitals, beginning with the Maria Callas gala in Paris, when this very aria brought instant stardom to the unknown singer.

There is an unmistakable match between the role and Bartoli's own personality, between the musical demands of the part and Bartoli's natural vocal capacity. Her ease in the role is clearly demonstrated in a story reported in *Classic CD*, by music critic Roger Mills.

"The version of [*Cenerentola*'s final, show-stopping rondo *"Non più mesta"*] that Bartoli recorded and does in concert, with variations prepared by musicologist Philip Gossett, offers every technical nightmare conceivable—frenetic coloratura, lightning scales, wild leaps from one extreme of the register to another. You would expect to need hours of recording to get such a daunting piece in the can. But on a memorable afternoon in Bologna in July 1992 Bartoli got it virtually note perfect in the one take. Recording sessions are seldom emotional occasions. But the atmosphere of stunned admiration around the Teatro Comunale after that particular take was palpable."

Bartoli has by now reached the stage in her career when critics, musicians, and music lovers no longer measure her accomplishments by reference to her own development as a singer, but compare what she does in a role to its other great interpretations. The music critic John Ardoin, for example, sees Bartoli as "the most accomplished, charming and captivating Cenerentola since Giulietta Simionata's first recording of the opera." He adds, "In fact, rarely since the magical Conchita Supervia has *Cenerentola*'s music been sung so ravishingly or with such finesse and point, such brio and clarity" (*Dallas Morning News*).

There is an interesting contemporary comparison available on video and laser disk. Another of today's most beloved Cenerentolas, Frederica von Stade, performs the role in the Jean-Pierre Ponnelle production from La Scala, with Claudio Abbado conducting (Deutsche Grammophon, 1981). Von Stade is the archetype of Germanic fairy-tale heroines: blond, angel-like, dreamy, starry-eyed, with the disembodied grace required of virgins, innocent princesses, and the like. Gentleness and tearful goodness are written all over her, building a moving contrast to the more rude and jolly comical elements of Rossini's "melodramma giocoso."

Rossini has in fact eliminated most of the supernatural elements and replaced them with a social set of miracles. The magical realm of nature and powerful women has given way to a world of powerful men: the evil stepmother is now a buffoonish stepfather, the fairy godmother the prince's tutor. The erotic symbol of the glass slipper is replaced by an innocuous matching pair of bracelets. In Rossini's cynical farce about social climbing, domestic violence, inheritance embezzlement, and royal retribution, von Stade's angelic Cenerentola preserves our childhood picture of a pure, long-suffering Cinderella.

Bartoli, by contrast, brings a whiff of modern air to her feisty, dark, Italian version of the abused girl. Her Angelina is the spirit of survival personified—a quality that evokes a comparison with another hot new contender, the Russian mezzo-soprano Olga Borodina, who recently began performing the role in the West, in San Francisco. Whereas Borodina stays placid throughout, Bartoli has a temperament and a temper; she pouts and pesters her bossy stepsisters. There is marked rebellion in the secret help she offers the beggar (the prince's tutor Alidoro, in disguise). She drags her steps when she is ordered about, but turns into a little engine of duty when she can do good. She has sensuous appetites: the prince (disguised as his manservant Dandini) enchants her, makes her weak, causes her voice to tremble.

This Angelina has a natural claim to fun and excitement: she, too, wants to dance. A mini melodrama ensues when she goes on pleading to go to the ball even if it means getting kicked and beaten.

But Bartoli's Angelina is never beaten into submission. Her feisty spirit prevails, and so does her faith. There is a childlike cuteness in Bartoli in this role —— in spite of her exaggerated décolletage. Her pudgy body, big radiant eyes, and comical grace all lend her the irresistible quality of a toddler who falls a hundred times and never hesitates to get up. This simple innocence and childlike optimism make it believable that Angelina is unwilling to give herself airs. Grateful joy is her reaction to anything good that happens to her. When Bartoli sings the word *"gioia"* ("joy"), she seems to chew the word as if it were a delicious fruit. Her voice vibrates with feeling, her eyes sparkle, her whole face and body seem to experience joy for the first time. Following her, we are taken into a child's belief in miracles untainted by self-conscious doubts or pride. This is a faith that has no need for retribution.

In an interview with the *Dallas Morning News,* Bartoli compared the role of Cenerentola with that of Rosina in *The Barber of Seville:* "Cenerentola is a more interesting character for me because she has a greater range. Rosina undergoes very little change. She is the same from first to last. She is more calculating. But Cenerentola is a more simple and honest girl. She has more character. I prefer her."

The character range Bartoli alludes to comes across as impressively in the videotaped live performance as it does onstage. This time, Bartoli manages to avoid almost all of the nervous facial tics that have occasionally detracted from her performances. She appears perfectly natural and relaxed in closeup. Angelina's joie de vivre (what Bartoli calls *"spumante"*—the champagnelike sparkle of the character) is as convincing as her romantic daydreaming and falling in love. Her fearful disbelief during the dramatic abuse scene looks and sounds as real as the calm authority Cenerentola takes on in her final redemption.

The music of her concluding aria, with its coloratura drama of emotions, drives her one more time through her entire story of suffering and redemption. The music takes her to vertiginous peaks, followed quickly by heart-wrenching abysses. Rescued from her family, securely united with the prince, decked out in her elaborate wedding gown, Bartoli's Angelina rises to the extreme emotions of the moment. At the line, "And then my whole destiny changed!" there is wonder, disbelief, ecstasy in her voice, there is the full recognition of the pain she leaves behind. And there is the surrender to the all-encompassing *"gioia,"* which in Bartoli's expression of it becomes synonymous with an ecstatic celebration of life's inherent goodness.

"This shall be my revenge:/It will be to forgive them," Angelina decides. In the way Bartoli sings and acts her "revenge," we are made to understand Cenerentola's forgiveness of her cruel family as something other than a gratuitous gesture, or even a self-congratulatory demonstration of the power she has achieved. On the one hand, Bartoli's happy radiance gives the impression that the forgiveness is a spontaneous event; it has happened to her even as much as she has made it happen. But her self-assured, solidly "regal" air seems to raise the personal generosity into a public statement of moral virtue. Her own faith has been confirmed, goodness is established and rises with her to the throne.

When Angelina takes on moral stature, we understand that Alidoro embodies the divine providence comic opera salutes and celebrates through its happy endings. In this sense, Bartoli's interpretation, her ability to make us feel the power of elemental joy and faith, establishes the fundamental seriousness of Rossini's work even in its ebulliently comic fairy-tale disguise.

L'ANIMA DEL FILOSOFO (OSSIA ORFEO ED EURIDICE)

JOSEPH HAYDN

Wiener Festwochen, Theater an der Wien, Wien

1995

CAST: Conductor: Nikolaus Harnoncourt/Concentus musicus Wein/
Arnold Schönberg Chor. Production: Jürgen Flimm/George Tsypin,
Florence von Gerkan. Orfeo: Roberto Saccà; Euridice: Cecilia Bartoli;
Creonte: Wolfgang Holzmair; Genio: Eva Mei.

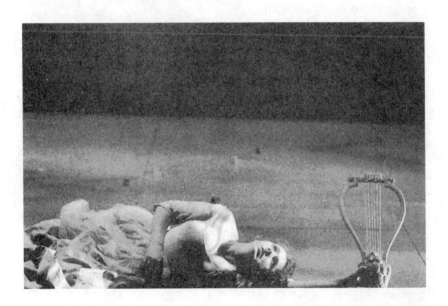

In 1995, Bartoli again worked with Nikolaus Harnoncourt and his famous
ensemble of period instrumentalists, Concentus musicus Wien. This time, as
Bartoli has said, she was given "the privilege not only of working with such fine
musicians, and in such a great theater as the Theater an der Wien, but the
privilege of singing my first tragic role."

The event that opened the 1995 Wiener Festwochen was a very rarely
performed opera, the thirteenth and last opera by Joseph Haydn. Haydn wrote

L'Anima del filosofo right after his arrival in England, in 1791, for the Italian (Haymarket) Theater in London. Taking up the classical myth of Orfeo and Euridice, Haydn intended to write an opera "of a very different kind than that by Gluck," the main difference being the tragic ending, with which Haydn leaned toward an opera seria treatment of the myth. The ending is shockingly unconventional for an eighteenth-century opera: Orfeo dies, there is no apotheosis of art, nor of philosophy, no redeeming victory for either gods or humans. Nature, with a raging thunderstorm, seems to drown the hero, the Bacchae, the myth itself. It all ends in incertitude. As though washed to the shores of the twentieth century, Haydn's music evaporates into a small, muted drum roll. Harnoncourt has said that this is "the most terrifying opera ending that I know."

We don't know, however, if this was the intended ending, although it seems unlikely. Haydn probably never finished the opera, or the last part may have been lost. The planned opening of *L'Anima del filosofo* at the Italian Theater in 1791 never took place. King George III suddenly withdrew the Royal Patent for the performance of operas from the theater. By order of the king, rehearsals had to be broken off, and Haydn's subsequent attempts to bring the opera to the stage failed. We know that the libretto, written in Italian by Carlo Francesco Badini and based on Virgil and Ovid, originally contained five acts. The rest is left to speculation—what happened to the fifth act, what might have happened in that act, and what the mysterious "philosopher's soul" (from the working title of the opus) referred to.

It took 160 years before the opera was finally performed at the Maggio Musicale Fiorentino in 1951. Erich Kleiber conducted and Maria Callas created the role of Euridice. Another sensational production followed in 1967 at the

Wiener Festwochen, featuring Nicolai Gedda and Joan Sutherland.

The surprise and sensation of the 1995 production was the dramatic and tragic intensity Harnoncourt coaxed from Haydn's music, presenting a stormy, emotional composition that was, in this sense, a doubly unknown Haydn opera. He could not have made a better choice for his tragically intense Euridice than Cecilia Bartoli.

The opera begins with Euridice alone onstage. She has escaped from an unwanted marriage arranged by her father, the king Creonte, and has lost her way in a wild forest. The chorus warns her to turn back: there is danger that savages will kill her for their blood sacrifice.

"Leave me alone," is Euridice's angry response to them. In her long, accompanied recitative, she complains with passionate indignation that she still has to live when her chance for love is dead. She wants to die; when the "savages" surround her with their spears, she is crippled with terror but faces them: "I fear no further sacrifice. Can prayer help me? I fear no death!" Her first aria, *"Filomena abbandonata"* ("Philomena, sad, deserted"), has the eerie, nostalgic atmosphere of a goodbye to life, forecasting in musical intention and atmosphere Desdemona's haunting *"Salce"* in Rossini's *Otello*. But here all similarity between the two heroines ends. Euridice is taken over by desperate protest. Bartoli launches her defiance at the *"crudeltà"* of destiny on hands and knees in the rapid fury of a coloratura passage, throwing herself into the extreme high and low notes with a vengeance. On the highest note she almost breaks loose from the grip of her captors; she is practically in tears, then she fights again; the end is bitter rage before they overwhelm her.

It is a strangely liberating experience to see and hear Bartoli in this first tragic role. She seems set loose, an elementary force that has finally shaken off the fetters of comedy, charm, seductive smiles, and feminine graces. She dives into the ravages of despair with a relish, a woman coming home after a long exile. She gives the impression that she belongs in this country of dark outcries, rapid, rageful scales, long-drawn legato lines of sighing pain, rising and falling.

When Orfeo appears in the last minute to save her, Bartoli's Euridice seems to have a hard time reentering the realm of human happiness. Here, her acting has a forced edge, as though she tries but does not quite find her place in the happy exchanges and vows of love. Perhaps Bartoli's Euridice has a foreboding that she *is* the sacrifice, that nothing will save her from death.

One can well imagine that Callas sang the end of act 1 with precisely this shadowed intensity and that Bartoli may have preferred to keep Euridice's happiness in question. The dark drama brought out in Harnoncourt's conducting and Bartoli's interpretation of the tragic heroine clashes with the rest of the production. Euridice and Orfeo have to roll and crawl over a steeply raked plateau as though the stage direction wants to show the couple crushed by the forces of destiny. It doesn't work. In addition to the steep plateau, Bartoli has to negotiate the steepest imaginable décolletage on Euridice's wedding dress. She moves, as always, with the physical agility of a dancer, but one wishes she might one day be liberated from wedding gowns solely designed to show off her breasts.

Consistently, no one else onstage matches the intensity of either the music or Bartoli's acting. Beautifully voiced Roberto Sacca, with his light and smiling trustiness, is a perfect Tamino, as one critic remarked, right out of Mozart's *Magic Flute*. Similarly, Holzmair's Creonte, with his modern, playfully cynical relaxedness, seems on temporary loan from Strauss's *Capriccio*. Eva Mei, the spirit who leads Orfeo into the underworld, has the look and air of the serious student Niklausse, in Offenbach's *Tales of Hoffmann*. The chorus, with their long, pointed noses, stiff long hair, and long cardboard arms seem to have stepped from a medieval miracle and morality puppet play; the "savages" sporting their oversized head masks and camouflage body paint might have leapt out of a 1920 production of Alfred Jarry's *Ubu Roi*. The Bacchae throwing themselves against the walls in long evening dresses and society wigs come straight from Pina Bausch's German dance theater. The Amorini Divini (a Baroque form of Cupids) in turn have become two dozen Erdas with long white wigs and rags, each keeping her failing body up with the help of a Wotan-speer.

Through all this, Bartoli's Euridice moves with a fine balance of classical poise and elemental power. It hardly matters that she is made to appear to Orfeo in the underworld standing in a boat like a forlorn Sylphide, "reminding us *nolens volens* of Christine in *Phantom of the Opera*," as critic Thomas Voigt remarked in *Opernwelt*. The moment she addresses Orfeo, the soulful beauty and longing of her singing are spellbinding. Nothing apart from her voice is needed to convince us that any lover would inevitably break the divine rule and turn around to face her. In the other operas about the Orpheus myth, this crucial moment, when Orpheus turns around and loses Euridice for the second and last time, requires arias, duets, long pleadings (as in Gluck's *Orfeo ed Euridice*). In Haydn's unconventional *L'Anima del filosofo*, the culmination of the tragedy is treated in a mere recitative and only takes one shocking moment, the literal blink of an eye.

Bartoli's performance has its peak early on in the scene of Euridice's death, after she is bitten by the snake. Once again, Bartoli is alone onstage. Her voice, in the awareness of death spreading through her body, narrows, the vibrato recedes until the poison has reduced her voice to the helpless purity of a child's. She is suddenly lost to the world; all her attention is focused on the mysterious process inside her. "*M'abbandona il respiro*" ("My breath abandons me"), she sings in the pianissimo realization of terror. A small tremor marks her words "*Io morò*" ("I die") as she sinks down near the place where Orfeo has left his lyre. The following cavatina, "*Del mio core il voto estremo*" ("The last desire of my heart"), draws a plaintive, increasingly dark and painful timbre from her. She struggles to reach the lyre. Her repeated *"ultimo sospir,"* the last breath she vows to Orfeo, is a halting, aspirated string of pianissimo syllables. Her eyes turn. A last trembling in her voice, her eyes open wide in the grip of death, her hand with the lyre sinks.

It is hard to imagine that Callas could have done it better. For Bartoli, as Euridice, everything comes together: the sheer vocal beauty of her voice, her dramatic intensity and soulfulness, the subtle support of Harnoncourt's conducting, and the perfect acoustic conditions of the house where even a pianissimo whisper carries. Most critics have professed sheer amazement at Bartoli's performance. Having proved herself in opera buffa and dramma giocoso roles, Bartoli, with this dramatic Euridice, has surpassed the promise of her first ten years as a singer.

The entire seventeenth and eighteenth centuries of operatic music are now written on the horizon of Bartoli's future career: the operas of Haydn, Monteverdi, Händel, and Vivaldi are waiting to be brought back into prominence by her. We, her audience, need only wait—Bartoli's first tragic role clearly opens into this future.

Discography

1996 Cecilia Bartoli: *Chant d'Amour. Mélodies Françaises*
   Bizet:

    Chant d'amour

    Ouvre ton cœur

    Adieux de l'hôtesse arabe

    Tarentelle

    La Coccinelle

   Delibes:

    Les Filles de Cadix

   Viardot:

    Hai luli!

    Havanaise

    Les Filles de Cadix

   Berlioz:

    La Mort d'Ophélie

    Zaïde

   Ravel:

    Chants populaires

    I Chanson française

    II Chanson espagnole

    III Chanson italienne

    IV Chanson hébraïque

    Vocalise-étude (en forme de habanera)

    Deux Mélodies hébraïques

    I Kaddisch

    II L'Enigme éternelle

    Tripatos

   Myung-Whun Chung, piano

   [London 452 667-2]

Cecilia Bartoli: Mozart Arias
From: *Lucio Silla* (K135)*
   "Il tenero momento" (aria)
   "Pupille amate" (aria)
   "D'elisio in sen m'attendi" (duetto)
   "Cecilio, a che t'arresti" (accompagnato)
   "Quest'improvviso tremito" (aria)
From: *Le Nozze di Figaro* (K492)
   "Voi, che sapete che cosa è amor" (arietta)
   "Non so più cosa son, cosa faccio" (aria)
From: *Così fan tutte* (K588)
   "Ah guarda, sorella" (duetto)
   "E amore un ladrocello" (aria)
   "Soave sia il vento" (terzettino)
   "Prendero quel brunettino" (duetto)
   "Ah, scostati!" (recitativo)
   "Smanie implacabili" (aria)
Gruberova*, Kenny*, Cunerli***, Furlanetto***, Tomlinson***
Harnoncourt; Concentus Musicus Wien*
Barenboim; Berliner Philharmoniker**/***
[Erato 0630-14074-2] (Teldec 1990. Erato classics, 1990, 1991)

1995   *Cecilia Bartoli: A Portrait*
   Mozart:
   From: *La Clemenza di Tito*
     "Parto, parto, ma tu, ben mio" (Sesto)
     Schatzberger, basset clarinet obbligato
     Hogwood; The Academy of Ancient Music
   From: *Così fan tutte*
     "Temerari! . . . Come scoglio" (Fiordiligi)
     "In uomini, in solidati" (Despina)
   From: *Le Nozze di Figaro*
     "Voi che sapete" (Cherubino)

"*Giunse alfin il momento . . . Deh vieni*" (Susanna)

From: *Don Giovanni*

"*Batti, batti, o bel Masetto*" (Zerlina)

Concert aria (K505), *Ch'io mi scordi di te*

Schiff, Bösendorfer piano

Fischer; Wiener Kammerorchester

Parisotti (attrib. Pergolesi): *Se tu m'ami*

Giordani: *Caro mio ben*

Caccini: *Amarilli*

Fischer, piano

Schubert:

La pastorella (D528)

Goldoni

"*Vedi quanto adoro ancora ingrato!*" (D510)

Metastasio, from *Didone Abbandonata*

Schiff, piano

Rossini:

"Beltà cudele"

Spencer, piano

From: *Semiramide*

"*Bel raggio lusinghier*" (Semiramide)

Marin; Orchestra del Teatro La Fenice

From: Maometto II

"*Giusto ciel, in tal periglio*" (Anna)

Marin; Orchestra del Teatro La Fenice

From: *La Cenerentola*

"*Naqui all'affano . . . Non più mesta*" (Cenerentola)

Chailly; soloists with Orchestra e coro del Teatro Comunale di Bologna

[London 448 300-2] (1991–1995)

1995   Mozart: *La Clemenza di Tito*

Heilmann (Tito), Bartoli (Sesto), Jones (Vitellia), Bonney (Servilia), Montague (Annio), Cachemaille (Publio)

Hogwood; The Academy of Ancient Music Orchestra and Chorus
[L'Oiseau-Lyre 444 131-2]

1994   Mozart: *Don Giovanni*

Bartoli (Zerlina), Cuberli (Donna Anna), Furlanetto (Don Giovanni), Malfitano (Donna Elvira), Seifert (Ottavio), Terfel (Leporello)

Barenboim; Wiener Philarmoniker/Wiener Staatsopernchor; live performance at Salzburg

[Serenissima 360176]

1994   Mozart: *Le Nozze di Figaro*

Skovhus (Count Almaviva), Studer (Countess Almaviva), McNair (Susanna), Gallo (Figaro), Bartoli (Cherubino), Antonacci (Marcellina), D'Arcangelo (Bartolo), Allemano (Basilio), Jelosits (Curzio), Gati (Antonio), Rost (Barbarina)

Abbado; Vienna Philharmonic

[Deutsche Grammophon 445 903-2]

1994   Mozart: *Mozart Portraits* (Operatic arias; *Exsultate, jubilate*)

From: *Così fan tutte*

     "*Temerari! . . . Come scoglio*"

     "*Ei parte . . . Per pietà, ben mio*"

     "*In uomini, in soldati*"

From: *Le Nozze di Figaro*

     "*E Susanna non vien! . . . Dove sono i bei momenti*"

     "*Giunse alfin il momento . . . Al desio*"

From: *Don Giovanni*

     "*Batti, batti, o bel Masetto*"

     "*In quali eccessi . . . Mi tradì quell'alma ingrata*"

From: *Davidde penitente* (K469)

     "*Lungi le cure ingrate*"

     Exsultate, jubilate (K165)

Fischer; Vienna Chamber Orchestra

[London 443 452-2]

1993   Puccini: *Manon Lescaut*

Freni (Manon), Pavarotti (Des Grieux), Croft (Lescaut), Taddei
(Geronte), Vargas (Edmondo), Bartoli (Un musico)

Levine; Metropolitan Opera Orchestra and Chorus

[Decca 440 200-2]

1993   Italian Songs (Beethoven, Schubert, Haydn, Mozart)

Beethoven:

   La partenza (WoO 124)

   L'amante impaziente I (op. 82 no. 3) *Stille Frage*

   L'amante impaziente II (op. 82 no. 4) *Liebes-Ungeduld*

   Liebes-Klage (op. 82 no. 2)

   Hoffnung (op. 82 no. 1)

   In questa tomba oscura (WoO 133)

Mozart:

   Ridente la calma (K152 [210a])

Schubert:

   Vedi quanto adoro (D510)

   Nel boschetto (D738)

   Alla cetra (D737)

   La pastorella (D528)

   Non t'accostar all'urna (D688 no. 1)

   Guarda, che bianca luna (D688 no. 2)

   Da quel sembiante appresi (D688 no. 3)

   Mio ben ricordati (D688 no. 4)

   Pensa, che questo istante (D76)

   Felice arrivo e congedo (D767)

Haydn:

   Arianna a Naxos

András Schiff, piano

[London 440 297-2]

1993   Pergolesi: *Stabat Mater, Salve Regina*; A. Scarlatti: *Salve Regina*
        Anderson, Bartoli
        Dutoit; Sinfonietta de Montréal

1993   Rossini: *La Scala di Seta*
        Di Credico (Dormont), Serra (Giulia), Bartoli (Lucilla), Matteuzzi
            (Dorvil), De Carolis (Blansac)
        Ferro; Orchestra del Teatro Comunale di Bologna; Rossini Opera
            Festival in Pesaro, live recording, September 1988
        [Ricordi 2003]

1992   Rossini: *Rossini Heroines*
        From: *Zelmira*
            "*Riedi al soglio*"
        From: *Le Nozze di Teti e di Peleo*
            "*Ah, non potrian resistere*"
        From: *Maometto II*
            "*Giusto ciel, in tal periglio*"
        From: *La Donna del lago*
            "*Tanti affetti in tal momento*"
        From: *Elisabetta regina d'Inghilterra*
            "*Quant'è grato all'alma mia*"
        From: *Elisabetta regina d'Inghilterra*
            "*Fellon la pena avrai*"
        From: *Maometto II*
            "*Ah! che invan su questo ciglio*"
        From: *Semiramide*
            "*Serena i vaghi rai . . . Bel raggio lusinghier*"
        Marin; Orchestra and Chorus of the Teatro la Fenice
        [London 436 075-2]

1992   *If You Love Me (Se tu m'ami)*; 18th-century Italian songs
        A. Scarlatti:
            Già il sole dal Gange

Son tutta duolo

Se Florindo è fedele

O cessate di piagarmi

Spesso vibra per suo gioco

Giordani: *Caro mio ben*

Lotti: *Pur dicesti, o bocca bella*

Cesti: *Intorno all'idol mio*

Paisiello: *Nel cor più non mi sento*

Paisiello: *Il mio ben quando verra*

(Anon.): *O leggiadri occhi belli*

Marcello: *Quella fiamma che m'accende*

Caldara: *Selve amiche*

Caldara: *Sebben, crudele*

Caccini: *Tu ch'hai le penne, Amore*

Parisotti (attrib. Pergolesi): *Se tu m'ami*

Paisiello: *Chi vuol la zingarella*

Caccini: *Amarilli*

Cavalli: *Delizie contente*

Vivaldi: *Sposa son disprezzata*

Carissimi: *Vittoria, vittoria*

Fischer, piano

[London 436 267-2]

1991   Mozart: *Mozart Arias*

From: *Le Nozze di Figaro* (K492)

   "*Non so più*"

   "*Voi che sapete*"

Concert aria (K582) *Chi sa, chi sa, qual sia*

From: *Così fan tutte* (K588)

   "*E'amore un ladroncello*"

Concert aria (K578) *Alma grande e nobil core*

From: *Don Giovanni*

   "*Vedrai carino*"

From: *Le Nozze di Figaro* (K492)
　"*Giunse alfin il momento . . . Deh vieni*"
From: *La Clemenza di Tito* (K621)
　"*Parto, parto*"
　"*Deh, per qesto*"
　"*Ecco il punto, o Vitellia . . . Non più di fiori*"
Concert aria (K505) *Ch'io mi scordi di te?*
Fischer; Vienna Chamber Orchestra
[London 430 513-2]

1991　Mozart: *Le Nozze di Figaro* (KV 492)
Schmidt (Count Almaviva), Cuberli (Countess Almaviva), Rodgers (Susanna), Tomlinson (Figaro), Bartoli (Cherubino), Pancella (Marcellina), Clark (Basilio), Brunner (Don Curzio), von Kannen (Bartolo), Rose (Antonio), Leidland (Barbarina)
Barenboim; Berlin Philharmonic
Creed; Rias Kammerchor
[Erato 2292-45501-2]

1991　Mozart: *Requiem in D minor* (K626)
Auger, Bartoli, Cole, Pape
Solti; Vienna Philharmonic
Burian; Konzertvereinigung Wiener Staatsopernchor
Recorded live in St. Stephen's Cathedral, Vienna, December 5, 1991
[London 433 688-2]

1991　Rossini: *Rossini recital*
La pastorella
Beltà crudele
Il trovatore
La regata veneziana
　I. Anzoleta avanti la regata
　II. Anzoleta co passa la regata
　III. Anzoleta dopo la regata

Mi lagnerò tacendo (A Major)

Mi lagnerò tacendo (D Major)

Mi lagnerò tacendo "*Sorzico*" (G Major)

Mi lagnerò tacendo "*Stabat Mater*" (E Major)

Mi lagnerò tacendo (G Major)

Il risentimento (D Minor)

La Grande Coquette (Ariette Pompadour)

Ariette à l'ancienne

L'Orpheline du Tyrol (Ballade élégie)

La Légende de Marguerite

Nizza

L'âme délaissée

Canzoncetta spagnuola "*En medio a mis colores*"

Cantata: *Giovanna d'Arco*

Spencer, piano

[London 430 518-2]

1990   Mozart: *Così fan tutte*
Cuberli (Fiordiligi), Bartoli (Dorabella), Rodgers (Despina), Streit
    (Ferrando), Furlanetto (Guglielmo), Tomlinson (Don Alfonso)
Barenboim; Berlin Philharmonic
Creed; Rias Kammerchor
[Erato 2292-45475-2]

1990   Rossini: *Stabat Mater*
Vaness, Bartoli, Araiza, Furlanetto
Bychkov; Symphonie-Orchester des Bayerischen Rundfunks
Weigle; Chor des Bayerischen Rundfunks
[Philips 426 312-2]

1989   Mozart: *Lucio Silla* (KV 135)
Schreier (Lucio Silla), Gruberova (Giunia), Bartoli (Cecilio), Upshaw
    (Celia), Kenny (Cinna)
Harnoncourt; Concentus musicus Wien
Ortner; Arnold Schönberg Chor

1989   Rossini: *Il Barbiere di Siviglia*
        Matteuzzi (Count Almaviva), Fissore (Bartolo), Bartoli (Rosina), Nucci
            (Figaro), Burchuladze (Basilio), Pertusi (Fiorello), Anepata (Ambrogio),
            Banditelli (Berta), Tadeo (Un ufficiale), Arbace (Un notario)
        Patanè; Orchestra e coro del Teatro Comunale di Bologna
        [London 425 520-2]

1989   Rossini: *La Cenerentola*
        Bartoli (Cenerentola), Matteuzzi (Don Ramiro), Corbelli (Dandini),
            Dara (Don Magnifico), Costa (Clorinda), Banditelli (Tisbe), Pertusi
            (Alidoro)
        Chailly; Orchestra e coro del Teatro Comunale di Bologna
        [London 436 902-2]

1988   Rossini: *Rossini Arias*
        From: *L'Italiana in Algeri*
            "Cruda sorte! Amor tiranno!"
            "Pronti abbiamo . . . Amici in ogni evento . . . Pensa alla patria"
        From: *La Donna del lago*
            "Mura felici"
        From: *Tancredi*
            "Oh! patrial . . . Di tanti palpiti"
        From: *Otello*
            'Assisa a piè d'un salice"
        From: *Stabat Mater*
            "Fac ut portem"
        From: *La Pietra del paragone*
            "Se l'Itale contrade . . . Se per voi, le care, io torno"
        From: *La Cenerentola*
            "Nacqui all'affanno . . . Non più mesta"
        Patanè; Wiener Volksopernorchester; Arnold Schönberg Chor
        [London 425 430-2]

Index

Page 1: As Dorabella in *Così fan tutte*, 1990 (Archivio fotografico del Teatro Comunale di Firenze/Maggio Musicale Fiorentino).

Page 39: (Jose R. Lopez/*New York Times* Pictures)

Page 39: (Jose R. Lopez/*New York Times* Pictures)

Page 67: At a lake near Salzburg, 1993 (Stephen Ellison/Outline).

Page 109: Bartoli and her mother, Silvana Bazzoni, giving a master class in Braunschweig, 1996 (Renate Stendhal).

Page 139: As Cherubino in *The Marriage of Figaro*, with Renée Fleming as the Countess. Paris, 1990 (Kleinefenn-Moatti, Opéra de Paris).

Page 150: (Agence Bernand)

Page 157: With Gino Quilico (Süddeutscher Rundfunk).

Page 162: With Natale de Caroli's (Amati-Bacciardi).

Page 167: With Barbara Ronney (Peter Schlegel).

Page 168: (Kleinefenn-Moatti, Opéra de Paris)

Page 175: (Lelli & Masotti, Teatro alla Scala).

Page 179: With Lella Cuberli and Joan Rodgers (Archivio fotografico del Teatro Comunale di Firenze/Maggio Musicale Fiorentino).

Page 187: With Paolo Gavanelli: (Mass Photo Co.).

Page 188: (Jim Caldwell)

Page 194: (Winne Klotz, courtesy Metropolitan Opera)

Page 195: (Winne Klotz, courtesy Metropolitan Opera)

Page 198: With Thomas Allan (Lelli & Masotti, Teatro alla Scala).

Page 199: With Ferrucio Furlanetto (Winifred Rabanus).

Page 203: Jim Caldwell

Page 204: With Raul Giménez (Jim Caldwell).

Page 207: (Clärchen Baus-Mattar)

Page 208: (Herman und Clärchen Baus)

"Portraits"

Plate 1: (*San Francisco Focus*)

Plate 2: *Top:* Zellerbach Hall, Berkeley, 1993 (Sarah Fawcett/*San Francisco Chronicle*). Bottom: 1995 (Liz Hafilia/*San Francisco Chronicle*).

Plate 3: *Top:* Lincoln Center, New York 1993 (Jack Manning/*New York Times* Pictures). *Bottom:* Rehearsal with Sir Neville Marriner and the Academy of St. Martin-in-the-Fields for a Carnegie Hall concert in 1994 (Stephanie Berger/*New York Times* Pictures).

Plate 4: Zellerbach Hall, Berkeley, 1994 (*San Francisco Chronicle*).

Plate 5: *Top:* (Erica Lanser, Black Star) *Bottom:* Teatro alla Scala, Milano, 1992 (Lelli & Masotti, Teatro alla Scala).

Plate 6: (J. Henry Fair)

Plate 7: (Stephen Ellison/Outline)

Plate 8: (J. Henry Fair)

Plate 9: Rehearsal for *The Barber of Seville* at the Houston Grand Opera, 1993 (Jim Caldwell).

Plate 10: Top: Rehearsing with György Fischer. Bottom: With her mother (Erica Lanser, Black Star)

Plate 11: With her mother (Erica Lanser, Black Star).

Plate 12: Silvana Bazzoni during her first master class at the Kammermusikpodium in Braunschweig (with Ukrainian soprano Rita Bieliauskaite), 1996 (Renate Stendhal).

Plate 13: Mother and daughter teaching together in Braunschweig, shown here with a translator, pianist Volker Link, and German mezzo-soprano Ulrike Jäger (Renate Stendhal).

Plate 14: Signing records in Braunschweig, 1996 (Anthony Pansch).

Plate 15: (Anthony Pansch)

Plate 16: Silvana Bazzoni and her daughters (Erica Lanser, Black Star).